Is there a link between creativity and psychosis or is it a middle class delusion that one's son or daughter has some cross to bear for being sensitive and intelligent? Do people become mentally ill spontaneously or are they upset about something? Should we treat mental illness medicinally or, with the patient, try to understand it? *Creativity and Psychotic States in Exceptional People* provides many clues and is a great starting point if you are interested in learning about psychoanalytic approaches to psychosis from scratch.

Dr Clive Hathaway Travis, from the Foreword

The beauty of this book is that it is written in a style accessible to the lay public as well as to psychoanalytically informed professionals. Murray Jackson in collaboration with Jeanne Magagna investigates how unconscious mental processes underlying both creative and psychotic phenomena can lead to a lessened capacity to distinguish between the two. He traces the development of psychotic phenomena in the external and internal complex 'histories' of well-known artists, and he extracts from these explorations of the minds of exceptional lives a world of wisdom that is useful not only for professionals but also for those interested in a deeper understanding of the human mind when it goes astray.

Bent Rosenbaum, Department of Psychology, University of Copenhagen, and Leading Senior Researcher at the Clinic of Psychotherapy, Psychiatric Centre Copenhagen

Van Gogh, Nijinsky, Nash and Saramago. Murray Jackson, the late distinguished psychoanalyst, investigates their formative lives in depth, giving much needed insights into the roots of adult creativity and of psychosis. A book for a very wide readership.

Brian Martindale, Chair of the ISPS

This book is a very serious contribution to this area of study and will be of lasting interest to a broad readership – obviously all working in the field of mental health will find themselves drawn into thinking deeply about this field and will see the relevance broadly both within their work and in terms of the theoretical/conceptual issues it raises – they will also gain a great deal from the discussion of theoretical and technical issues as regards psychotherapeutic treatment of this kind of disturbance, in the latter part of the book. But the work presented here will be of much broader interest – that is to anyone who can allow themselves to be fascinated by serious psychological disturbance and who has a serious interest in understanding exceptional creativity.

Dr David Bell, Former President of the British Psychoanalytic Society, Consultant Psychiatrist at the Tavistock and Portman NHS Foundation Trust, Visiting Professorial Fellow, Birkbeck College London

To Cynthia and Christiane

CREATIVITY AND PSYCHOTIC STATES IN EXCEPTIONAL PEOPLE

Creativity and Psychotic States in Exceptional People tells the story of the lives of four exceptionally gifted individuals: Vincent van Gogh, Vaslav Nijinsky, José Saramago and John Nash. Previously unpublished chapters by Murray Jackson are set in a contextual framework by Jeanne Magagna, revealing the wellspring of creativity in the subjects' emotional experiences and delving into the nature of psychotic states which influence and impede the creative process.

Jackson and Magagna aim to illustrate how psychoanalytic thinking can be relevant to people suffering from psychotic states of mind and provide understanding of the personalities of four exceptionally talented creative individuals. Present in the text are themes of loving and losing, mourning and manic states, creating as a process of repairing a sense of internal damage and the use of creativity to understand or run away from oneself. The book concludes with a glossary of useful psychoanalytic concepts.

Creativity and Psychotic States in Exceptional People will be fascinating reading for psychiatrists, psychotherapists and psychoanalysts, other psychoanalytically informed professionals, students and anyone interested in the relationship between creativity and psychosis.

Murray Jackson was a psychoanalyst with the British Institute of Psychoanalysis. He is well known as a teacher and writer who has applied psychoanalytic understanding to adults suffering from psychotic states. In 1994 he was given the International Society for Psychological and Social Approaches to Psychosis (ISPS) Lifetime Achievement Award for Outstanding Contribution to the Psychotherapy of Schizophrenia. He died in 2011.

Jeanne Magagna is a child, adult and family psychotherapist. She was formerly Head of Psychotherapy Services at Great Ormond Street Hospital for Children and for many years she headed the child psychotherapy training at Centro Studi Martha Harris in Florence and Venice, Italy. She teaches and publishes internationally.

THE INTERNATIONAL SOCIETY FOR PSYCHOLOGICAL AND SOCIAL APPROACHES TO PSYCHOSIS BOOK SERIES
Series editors: Alison Summers and Nigel Bunker

ISPS (The International Society for Psychological and Social Approaches to Psychosis) has a history stretching back more than 50 years, during which it has witnessed the relentless pursuit of biological explanations for psychosis. The tide has been turning in recent years and there is a welcome international resurgence of interest in a range of psychological factors that have considerable explanatory power and therapeutic possibilities. Governments, professional groups, people with personal experience of psychosis and family members are increasingly expecting interventions that involve more talking and listening. Many now regard practitioners skilled in psychological therapies as an essential component of the care of people with psychosis.

ISPS is a global society. It aims to promote psychological and social approaches both to understanding and to treating psychosis. It also aims to bring together different perspectives on these issues. ISPS is composed of individuals, networks and institutional members from a wide range of backgrounds and is especially concerned that those with personal experience of psychosis and their family members are fully involved in our activities alongside practitioners and researchers, and that all benefit from this. Our members recognize the potential humanitarian and therapeutic potential of skilled psychological understanding and therapy in the field of psychosis and ISPS embraces a wide spectrum of approaches, from psychodynamic, systemic, cognitive, and arts therapies to the need-adapted approaches, family and group therapies and residential therapeutic communities.

We are also most interested in establishing meaningful dialogue with those practitioners and researchers who are more familiar with biological-based approaches. There is increasing empirical evidence for the interaction of genes and biology with the emotional and social environment, and there are important examples of such interactions in the fields of trauma, attachment relationships in the family and in social settings and with professionals.

ISPS activities include regular international and national conferences, newsletters and email discussion groups. Routledge has recognized the importance of our field in publishing both the book series and the ISPS journal, *Psychosis – Psychological, Social and Integrative Approaches*, with the two complementing one another. The book series started in 2004 and by 2012 had 13 volumes with several more in preparation. A wide range of topics is covered and we hope this reflects some success in our aim of bringing together a rich variety of perspectives.

The book series is intended as a resource for a broad range of mental health professionals as well as those developing and implementing policy and people whose interest in psychosis is at a personal level. We aim for rigorous academic standards and at the same time accessibility to a wide readership, and for the books to promote the ideas of clinicians and researchers who may be well known in some countries but not so familiar in others. Our overall intention is to encourage the dissemination of existing knowledge and ideas, promote productive debate, and encourage more research in a most important field whose secrets certainly do not all reside in the neurosciences.

For more information about ISPS, email isps@isps.org or visit our website, www.isps.org.

For more information about the journal *Psychosis* visit www.isps.org/index.php/publications/journal

MODELS OF MADNESS
Psychological, social and biological approaches to schizophrenia
(1st edition)
Edited by John Read, Loren R. Mosher and Richard P. Bentall

PSYCHOSES
An integrative perspective
Edited by Johan Cullberg

EVOLVING PSYCHOSIS
Different stages, different treatments
Edited by Jan Olav Johanessen, Brian V. Martindale and Johan Cullberg

FAMILY AND MULTI-FAMILY WORK WITH PSYCHOSIS
Gerd-Ragna Block Thorsen, Trond Gronnestad and Anne Lise Oxenvad

EXPERIENCES OF MENTAL HEALTH IN-PATIENT CARE
Narratives from service users, carers and professionals
Edited by Mark Hardcastle, David Kennard, Sheila Grandison and Leonard Fagin

PSYCHOTHERAPIES FOR THE PSYCHOSES
Theoretical, cultural, and clinical integration
Edited by John Gleeson, Eión Killackey and Helen Krstev

THERAPEUTIC COMMUNITIES FOR PSYCHOSIS
Philosophy, history and clinical practice
Edited by John Gale, Alba Realpe and Enrico Pedriali

MAKING SENSE OF MADNESS
Contesting the meaning of schizophrenia
Jim Geekie and John Read

PSYCHOTHERAPEUTIC APPROACHES TO SCHIZOPHRENIA PSYCHOSIS
Edited by Yrjö O. Alanen, Manuel González de Chávez, Ann-Louise S. Silver and Brian Martindale

BEYOND MEDICATION
Therapeutic engagement and the recovery from psychosis
Edited by David Garfield and Daniel Mackler

CBT FOR PSYCHOSIS
A symptom-based approach
Edited by Roger Hagen, Douglas Turkington, Torkil Berge and Rolf W. Gråwe

EXPERIENCING PSYCHOSIS
Personal and professional perspectives
Edited by Jim Geekie, Patte Randal, Debra Lampshire and John Read

PSYCHOSIS AS A PERSONAL CRISIS
An experience-based approach
Edited by Marius Romme and Sandra Escher

MODELS OF MADNESS
Psychological, social and biological approaches to psychosis
(2nd edition)
Edited by John Read and Jacqui Dillon

SURVIVING, EXISTING, OR LIVING
Phase-specific therapy for severe psychosis
Pamela Fuller

PSYCHOSIS AND EMOTION
The role of emotions in understanding psychosis, therapy and recovery
Edited by Andrew Gumley, Alf Gillham, Kathy Taylor and Matthias Schwannauer

INSANITY AND DIVINITY
Studies in psychosis and spirituality
Edited by John Gale, Michael Robson and Georgia Rapsomatioti

PSYCHOTHERAPY FOR PEOPLE DIAGNOSED WITH SCHIZOPHRENIA
Specific techniques
Andrew Lotterman

CREATIVITY AND PSYCHOTIC STATES IN EXCEPTIONAL PEOPLE
The work of Murray Jackson
Murray Jackson and Jeanne Magagna

CREATIVITY AND PSYCHOTIC STATES IN EXCEPTIONAL PEOPLE

The work of Murray Jackson

Murray Jackson
Edited by Jeanne Magagna

LONDON AND NEW YORK

First published 2015
by Routledge
27 Church Road, Hove, East Sussex BN3 2FA

and by Routledge
711 Third Avenue, New York, NY 10017

Routledge is an imprint of the Taylor & Francis Group, an informa business

© 2015 Murray Jackson and Jeanne Magagna

The right of Murray Jackson to be identified as author of this work and of Jeanne Magagna to be identified as the author of the editorial material has been asserted by them in accordance with sections 77 and 78 of the Copyright, Designs and Patents Act 1988.

All rights reserved. No part of this book may be reprinted or reproduced or utilised in any form or by any electronic, mechanical, or other means, now known or hereafter invented, including photocopying and recording, or in any information storage or retrieval system, without permission in writing from the publishers.

Trademark notice: Product or corporate names may be trademarks or registered trademarks, and are used only for identification and explanation without intent to infringe.

British Library Cataloguing in Publication Data
A catalogue record for this book is available from the British Library

Library of Congress Cataloging in Publication Data
Jackson, Murray.
Creativity and psychotic states in exceptional people: the work of Murray Jackson / Murray Jackson; edited by Jeanne Magagna.
  pages cm.—(The international society for psychological and social approaches to psychosis book series)
1. Genius and mental illness—Case studies. 2. Creative ability—Psychological aspects—Case studies. 3. Creation (Literary, artistic, etc.)—Psychological aspects—Case studies. 4. Artists—Psychology—Case studies. 5. Psychoanalysis and the arts—Case studies. I. Magagna, Jeanne. II. Title.
  BF423.J33 2015
  153.9'8—dc23
  2014034240

ISBN: 978-0-415-70385-7 (hbk)
ISBN: 978-0-415-70386-4 (pbk)
ISBN: 978-1-315-72642-7 (ebk)

Typeset in Times
by Book Now Ltd, London

CONTENTS

Contributors		xiii
Foreword		xvii
PAUL WILLIAMS		
Commentary		xix
CLIVE HATHAWAY TRAVIS		
Acknowledgements		xxiii
	Introduction	1
	JEANNE MAGAGNA AND MURRAY JACKSON	
1	John Nash: reason's approach to an alternative reality	5
	MURRAY JACKSON	
2	Vaslav Nijinsky: living for the eyes of the other	25
	MURRAY JACKSON	
3	José Saramago: sanity and the overcoming of adversity	67
	MURRAY JACKSON	
4	Vincent van Gogh: enduring unrequited love	91
	JEANNE MAGAGNA AND MURRAY JACKSON	
	Conclusion	114
	JEANNE MAGAGNA AND MURRAY JACKSON	
	Glossary: useful psychoanalytic concepts	127
	Appendix: list of publications by Murray Jackson	134
	Bibliography	137
	Index	148

CONTRIBUTORS

Author

Murray Jackson trained as a Jungian psychoanalyst and subsequently as a psychoanalyst with the British Institute of Psychoanalysis. He worked for ten years as a Consultant Psychiatrist at University College Hospital before being appointed as a Consultant Psychiatrist, co-directing a ten-bedded in-patient unit at Ward Six of the Maudsley Hospital. Dr Jackson is well known in the United Kingdom and abroad, both personally as a speaker and teacher and through his publications regarding his application of psychoanalytic understanding to the treatment of a wide range of psychotic and borderline psychotic patients. After a long, distinguished and internationally recognized career writing, teaching and making clinical contributions towards the understanding of psychotic disorders at the Maudsley Hospital and in Scandinavia, Dr Jackson was given the ISPS (International Society for Psychological and Social Approaches to Psychosis) Lifetime Achievement Award for Outstanding Contribution to the Psychotherapy of Schizophrenia.

Through regular teaching and supervision he supported the development of 'nurse-therapists', thus positively influencing the direction of psychiatric nursing in the UK National Health Service and in Scandinavian mental health services. 'Nurse-therapists' were taught by Dr Jackson to engage with and try to understand the unconscious fears, anxieties, irrational beliefs and conflicts in people suffering from psychosis. The clinical work of Melanie Klein, Wilfred Bion, Herbert Rosenfeld, Henri Rey and Harold Searles was central to Dr Jackson's work with such individuals.

Dr Jackson co-authored *Unimaginable Storms: A Search for Meaning in Psychosis* (Murray Jackson and Paul Williams, 1994) and he also wrote *Weathering the Storms: Psychotherapy for Psychosis* (2001). In addition, Dr Jackson published over 45 papers and/or chapters on psychoanalytic topics. Three years before his death, and before Paul Williams' publication of *Invasive Objects* (2010), Dr Jackson gave his papers on John Nash, Nijinsky and Saramago to some of his psychoanalytic colleagues to read and discuss.

CONTRIBUTORS

Editor

Jeanne Magagna was Head of Psychotherapy Services at Great Ormond Street Hospital for Children in London for 24 years. She also worked for 11 years as a Consultant Psychotherapist in an inpatient centre for young people suffering from anorexia nervosa, and as a clinical consultant to the staff group at Family Futures Adoption and Fostering Consortium in London. She formally completed three trainings at the Tavistock Clinic to become a Child and Adolescent Psychotherapist (PhD level), Family Therapist and Adult Psychotherapist. Jeanne has been the vice-president and joint coordinator of training for the Centro Studi Martha Harris Tavistock Model Psychotherapy Training in Florence and regularly teaches in various Italian cities and in Istanbul. She has edited Henri Rey's *Universals of Psychoanalysis* (1994) and jointly edited *Psychotherapy with Families, Crises in Adolescence* and *Intimate Transformations: Babies with their Families* (2004) and *Observacion de Bebes* (2012). She also edited *The Silent Child: Communication without Words* (2012) and co-edited *Being Present for Your Nursery Age Child: The Tempo Lineare Project* (2014). For many years she worked with Dr Herbert Rosenfeld, Dr Donald Meltzer and Dr Anne Alvarez discussing young people with borderline personality disorders and psychosis.

Foreword author

Paul Williams is a psychoanalyst who trained initially as a social anthropologist. He completed his doctorate at the Maudsley Hospital, London, where he studied Ward 6 and worked there with Murray Jackson, with whom he was to collaborate for the next 30 years. He has written widely on the psychoanalytic understanding and treatment of severe disturbance. From 2001 to 2007 he was, with Glen Gabbard, Joint Editor-in-Chief of the *International Journal of Psychoanalysis*. He now works as a psychoanalyst in private practice in Hampshire.

Commentary author

Clive Hathaway Travis has an honours degree in physics from University College London, a master's degree in Applied Optics from Imperial College London and a PhD from Surrey University on *The Inverse Problem and Applications to Optical and Eddy Current Imaging* sponsored by RAE Farnborough. From 1990 he worked in the defence arena on classified military projects. He developed paranoid schizophrenia in 1994 and spent the next ten years in and out of hospital under the Mental Health Act before finally finding a medication that suited him in 2004. Since then he has worked as an expert patient in the health and social care field, with a special interest in the ending of forced treatment with antipsychotics and justice for those who took their lives as a result of these treatments.

He is a member of ISPS, a patron of Talking 2 Minds and the author of *Looking for Prince Charles's Dog*, the story of his journey to recovery and contribution to the peace process in Northern Ireland.

Cover artist

Ken Kiff, RA (London, 1935–2001), was a twentieth-century British painter. He studied at the Hornsey School of Art from 1955–1961. He became a Royal Academician in 1991. During 1991–1993, Kiff was Associate Artist at the National Gallery in London. In 2001 his paintings were presented in a book entitled *Ken Kiff* written by Andrew Lambeth and Robert Lynton (Thames & Hudson).

FOREWORD

Paul Williams

Murray Jackson had a long and distinguished career as a Consultant Psychiatrist at the Maudsley Hospital, London and as a psychoanalyst in private practice, and became a Life Member of ISPS (International Society for Psychological and Social Approaches to Psychosis). His work was marked, above all, by devotion to the clinical understanding of disturbed adults, many of whom suffered the most severe of psychotic illnesses. This quality of devotion to understanding in itself is not unique, but the form it took in Murray Jackson was especially notable. Throughout his life Murray held firmly to the view that individuals with psychotic illnesses were trying, often in confused or bizarre ways, to communicate essential information about the nature of catastrophic events that had resulted in destruction to or loss of relationships with vital others. Without these important relationships, life no longer held meaning. These 'significant others' were actual, external people, yet also their inner psychic variants which altered reality in confusing, perhaps terrifying, ways.

Following in the footsteps of Freud, Klein, Bion, Rosenfeld and Rey, among others, Murray placed well-founded faith in areas of the mind capable of non-psychotic thinking and amenable to receiving comments and ideas designed to clarify the significance of psychotically confused states, no matter how difficult this task might be. Colleagues and adults who consulted Murray will recall his combination of quiet warmth and vivid imaginative thinking as he pursued with interest, compassion and an alert sense of irony his explorations of mental illness through conversations that could be by turns moving, illuminating and therapeutically powerful. A blend of educated, imaginative speculation, human warmth and a solid grasp of the internal object world and the devastation that affects it in psychosis, distinguished Murray from his psychiatric peers. He was a clinician's clinician. The type of clinical approach that characterized Murray's work was not 'charismatic' – a term that has taken on somewhat pejorative overtones in the current dispassionate era of 'evidence-based' medicine: rather, it involved deployment of an unusually high level of intuitive skill. His intuition was assisted by many years of self-analysis following his various analytic trainings, filtered or refracted through a deep interest in concepts and theories considered as servants, not masters in his efforts to formulate meaningful ideas. These ideas originated with the person in psychotherapy with Murray yet allowed Murray to attain the limits of his own imaginative understanding in a form that was usable to the person consulting him.

To the untutored eye, conversations with adults in psychotherapy or psychoanalysis with him could at times seem odd, even baffling: closer examination revealed a keen sensitivity to the person's unconscious world about which Jackson seemed able to speak with unusual fluency, using everyday language. A moving picture emerged of two people talking in a sane way about what it feels like to have gone mad, and the relief that this way of talking gave to people in therapy was frequently profound. One example of many illustrates this: a young woman suffering from a bipolar disorder declared midway through the interview with Murray that the only problem she had was that she had a psychiatrist who was insane. She stood up and informed Murray that she was leaving the interview and the hospital. Instead of turning toward the door, she hovered instead, as though searching within herself for one final denunciation. Then, at the top of her voice, she yelled 'It's ALL OVER, Dr Jackson!' She then proceeded to throw a full, fortunately lukewarm, cup of tea over Murray. He stood up, wiped himself down and, with complete seriousness, replied: 'I think you are right. It is all over Dr Jackson.' The woman's face gradually softened, as though she might laugh and then as though she might cry. She sat down, confused, and the conversation resumed in a different vein, on the lines of how terrified she was of recognizing how ill she felt and how understandable it was that she needed to locate her feelings of insanity, helplessness and hopelessness in others.

As well as being an excellent clinician himself, Murray Jackson was an advocate of the application of psychoanalytic ideas to psychiatric practice, nursing and to the activities of other mental health professionals who came into contact with a person suffering from psychosis. He never surrendered the view that every person suffering from a psychotic condition merited a psychoanalytically informed assessment interview as part of the admission procedure. He felt that, with guidance, supervision and support, many doctors, nurses and other mental health workers could, with the help of their own psychoanalytic therapy, become more thoughtful clinicians, influencing assessment, care plan development, treatment goals and after-care. He supported the development of 'nurse-therapists' who were taught to engage with unconscious fears in people suffering from mental illness. He believed that, at the very least, psychiatrists and nurses should be capable of recognizing anxieties, irrational beliefs and conflicts in people, and of talking about them rather than treating them as marginal events or, worse, debris. A complete absence of elitism, and a focus on creativity, marked his attitude to psychiatry and psychoanalysis in all their forms.

Murray enjoyed a creative life right up until the day he died. This book, edited by Jeanne Magagna with great care, represents the final piece of writing Murray Jackson undertook. The chapters delve into the nature of psychosis in certain exceptionally gifted individuals and they reveal not only the wellspring of creativity in the subjects under consideration, but also in the author himself. A theme of mourning, reparation and the need to nurture good objects is apparent in his writing, as was the case in his life.

COMMENTARY

Clive Hathaway Travis

So is there a link between creativity and psychosis or is it a middle-class delusion that one's son or daughter has some cross to bear for being sensitive and intelligent? Do people become mentally ill spontaneously or are they upset about something? Should we treat mental illness medicinally or, with the patient, try to understand it? I read this book hoping to find some clues, noting one of Nash's sons is no stranger to psychosis himself. Nor was van Gogh's brother.

The book is firmly set in the psychoanalytic field. In this field, it often seems, people don't become mentally ill spontaneously but rather due to adverse relationships, traumatic events/circumstances and disadvantageous levels of self esteem. For example in the case of John Nash (Chapter 1), it is held that infantile conflicts left a terrible legacy throughout life. If these causes are understood, says the psychoanalyst, then the prospect of recovery may be available to the sufferer by psychoanalytic intervention. Interestingly, for psychosis, in cognitive behavioural therapy (CBT) it is recommended that the therapist talk to the patient about their early life, and in family intervention (NICE 2014) it is also recommended that the sufferer discuss with the family how they understand their current experiences, so we see a little common ground. There is strong research evidence that both of these types of therapy, as well as arts therapies, are helpful (NICE 2014 guideline *Psychosis and Schizophrenia in Adults*). This is not to deny that other types of psychological treatments, like psychoanalysis, might seem to be, or actually be, helpful for some patients. Some might even swear by them. Any process that enables engagement with a psychotic patient, that gets them from A to B in one piece might well be regarded as efficacious.

For ten years of my life some of the best help I got, courtesy of the state, was the support of a Mental Health Act solicitor, that is a person who did not challenge my delusions. One of the things I learnt from reading this book is the possible value of working *with* the thoughts of the patient, be they dreams, delusions or memories. The only psychological therapy I got during this time was what I manufactured for myself, and that, I now feel, was effective. My stance would be that no treatment could be worse than the NHS regime I was subjected to over those ten years, and certainly not a scientifically proven psychological technique or even the artfulness of psychoanalytic therapy, though this is not widely available on the NHS. For, as Jackson holds, good psychoanalytic therapy is a creative process between the patient and the analyst. Although psychoanalytic and arts therapies do not have the same kind of research base as therapies such as CBT, there is research evidence, the community strongly argues, supporting the view that they can in some instances be effective. If a therapist aims to enable the patient to make sense of the world around them, then the proof of the pudding is partly whether the patient thinks they have. Your average psychiatric patient is not offered psychoanalytic approaches. Neither is it likely that the relationship between their 'conscious and unconscious thoughts' will be explored. The reader can decide for themselves if they believe in the ideas behind psychoanalysis rather than spontaneous mental illness. Not that most practitioners don't now believe in at least some of these ideas, and see them as part of understanding where problems may have begun, or are currently maintained. For those merely interested in the relationship between creativity and psychosis, the book is written mostly in lay terms with a terse introduction so you know what the book aims to say. Where it isn't expressed in lay terms, *Creativity and Psychotic States in Exceptional People* is a great starting point if you are interested in learning about psychoanalytic approaches to psychosis from scratch, as indeed I have done by reading this book, which has a useful glossary of the psychological/psychoanalytic and psychiatric terms used. It also contains a review of the rather dry book *A Beautiful Mind*, saving you from having to read it and, at the same time, complementing the film.

The first thing I understood from my reading of this warts-and-all analysis of the book's subjects (the all was not there in the film of *A Beautiful Mind*) is the very factors which successful artistic endeavour are oftentimes attributed to can also impede artistic endeavour. On the other hand we find that, as illustrated by Nash, intellect can be a useful weapon in the battle against psychosis, a psychosis which anyone could understand was not ameliorated by the persecution of Nash for his sexuality. You don't have to be a Nobel laureate or a famous dancer to believe you are a superhero on a mission to save the world, as many patients and mental health professionals will tell you. So don't imagine your more humble patient, perhaps on a bipolar high, cannot identify with the Nash portrayed here, the Nash who himself campaigns for a more psychotherapeutic rather than purely medicinal approach.

Like Nash and the film, Vaslav Nijinsky (Chapter 2) has had a rather, shall we say, incomplete version of his life story made – the heavily edited diary of 1935. Even then it is apparent that both studies bear little resemblance to the psychiatric notes of the typical modern psychiatric patient, only a small proportion of whom will receive CBT, let alone psychoanalysis.

Speaking as a person who has recovered from paranoid schizophrenia, who found ten medications entirely unacceptable to take, yet regards the one I am on now as a vital component of my ongoing recovery, I have found reading this book a useful exercise. There are dangers in exposing the psychotic core of the personality in the course of psychotherapy but God knows, as do many (often only just surviving) patients, medication brings its own risks! Her Majesty's Coroners please take note! 'You cannot know what it means to have eyes in a world in which everyone else is blind' says Saramago (Chapter 3), echoing my own feelings about my years being chewed up in an insane system. We also learn that the lives of famous talented people with mental illnesses, such as Nijinsky, are no more chaotic than those of lesser known mortals, it is just that they had the eyes of the world on them.

The book is an interesting read from an historical perspective, not least in the case of van Gogh (Chapter 4), with whom I can certainly, as a formerly psychiatrically challenged person, identify when Jackson says 'through painting as a kind of therapy Vincent, unconsciously and perhaps consciously, drew and painted in order to recover and recreate harmony in his damaged internal world and thus regain his mental balance'. Van Gogh's lifestyle anticipated the recommendation for art therapy in the NICE 2014 guideline, *Psychosis and Schizophrenia in Adults*, by more than a century!

Jackson hypothesizes that paranoid delusions originate as the best possible solution to an intolerable psychological situation. From my own experience it does seem that, in fact, such fantasies can be a means of protecting one's self by creating a tolerable scenario from an intolerable one: a strategy to find a way ahead and, in fact, a form of self protection. Whether they are *designed to be* is probably a question for a psychological anthropologist (or somebody). But Jackson seems quite sure that in each of the cases of Nash, Nijinsky, Saramago and van Gogh, their families moulded the direction and personality of these creative geniuses.

From a lay point of view one has confidence in Dr Jackson, who certainly sounds like he knew what he was 'on about' and was clearly a much loved and respected man. But how valuable it might have been to have him as a therapist during my lost decade as an unrecovered patient for, who knows, he might have facilitated a somewhat more rapid, even safer and a less painful route to recovery and that is the hope for psychiatry. For this book is really an appeal to complement psychiatric care with more extensive psychological therapy, whilst not replacing it, and to understand the patient's life, not just their illness. *Creativity and Psychotic States* demonstrates that a person might have a greater chance of recovery if their care team adopted a more eclectic approach and should be set reading on any psychology course.

ACKNOWLEDGEMENTS

We would like to acknowledge the contributions of Cynthia Jackson, Erin Hope Thompson, Michelle Scott, Isabel Owen, Roy Lowenstein, John Mason as well as the Routledge and ISPS editors, Brian Martindale, Alison Summers and Nigel Bunker. Also, we are particularly grateful to the people whose lives are explored in this book.

List of illustrations

Photograph of John Nash appears in this book courtesy of Princeton University.

Photograph of José Saramago is copyright of Carlos Alvarez/Getty Images and appears here with permission.

Photograph of Vaslav Nijinsky appears here courtesy of the Bibliothèque nationale de France.

Self-portrait by Vincent van Gogh is reproduced courtesy of Van Gogh Museum Enterprises BV; Vincent van Gogh (1853–1890), self-portrait, 1887, Paris, oil on canvas, 41 × 33 cm. Van Gogh Museum, Amsterdam (Vincent van Gogh Foundation).

INTRODUCTION

Jeanne Magagna and Murray Jackson

Many educated people lack understanding of the severe psychotic anxieties, irrational beliefs and conflicts present in creative people. The aim of this book is twofold: first, it is an attempt to lend deeper understanding to aspects of certain exceptionally talented creative people, namely, John Nash, Vaslav Nijinsky, José Saramago and Vincent van Gogh. Second, it tries to enhance the reader's understanding of severe psychotic anxieties by indicating where loving and destructive phantasies may both prompt and impede artistic endeavours and personality development.

The exploration of links between creativity and psychotic states is a subject of popular interest for readers, artists and cinema goers who will have seen films on Nash, Nijinsky, van Gogh and Saramago's book *Blindness*. The writings in this book should also be of great interest and value to people trying to understand and ameliorate psychotic functioning in very disturbed individuals.

The task of exploring creativity and psychotic anxieties will involve making links between sibling relationships, loss of love, and creative developments and psychotic breakdowns in the lives of these famous artists. Saramago did not suffer from a psychotic illness, but experienced overwhelming anxieties at times, and had psychosis-like experiences in childhood. He will be used as an illustration of psychological processes which prevent breakdown in the face of life crises.

Psychoanalysis is an activity which can only take place with the individual in the presence of a psychoanalyst or psychotherapist. For this reason the chapters provide only tentative psychoanalytic explorations of mental illness through exploring four emotionally painful lives dedicated to creativity.

The main body of the book is structured in four chapters, each of which details the life of a gifted individual. Chapter 1 is on John Nash, Nobel Laureate in economics, who may be understood as overwhelmed by the 'alternative reality of unconscious conflicts regarding destructiveness and creativity'. He expressed some of his conflicts through his mathematical endeavours. For 25 years he suffered from a paranoid psychosis. His Princeton colleagues' tolerance and containment enabled him to pursue his career and work through some of his most severe difficulties. This narrative of John Nash's life, including his relationship to siblings, illustrates how unresolved infantile conflicts can leave a terrible legacy throughout life. Nash eventually recovered, apparently through both his own courageous introspective efforts and the loving care of his wife, who seems to have been crucial to his recovery.

Chapter 2 examines the life of Vaslav Nijinsky, who illustrates a most extreme form of psychotic suffering. His enduring fame rests not only on his remarkable ballet career, but also on his detailed diary. He wrote this diary in the period when he was struggling to recover his sanity, which was being overwhelmed by psychotic processes. Dancing seems to have helped Nijinsky to remain sane by providing the public adulation which was essential to his mental well-being. When he was rejected by Sergei Diaghilev, his patron and lover, and thus denied the opportunity to continue dancing, he fell into a psychotic illness from which he never fully recovered. Nijinsky's personality appears to have been characterized by lack of empathy and communication skills, instability of mood and aloofness. He grew up in a family that stressed achievement at all costs. His early life was emotionally traumatic and unstable, as highlighted by his proneness to very destructive jealous rages. His difficulties could be understood as a failure to have and to introject loving compassionate parents, which predisposed him to use dancing as a means of gathering upon himself the eyes of an appreciative audience, representing 'the glow in the mother's eye'. He fell apart if he was not 'held' by the gaze of the audience.

Nijinsky's severe psychotic anxieties seem to have been often linked to both conscious and unconscious destructive jealousy of 'others' sharing maternal emotional space. He wished to be the most important and single focus of not only his mother and his wife, but also of ballet audiences. His possessive jealousy, as well as his sense of being rejected, appear to have been major factors contributing to his mental illness and, latterly, led to his remaining in a psychiatric hospital for a large part of his adult life. Nijinsky was keenly aware of both his love and his destructive possessive feelings, which seem to have prompted creativity in his sexually provocative dances. Unfortunately, in contrast to this, his destructive notions predominated over loving impulses in his personal life. His writings in *The Diary of Vaslav Nijinsky* (2006) helped to ensure his enduring fame. Chapter 2 describes aspects of his emotional difficulties and provides connections between his dancing, personal life and states of mind detailed in his personal diary.

Chapter 3 details the life of Nobel Laureate in Literature, José Saramago, who passed his early childhood in extreme poverty. Having been sexually abused in a most torturous way and overcome by subsequent severe nightmarish anxieties, Saramago found inspiration to struggle with his loving and destructive impulses. He developed moral concern for others and became creative in the context of an emotionally secure relationship with loving and understanding grandparents. His literary works show a Proustian recall of memories, and an intense mourning process filled with nightmarish destructiveness, denial and, subsequently, openness to love and hate. Through mourning his lost grandparents and his dead elder brother, Saramago is able to creatively evoke and bring to life dead and persecutory objects and restore valued lost relationships. This chapter demonstrates how, through this mourning process, Saramago managed to recover from some of the severe anxieties which beset him.

Chapter 4 suggests possible psychological contributions to both van Gogh's creative genius and his mental illness. In particular, there is a demonstration of the power of his love for his mother. Part of his life and work was influenced by the desperate, but hopeless, attempt to restore and repair the damage done to his mother through his conscious and unconscious hostility. Through offering deeper understanding of van Gogh, the chapter provides good reasons to admire his formidable skill as an artist and his determination to win his mother's exclusive love while sparing her from direct expressions of his hate.

Van Gogh's love for his mother was in many ways similar to Saramago's deep affection towards his grandparents. Like Nijinsky, van Gogh's ambition was to be 'the triumphant one winning first prize', to be the sole one catching the eye of 'the other', representing at times, the mother. Murderous competition towards Gauguin and a sense of abandonment by his brother and others seem to have led to van Gogh's self-harm.

Like Saramago and Nijinsky, van Gogh had a dead sibling. Van Gogh received the name of his dead sibling and suffered his mother's pathological bereavement over this child. His shooting himself could be linked to splitting-off his hatred from the external mother and projecting it into his internal mother whom he attacked by attacking his own body. Somehow van Gogh's act of dying also seemed an attempt to bring to his side 'the good mothering part' of his brother Theo, a consciously very much-loved brother, for whom he also perhaps had considerable unconscious envy and jealousy.

Like Nijinsky and Saramago, van Gogh lacked an emotionally responsive mother and somehow, in his artistic creations he attempted to portray sorrow, isolation, death and darkness and also their antitheses. Perhaps Nijinsky's sexualized dancing suggests a similar act of struggling against darkness, hate and loss. Once again, the love and hate of his siblings had a strong determining influence on van Gogh's life and his creativity. Through the study of van Gogh this chapter will explore connections between psychotic anxieties, family relationships and creative impulses.

In the book's concluding chapter, family relationships, particularly a person's internalized relationships with the parents and siblings, will be shown to vitally influence both creativity and the interplay between psychological health and illness (Magagna *et al.* 2004). Through this work it is hoped that the reader will appreciate the psychoanalytic method of inquiry and strive to compassionately comprehend the lives of these people and their creative endeavours.

Figure 1 John Nash.

1
JOHN NASH
Reason's approach to an alternative reality

Murray Jackson

The remarkable story of John Nash, Nobel Laureate, has received worldwide publicity through the success of Sylvia Nasar's biography *A Beautiful Mind* (Nasar 1998) and the film of the same name derived from it (Howard 2001). In 1958, at the age of 30, already recognized as a mathematician of genius, Nash began to suffer recurring psychotic states from which he recovered 25 years later. This chapter will explore the nature of Nash's illness from a psychoanalytic perspective, based on the public accounts of his life. Included will be a discussion of both the different factors that may have precipitated his move into psychotic thinking and those experiences which may have enabled Nash to take the steps necessary for his eventual recovery. Certain features of Nash's life, which are not explored in either the book or the film, have important implications for the treatment of people suffering from severe psychotic illness and these will be reflected upon in this chapter. The aim of this chapter is to illustrate how modern psychoanalytic concepts can contribute in a helpful and practical way to the psychotherapeutic treatment of people suffering from psychosis and other related problems.

The chief sources of information for this chapter are Sylvia Nasar's biography (Nasar 1998), Nash's own writing subsequent to his recovery, and his 1996 historical lecture in Madrid. The film *A Beautiful Mind* (Howard 2001) is also of considerable interest. Nash cooperated more extensively in the making of a later documentary *The American Experience: A Brilliant Madness* (Samels 2003) which adds further significant material. Nash's personal disclosures during and after his illness also corroborate much of the information included in this chapter.

Prologue

Nash came to understand his illness as an essentially psychogenic one, a view contrasting sharply with the reductionist 'biomedical' orientation of the biography and of much of contemporary psychiatry. The film script of *A Beautiful Mind* (Howard 2001) shows a certain acquaintance with psychoanalytic theory; for instance, it refers to Rosenfeld's 'destructive narcissism' (Rosenfeld 1971: 169–178). Nevertheless, it draws the same biomedical conclusion as the biography. Apparently, in the interests of opposing the social stigma attached to psychosis, the film promotes the seriously misleading message that psychosis is an organic illness like diabetes.

Nasar's biography (1998) describes Nash's colleague questioning him in a reasonable moment, soon after the acute onset of his psychosis: 'How could you, a mathematician, a man devoted to reason and logical proof, believe that extraterrestrials are sending you messages? How could you believe that you are being recruited by aliens from outer space to save the world?'

Nash replied: 'Because the ideas I had about supernatural beings came to me in the same way that my mathematical ideas did. So I took them seriously' (Nasar 1998: 11).

Nash's remarkable response demonstrates how unconscious mental processes underlying both creative and psychotic phenomena can lead to a loss of the capacity to distinguish between the two. His response might also suggest that Nash had an unusual ability to preserve the capacity for curiosity and intellectual exploration, a talent which may have served him well throughout his illness and contributed to his eventual recovery.

Why study John Nash?

All the psychological factors that will be considered in this essay are very familiar to modern-day psychoanalysts working with people suffering from psychosis, and such psychological descriptions can be found in psychoanalytic publications. For example, good clinical illustrations of successful psychotherapy with people suffering from psychotic states exist in Jackson and Williams (1994), Robbins (1993) and Lotterman (1996 and 2015 in press). Although Nash's recovery after such a long psychotic illness is not unusual (Bleuler 1978; Harding *et al*. 1987) there are features that make Nash's case exceptionally interesting to discuss. For example:

- the worldwide publicity arising from the award-winning film, *A Beautiful Mind* (Howard 2001), and its partial misrepresentation of the nature of psychotic states;
- Nash's remarkably high level of abstract thinking that led many of his peers to regard him as the greatest mathematician of the century;
- the fact that, upon recovery, Nash was able to resume creative work of a high order;
- Nash's considered decision to reject the anti-psychotic medication which had been effective in suppressing his symptoms, and his insistence that he find a way of recovering through his own efforts;
- the likelihood that a significant benign transformation and growth of Nash's immature personality occurred as a consequence of his attempt to work through some of his pathogenic unconscious conflicts.

Background history

For those who have not read the book, much of this history is contained in *A Beautiful Mind* (Nasar 1998). Born in 1928, Nash was a loved and wanted first child who was followed, two years later, by his sister, Martha. He was described as 'a singular little boy who was solitary and very introverted' (O'Connor and Robertson 2002: 7). Nash's mother and father were devoted and loving parents of exceptional intellectual stature, who unreservedly supported the development of their son's prodigious intellectual qualities and enquiring mind. Nash pursued his education mainly at home through encyclopaedias, science books and making scientific experiments. He was bored by the teachers at school and learning at school was troublesome because of Nash's marked disrespect for authority and his conflicts with his peers.

From early childhood onwards Nash's peer relationships were fraught with hostility. A contributory factor may have been his intense destructive jealousy towards his sister Martha, whom he once seated in a chair which he had wired up with batteries (O'Connor and Robertson 2002: 2). Nash often derived malicious pleasure by playing childish, sometimes cruel, tricks on his peers. Torturing animals and creating an explosion that badly hurt a classmate, as well as drawing antagonistic caricatures of his classmates, suggested Nash had an excess of unintegrated hostility to peers and to his sister, of whom he speaks very little. Few friendships resulted from Nash's eccentric, withdrawn behaviour and his underlying aggression.

At 14, Nash became particularly inspired by E. T. Bell's *Men of Mathematics* (1937) and he tried on his own to solve the mathematic problems presented in Bell's book. Nash had a strong competitive tendency to present himself as an unrivalled and superior thinker who denounced the work of others in his field. His arrogance and eccentricity were most pronounced in his early adult life. As a result he was often tormented by his contemporaries.

Aged 19, Nash burst onto the mathematical scene and over the next ten years established himself as one of the more remarkable mathematicians of the century. His ground-breaking work into the processes of human rivalry and his theory of rational conflict and cooperation are achievements which have sometimes been regarded in mathematical circles as having similar stature and importance to the ideas of Newton and Darwin. Nash worked for some years as a part-time consultant to the RAND Corporation, a privately funded 'think-tank' employed by the US military during the Cold War period. This post brought him into a certain, although limited, contact with the Central Intelligence Agency. At this time, US concern about Soviet nuclear development had a markedly paranoid quality, which found its most direct expression in the anti-communist activities of the 'McCarthy era'. A pre-emptive US military strike was being seriously considered (Milnor 1998). Simultaneously, Nash's 'game theory' was being seen as crucial to Cold War politics.

In 1951, Nash, aged 23, began a close and intense relationship lasting over several years with a colleague, 'Mr Jacob B' (Nasar 1998: 180). Nasar makes the interesting suggestion that it was Mr B's reciprocation of Nash's love which altered Nash's perception of himself in a fundamental and benign way (Nasar 1998: 181). During this period he also conducted a relationship with a young, attractive nurse,

Eleonor, who became his mistress. Shortly afterwards, while continuing his affair with Eleonor, he became involved in a relationship with his future wife, Alicia. In 1954, Nash's involvement with the RAND 'think-tank' came to an abrupt and humiliating end when he was arrested and charged with engaging in homosexual behaviour in public.

In 1954, around the time of this traumatic event, Eleonor became pregnant and gave birth to their son, John. For several years Nash kept ongoing life with Eleonor and John almost completely secret, maintaining it together with this longstanding and emotionally powerful relationship with his male colleague, 'Mr B'. Subsequently, Nash was filled shame when Eleonor shocked his parents with news of their affair and child. A further consequence of the exposure of his double life was that Nash's parents, horrified at his duplicity, at first pressed him to marry his mistress (Nasar 1998: 206). Nash father died in 1956 shortly after hearing of Nash's double life.

It was against the background of these personal and professional conflicts that in 1958 Nash, while continuing his affair with Eleonor, now married Alice, a physicist and former student. Eleonor was furious with him for rejecting her. Nash's wife quickly became pregnant in the context of all this turmoil. Nash thereupon abandoned his mistress and declined to give financial help to her and his son. This resulted in their suffering considerable financial hardship during his son's childhood. Shocked by what he regarded as Nash's 'callousness' towards Eleonor, and finding the threesome relationship too intense, 'Mr B' terminated his involvement with Nash, leaving Nash suffering an overwhelming sense of rejection. In 1959, Alicia, gave birth to their baby, named John; the same name as Nash's firstborn son conceived with Eleonor.

The biographer's views

Sylvia Nasar's book (Nasar 1998) is a masterpiece of meticulous research and of skilful and indefatigable, albeit intrusive, interviewing. Her biography was unauthorized, and because Nash declined to disclose any personal information that might cause embarrassment, the depth of Nasar's (1998) investigation was, of necessity, limited. Nonetheless, her perceptiveness is evident in her conclusions about the nature of Nash's vulnerability and her understanding of the factors precipitating his breakdown. She considers that his extraordinary sense of self-importance had its roots in his early childhood, and was a way of protecting himself from a sense of loneliness, isolation, jealousy and hostility, while at the same time obscuring his craving for love and affection.

Nasar (1998) suggests that Nash's impressively intellectual mother might have been excessively ambitious for Nash and thus possibly experienced by him as intrusively demanding in her educational endeavours with him. At the same time his father, a somewhat reserved, highly intelligent and scientifically minded man, might have been experienced as emotionally unavailable at important stages of Nash's development. When she searched through the historical information regarding Nash's parents and grandparents, Nasar (1998) could find no evidence of trans-generational pathological influences.

As well as acknowledging the importance of Nash's personal life experiences, Nasar (1998) lends great importance to the fact that, shortly before his breakdown, Nash had narrowly failed to win the Fields medal, the most prestigious prize for mathematics, to which he felt entitled. Nash had been shocked to discover that some months before he solved a crucial problem in mathematics, a rival had already resolved it. Retrospectively, Nash said that he believed that his rival's earlier resolution of the mathematical problem was the reason why the Fields medal had eluded him. Nasar (1998) considered Nash's setback to be an Icarus-like fall, combined with new emotional burdens occasioned by marriage, revelation of his affair and his parenthood, coupled with the death of his father. The cumulative effect of these factors interacting with his own internal experiences seemed to contribute to his psychotic states (Nasar 1998: 221). Nasar's (1998) uncontroversial conclusion leaves open such questions as the nature of Nash's pre-morbid vulnerability and the meaning of his psychotic experiences. Her omissions reflect the stance of well-known, primarily biomedically oriented psychiatrist-researchers who discredited psychoanalysis as a method of treating psychosis and maintained that psychosis is simply a brain disease, albeit with psychological concomitants (Nasar 1994).

The film: *A Beautiful Mind*

The film script, *A Beautiful Mind*, was written by Avika Goldsman, directed by Brian Gazer and produced by Ron Howard (2001). The film-makers set out to involve the audience in Nash's experience, inviting them to empathize with him, hoping in this way to contribute to the de-stigmatization of mental illness and to raise public awareness of the very often terrifying nature of his type of psychosis. The film-makers dramatically illustrate what it can be like to experience the invasion of the mind by alien forces and to lose the capacity to distinguish a hallucination from reality. The viewer also has the opportunity of experiencing Nash's confusion and perplexity by means of the director's device, explained in detail in the accompanying DVD, of offering many subtle clues which point to the fact that what is being seen is Nash's delusional reality.

The film-makers have created a remarkably authentic presentation of some of the important aspects of the inner life of Nash and many other people suffering from psychosis. The film's imaginative elaboration of Nash's dream-like psychotic experience is, in some respects, psychoanalytically sophisticated. The scriptwriter creates an imaginary companion, Charles, who at first gives him constructive encouragement, but eventually incites him with great seductive power to grandiosity and omnipotent thinking, thereby undermining Nash's sense of reality. The scriptwriter also invents a hallucinatory Mafia-like controller/supervisor of the CIA, William, who eventually reveals his sadistic potential and threatens to kill Nash and his wife and child if he tries to break free of the grip of the CIA 'gang'. Nash eventually courageously struggles to escape from William and the murderous gang's powerful and threatening influence.

These themes of being potentially protected and then powerfully coerced by compelling delusions are particularly well-documented in Kleinian psychoanalytic studies of psychotic conditions (Rosenfeld 1987; Steiner 1993b; De Masi 1997; Jackson 2001). The destructive delusional organization, described by Rosenfeld (1987), lends meaning to the narcissistic omnipotent object relations characteristic of certain psychotic states of mind. In his book *Impasse and Interpretation*, Rosenfeld (1987) describes the nature of narcissistic omnipotent object relations. He suggests that a narcissistic character structure arises in infancy as a protection against the sense of helplessness but subsequently such a character structure may lead to many pathogenic consequences. Rosenfeld goes on further to explain that:

> Once a firm narcissistic way of living has been established beyond infancy, relations to self and object will be controlled in order to try to maintain the delusional omnipotent belief. Any contact with reality or self-observation inevitably threatens this state of affairs and is felt as very dangerous ... this omnipotent way of existing is experienced and even personified as a good friend or guru who uses powerful suggestions and propaganda to maintain the status quo, a process which is generally silent and often creates confusion. Any object, particularly the analyst, who helps the patient to face the reality of his need and dependence is experienced as dangerous by this good friend, who is afraid of being exposed as a phantom.
>
> When the patient's capacity for self-observation improves ... and he tries to free himself from being controlled, the persuasive, seductive nature of the omnipotent structure changes: it becomes sadistic and threatens the patient with death. Only then does one become aware that hidden in the omnipotent structure there exists a very primitive superego, which belittles and attacks the patient's capacities, observations, and particularly the acceptance of his need for real objects. The most confusing element in this process is the successful disguise of the omnipotent structure of omnipotent relating and the envious destructive superego as benevolent figures; this disguise makes the patient feel guilty and ungrateful towards them when he tries to improve.
>
> (Rosenfeld 1987: 87)

The scriptwriter's psychoanalytically sophisticated interpretation of Nash's inner object relationships can fairly be considered as a brilliant depiction of Rosenfeld's (1987) work on borderline and psychotic destructive narcissism.

Other subtle features in the film further illustrate psychoanalytic themes. Nash's wife is shocked when she enters Nash's study. She discovers that the study wall, covered with his press cuttings, demonstrates that her husband, whom she thought to be well at the time, had been pursuing his paranoid preoccupations in secret. Most of the items on which the camera slowly re-focuses refer specifically to the Oedipal and pre-Oedipal content of these preoccupations, either directly, such as the birth of the first 'test-tube' baby, or symbolically, such as that of a happily retired couple living on a $300 pension, the recurrence of the numbers 2 and 3 representing coupling and Oedipal relationships, and other significant, near-subliminal artefacts.

The film shows the dramatic change that gradually took place in Nash's personality, transforming him from a narcissistic, isolated and haughty young man, into a more normal human being, able to accept help and acknowledge dependence with humility. Nash's remarkable capacity to survive his delusional experiences and his determination to recover his grasp on reality are also poignantly conveyed in the film. In a convincing manner it depicts how the psychotic confusion in the dream-like inner world of phantasies gets mixed up with external reality. The audience is also presented with a vivid portrayal of the devastating power of both wishful and terrifying delusional beliefs and the persuasiveness of the psychotic mental processes, which struggle to undermine sanity.

The decision to portray Nash's world of psychotic thinking in visual terms, which is somewhat uncommon in psychosis rather than in Nash's actual auditory hallucinatory mode, is an artifice which might have been designed to compel the interest of the viewers in a way that a story about hallucinatory voices might not. The film-makers have thus created Goldman's own speculative version of the nature of Nash's internal object relationships. These portrayals were based upon Nash's personal account of his hallucinations and his method of success in gradually opposing 'the delusionally influenced lines of political thinking' which had been characteristic of his orientation (Nash 2002a).

This chapter will supplement some of the issues which the remarkable film did not sufficiently highlight. Addressing the issue of destructive and reparative motivations underlying Nash's psychotic states, however difficult this might have been in the film, could have avoided the idealization of Nash and the thread of superficial sentimentality that runs through the film. In contrast to the film, this chapter attempts to give a more balanced picture of the true nature of psychotic illness and draw the missing connections between paranoid states and unconscious hostility.

Evolution of Nash's psychosis

In 1958, although celebrated in the media as the most successful mathematician of the century, Nash was showing a marked instability of mood. His excitement over yet more imminent triumphs was marred by increasing self-doubt and intense resentful rivalry experienced when someone else received the Fields medal.

Nash's homosexual relation with 'Mr B' may have been his first, or at least most powerful, experience of finding the exclusive love that treacherous pregnant women, representing his mother, denied him. He did, however, feel intense jealousy when 'Mr B' showed interest in another man. Both the manner of 'Mr B's' break-up with him and his own resulting experience of bitterness, revenge and loss, were to have profound consequences for Nash's mental stability. The loss of 'Mr B' was particularly emotionally devastating to Nash who some years later described him as the person in his life who had caused him the greatest personal injury. Being traumatized by both his father's death and 'Mr B's' rejection, Nash felt a deep mistrust of people, feeling that intimacy with neither a man nor a woman was safe. He also later incorporated 'Mr B' into his delusional world, considering him as his supremely malevolent betrayer (Nasar 1998: 326) calling him 'Satan' and 'Jacob, the thief of his birth-right'.

As Nash's mood instability became more pronounced, he had sudden transient homosexual infatuations. His friends became worried when, at a fancy dress New Year's Eve party in 1958, he arrived carrying a baby's bottle of milk, clad only in a diaper and a sash and proclaiming the arrival of the New Year (Nasar 1998: 239). Although his astonished fellow guests accepted this as his wife's witty idea, some found the charade bizarre and disturbing, particularly since Nash spent much of the evening sitting on his pregnant wife's lap, sucking the bottle.

Psychotic confusion can be extremely distressing for other family members, friends and colleagues. Nash's attitude towards Alicia, which included frequently accusing her and threatening her if she didn't tell him who made her pregnant, made her anxious. She became even more worried when Nash painted black spots all over their bedroom walls and at one point threatened her and their son in the middle of the night. Although Alicia was sometimes confused and frightened by her husband's behaviour, out of loyalty to him she concealed some of his threatening behaviour towards her.

In March 1959, Alicia felt compelled to have Nash compulsorily admitted to McLean Hospital in Boston, Massachusetts. At that time, McLean Hospital had a widely recognized psychoanalytic orientation. Some aspects of the combination of Nash's leaving his work and home environment, and his taking medication and being involved in group therapy, family discussions and individual psychoanalytic psychotherapy seemed to contribute to his improvement. Fifty days after his hospital admission, in May 1959, with the help of a lawyer, Nash formally left the hospital. At this time he was deliberately concealing his still active psychological disturbance and he later regretted his decision to cut short his hospital admission. His departure from hospital was the week after his wife Alicia gave birth to their baby.

Over the next few years, Nash's illness followed a course of remission and relapse. After leaving McLean Hospital he was able to cling to his remaining sanity for the two months following Alicia giving birth. Subsequently he went on to be repeatedly admitted to mental hospitals where anti-psychotic medication and eventually insulin coma therapy brought improvement and helped him recover some stability, but after some time he regularly relapsed. However, in the Carrier hospital, where he spent six months under a compulsory order, Nash engaged in supportive psychotherapy with a psychiatrist accompanied by a helpful control medication and after he left hospital he continued psychotherapy for two years.

He was well enough to resume work and an appointment at Princeton University was found by his colleagues, who regarded him as recovered. Then, abruptly, against his psychiatrist's advice, although he was still emotionally troubled, Nash stopped the medication and psychotherapy and decided to depart for Europe. At this time he was again imagining himself to be the Messiah who had a mission to save the world.

In August 1963, Nash was divorced by his wife, Alicia, who was both exhausted by three years of turmoil and feeling hopeless about the possibility of Nash recovering from his ongoing psychotic states. Nash lived with his mother from 1963, when he got divorced, until 1969, when his mother died. When Nash returned from the West Coast to Boston he felt depressed and lonely without his wife and his second-born son. He again made contact with his mistress, Eleonor, and his firstborn son, in whom he began to take an interest, treating him with fatherly kindness and support. Filled with a deep sense of regret Nash wrote a 'poignant and introspective' letter to his sister, referring to the struggle between his 'merciless superego' and his 'old simple' self (Nasar 1998: 317). At this time he was able to resume his Princeton teaching and research activities.

In 1965, while in Rome, some six years after the onset of the psychosis, Nash began to hear voices, in the form of telepathic phone calls from individuals. He felt they had been inserted into his brain by a central machine. Some voices he considered to come from mathematicians opposed to his ideas. He soon returned to Princeton, New Jersey where his disturbance quickly escalated and he was readmitted to Carrier Hospital, where he remained for four months, under the care of his previous psychiatrist. He left hospital only when his psychiatrist was satisfied that he was in a stable state of remission.

However, this period of relatively good mental functioning, which occurred within the stable hospital setting, did not survive when he was at home and in the less predictable environment of the outside world. Shortly after he left hospital Nash became excited, talking incessantly and making no sense. The return of his long-suppressed delusions and intense confusion may be linked with his possible refusal to take his medication as well as the stressors outside the hospital.

Once again Nash felt himself to be the saviour of the doomed world. He was preoccupied with great leaders' political behaviour, issues of morality concerning what was good and what was bad and the presence of magically good and dangerously bad numbers. Simultaneously, he felt he was receiving coded messages from the *New York Times*. He began accumulating household garbage. In an elated state, Nash travelled to the West coast and contacted 'Mr B', who found him almost incoherent, and he also visited RAND, where old colleagues refused to see him. In addition, Nash also visited his cousin who found his behaviour to be pleasant and rational, but punctuated by moments of incoherent talk.

Conventional treatment produced many remissions in Nash's symptoms but did not reach the core of his psychotic psychopathology. It was not until he had been ill for ten years (1970) that he permanently renounced the use of the anti-psychotic drugs which had reliably suppressed his hallucinatory voices.

At this point a temporary stability allowed him to begin to follow a new and different pathway.

Some conflicts underlying Nash's psychotic states

It seems that Nash originally needed to model himself on the hero of *Star Trek* (1966), hominid Mr Spock, whose super-rational approach left him feeling very alienated from humans and the emotions which arise in intimate and dependent relationships. In this armoured state, Nash had been somewhat insulated against the pain of human feelings of inferiority, loss, envy, jealousy, guilt and shame.

Humiliation over RAND's dismissal of him for police charges relating to his homosexual activity in public must have been a shock that severely threatened this emotional insulation. Overtly, the catastrophe of being rejected by RAND did not appear to have upset him severely, but there was cumulative trauma linked with further setbacks and professional disappointments.

The sudden death of Nash's father in September 1956 led his mother to write to Eleonor blaming her for being the cause of her husband's death. Nash's mother was probably also indirectly imputing the death-provoking blow to Nash himself (Nasar 1998: 209). Perhaps as a consequence, feeling his 'perfect little world' had been destroyed, Nash became overwhelmed and increasingly disturbed (Nasar 1998: 201).

Nash's marriage to Alicia demanded maturity to fulfil his responsibilities as a husband, but Nash felt a cumulative sense of rejection by Eleonor, by 'Mr B' (Nasar 1998: 182) and by his wife, Alicia, for she now had his rival, the baby, in her womb. Nash's psychotic states seem to have been partially precipitated by 'fetus envy' (Berke 1989). His wife's pregnancy seems to have revived the deeply defended and guilt-laden conflicts of his early life linked with feeling abandoned, distressed and hostile towards his sister, Martha, with whom he had to share his parents.

Present in Nash's psychotic states were unconscious feelings of love, his need for love and his possessive wish to be the only one in both the eyes of his mother and then in the eyes of 'Mr B' and his wife. It is possible that his destructive jealousy towards his new baby contained his jealousy of his sister, Martha, and his envy of peers, representing siblings. Being forced to realize that he was not mother or wife's 'number one' priority may have obliged him to confront his dyadic/rivalrous and triadic/Oedipal world of painful and complex emotional relationships. Phantasies of hatred of a mother who conceived someone other than himself may have found expression in his aggressive behaviour towards his pregnant mistress and his wife, both during their pregnancies and subsequently.

Thus a chain of events, beginning with the collapse of Nash's strategy of having a double life, had the cumulative effect of generating an increasing load of persecutory guilt. This, in turn, seems to have created a seriously unstable inner situation. As time progressed, Nash's regressed behaviour signalled the advent of other clear signs of psychosis. His elaborate protective capsule had broken open, releasing his long-banished destructive feelings and his accompanying terror of disintegration.

Nash struggled to avoid the imminent inner catastrophe by projecting the whole apocalyptic drama into the environment (Segal 1972). This unconscious emergency defensive enterprise established the content of much of his subsequent psychotic thinking. This was a typical example of a psychotic defence against the terror of total dissolution of the sense of self, a most extreme form of anxiety variously termed 'traumatic anxiety' or 'organismic panic' (Pao 1979; Volkan 1995), leading to the adoption of new, delusional, identities.

Nash began speaking about threats to world peace, warning that powers from outer space were communicating with him through encrypted messages in the newspapers. This mental process is similar to that of a psychotic person who may suddenly switch his attention to some hallucinated element in some other part of the room, thus using his mind as a muscle or bowel to rid it of the unwanted omnipotent destructiveness and intolerable psychic pain (Bion 1967; Lucas 2003). Freud (1911) saw paranoia as the consequence of projecting into the external world ideas that are incompatible with the ego. He considers the subsequent delusional elaborations as representing a 'patch over the ego', an attempt to recover meaning in a world that had become disintegrated and meaningless.

Persecutory delusions

The most terrifying consequence of this unconscious defensive struggle seems to be that Nash felt he was the victim of Communist assassins. One way to understand the extreme violence of his Communist and 'bad extraterrestrial' persecutors would be to regard them as mental structures (internal part-objects) created by projection of his infantile unconscious murderous jealousy, felt as omnipotently powerful in early life, thereby reversing the psychological reality. His omnipotent unconscious belief that his aggressive impulses of envy and jealousy were limitlessly destructive brought the dread of destroying his mother-world, and his psychotic identifications brought him terror.

Using this perspective, the identity of the victims can, in the same way, be considered as unborn babies (Meltzer 1992), rival siblings (Freud 1900) or offspring, containing the projection of unconscious invasive and polluting attacks on the maternal body of infancy (Jackson and Williams 1994; Jackson 2001; Willoughby 2001).

Manic delusions of omnipotence

Nash was both desperate to save the rival babies from the assassins and, at the same time, he was putting them at risk. Nash's state of persecution, resulting from his aggression to rival babies, was quickly joined by delusions of self-importance. In response to the terror of 'damaged babies' there arose a manic omnipotence in which Nash delusionally believed he was 'the saviour' who would prevent 'world disasters' from occurring. Once Nash began using omnipotent identifications, as in his 'becoming the Prince of Peace', he lost his capacity for the symbolic thinking that was essential to his creativity in mathematics. He was then plunged into a world of omnipotent phantasy in which he experienced his worst fears and greatest ambitions as actually taking place in the immediate present.

At other times Nash heard voices saying he had a unique mission to save the world from its impending destruction by foreign governments or alien extraterrestrial entities. He then became an agent, manically excited, pathologically triumphant and gratified by his assumed self-importance. On these occasions he sometimes became 'the Messiah', left-foot of God or the Pope. These delusional identities quickly strengthened his new psychotic equilibrium.

When his powerful unconscious phantasies were massively projected into the external world, Nash lost touch with the difference between the external world and his internal world and started writing letters to the Department of Defence, heads of state, foreign ambassadors and the Pope (Nasar 1998: 249) warning them that the world was in imminent danger of destruction by Communist Russia, or by alien extraterrestrial forces. He announced to them that he was forming an organization for promoting world peace. As the psychotic process progressed, Nash's periods of relative rationality and lucidity were increasingly interrupted by these delusional preoccupations. In his delusional existence he often fluctuated between pride at being selected by good extraterrestrial entities as the world's only hope of salvation, and terror at being in imminent danger, along with the whole world, of annihilation by Communist agents or bad extraterrestrials.

Nash was determined to convince the world leaders that the only way to avoid the coming destruction of the world was to create a world government devoted to universal brotherly love. This was in itself a sane ambition but the methods that he used to promote his cause revealed that his unconscious concern was to protect his mind, his inner world, from catastrophic destruction. The unconscious process by which Nash did this was to project his 'brotherly hatred' into the destructive forces in the world and endeavour to control it by being 'the Messiah' trying to create peace and save the world.

The search for sanctuary and the claustro-agoraphobic dilemma

In a tormented and confused state of mind, Nash's imagination took him all over the world as he sought refuge in remote places from murderous pursuers. In these imagined structures he lived for a time in one place (such as a foreign embassy, bomb shelter, prison or refugee camp), moving from one to the next. This search for a 'containing' space in which he might hope to feel safe was replaced at other times by an entrapment in an 'Inferno' (Nasar 1998: 324).

A detailed consideration of the significance of house as a symbolic derivative of mother's body, its spaces and contents can be found in Meltzer (1967) and Rey (1994). Nash's state in running away could be regarded as 'claustrophilia'; the latter state of entrapment, as 'claustrophobia'. At other times, Nash was living with a perpetual fear of annihilation, as in a state of 'agoraphobia' (Rey 1994).

Auditory hallucinations

Although hearing voices is not necessarily problematic (Romme *et al.* 1992; Johns *et al.* 2002), Nash's voices certainly were. Nash wrote a letter to his colleague sharing how frightening his voices were, saying 'My head is as if a bloated windbag with Voices which dispute within' (Nasar 1998: 328). This metaphorical description of alarming experiences demonstrated that Nash's loss of symbolic functioning was not pervasive.

When Nash began to improve, his voices exerted powerful pressure to try to convince him that his delusional 'political' thinking was sane and realistic. This phenomenon was described earlier in the chapter when referring to the work of Rosenfeld (1987: 87) and very dramatically personified in the film, *A Beautiful Mind* (Howard 2001).

Final relinquishment of medication and entry into 'The Inferno'

Nash felt that his remissions while on medication, far from being happy returns to normality were 'enforced interludes of rationality' (Nasar 1998: 295). In his address to the 1996 World Psychiatric Congress, Nash described how 'return to rationality after being irrational, can be a source of agonizing pain' (Nash 1996).

Finally, after years of mental illness, Nash discontinued anti-psychotic medication because he found it created intolerable physical side effects and also left his mental functioning at such a distressingly superficial, sluggish level that he was unable to think creatively. The medication also silenced his voices, which he found important to him. Perhaps Nash valued them as friendly companions in his lonely isolation but he also believed that they had a point of view that he respected. At the same time he was progressively opposing them in a scientific manner, labelling them as 'delusional hypotheses'.

Without the medication, Nash subsequently entered a long period of confusion marked by bursts of delusional thinking, auditory hallucinations and a recurrent terror, in which he felt he was inhabiting a life which he described as hell, an 'Inferno, a purgatory, a polluted heaven', 'a decayed rotting house infested by rats and termites and other vermin' (Nasar 1998: 324).

'Repentingness oscilloscope' – moving towards depressive concern

Some ten years after the onset of his psychosis, although still dominated by his psychotic thinking, Nash developed ideas about the possibility of constructing an oscilloscope that could display a 'repentingness function' (Nasar 1998: 326). This, together with the development of a painful sense of loneliness and pining for the people who loved him and who were now lost (his male intimates, his wife, by enforced separation followed by divorce, his mistress by her disillusionment with him), suggests a remarkable increase in integration, characteristic of the 'threshold' of the depressive position (Meltzer 1967).

Consequently, Nash developed a sense of regret, remorse, sorrow, a sense of personal responsibility and desire to make amends characteristic of depressive concern. This increased maturity led to the attenuation of his 'merciless' superego, prompting persecutory guilt and terror (Rey 1979, 1994; Steiner 1993b), and fostered a more normal sense of guilt, a tolerance for painful feelings of shame, humiliation and damaged self-esteem and to a new capacity for concern for fellow sufferers. This creative achievement found expression in Nash's subsequent commitment to promoting an improved, psychotherapeutically based treatment of fellow-sufferers.

'Self-cure' and a return to sanity

Over two decades Nash's capacity for rational thinking gradually returned. His creativeness and his claim for self-cure can be compared with that of August Strindberg, whose story *The Inferno* (Strindberg 1979) is an essentially autobiographical account of his paranoid psychosis (Lidz 1964; Cullberg 2006). Still remaining unprotected by medication, Nash had sufficient sanity to return for part of each day to Princeton University's mathematics department. In this period he became a familiar eccentric whose bizarre behaviour led him to be referred to as the 'Phantom of Fine Hall' (Nasar 1998: 332) for he was preoccupied with apparently meaningless numerical calculations.

A colleague later recorded that during this time Nash was actually 'pretty sane' as though he had seemingly undergone a transformation in personality. The colleague suggested that Nash's arrogance and obvious pleasure in humiliating others had disappeared. In fact, said his colleague, Nash seemed 'nice, gentle, lots of fun to talk to' and 'this old ego stuff was gone' (Nasar 1998: 317). Nasar (1998) suggests that Nash emerged from his psychosis as a transformed personality, more emotionally mature and free of his previous arrogance and other disagreeable personality traits.

When Nash's mother died, his ex-wife, Alicia, took him back into her care. Her loving concern seems to have enabled him to slowly recover his capacity for normal social relationships and resume both previously lost friendships and creative work of a high order.

In 1994 Nash shared a Nobel Prize in economics with two others. His prize-winning work on game theory had been accomplished before his first breakdown. The famous 'Nash Equilibrium' demonstrated for the first time how non-cooperating players – at individual, group and national levels – might share benefits, by empathically reflecting on the motives of competitors, rather than pursuing the destructive 'win–lose' of 'zero-sum' games.

At the time of publication of *A Beautiful Mind* (Nasar 1998), Nash was living with his wife and apparently functioning normally. He had restored his relationship with his firstborn son, John. Nash and his wife were also occupied in caring for Nash's second son, John, who, after an initially brilliant career as a young mathematician, had had a psychotic breakdown somewhat similar to his father's.

Since his own recovery, Nash has lectured widely about severe mental illness, pointing out the limitations of the exclusive use of medication in treatment and campaigning for the importance of a psychotherapeutic approach in the treatment of psychosis. In 1996 he delivered a memorable lecture at the World Congress of Psychiatry entitled 'Rational thinking: is it easy or hard?' (Nash 1996). In an interview, Nash (2002b) made a remarkable, albeit controversial, claim that if his life had been different, he would have become a leader in the field of psychotherapy! In view of this respect for psychotherapy, one can wonder why Nash frequently discontinued his own psychotherapy.

Hope, relief and new beginnings

Many individuals suffering from psychotic states of a paranoid nature reach a stable adjustment by recognizing that their behaviour is socially unacceptable and keeping their delusional state hidden. They seem to function relatively normally. A majority of individuals suffering from psychoses will achieve varying degrees of remission, sometimes amounting to permanent recovery (Harding 2002). In the right circumstances, for example with access to 'need-adapted' or 'Open Dialogue' approaches (Alanen 1997; Seikkula *et al.* 2011), it will be found that people with a first episode of psychosis may require little or no medication. In some cases remission may, from a psychoanalytic perspective, represent a sealing-over of psychopathology with greater or lesser degrees of stabilization, and in others a working-through to a higher level of integration and maturity, perhaps even spontaneously (Rey 1994).

By renouncing the symptom-relieving medication Nash may have deliberately confronted the worst of his psychotic experience, a move necessary to allow the core of his disturbance to be reached and for the eventual resumption of the arrested growth process. Whether or not this was the case, during his crises it seems to have been the loyalty and devotion of Nash's wife, and the remarkable tolerance of his professional colleagues who provided something resembling a therapeutic community for him – a containing environment which allowed him to take the pathway towards recovery. Nash has subsequently claimed that his recovery was achieved largely due to the support of his loving wife and by his own intellectual efforts rather than through the help of medication.

We do not know whether the group and individual psychotherapy that Nash received played a part in the resolution of his unconscious problems. What we do know, however, is that over a very long period of time he gradually succeeded in opposing the seductive and tyrannical intimidations of the hallucinated omnipotent elements in his mind (De Masi 1997), slowly regained his lost capacity for reality testing, and recovered the normal use of numerical symbols, the 'ultra-logical thinking' necessary for functioning in the abstract world of mathematics (Nash 1996).

Nash certainly seems to have become a happier and more mature, loving person. His 'recovery' could be regarded as a 'discovery' of new aspects of his personality, a re-growth of development that was arrested in his childhood. This may be considered to be true despite the fact that he still sometimes hears his voices and has occasional paranoid thoughts. Reflecting on the meaning of 'recovery', Nash (1996) observed: 'Can a musician be said to have recovered if he cannot compose great works? I would not treat myself as recovered if I could not produce good things in my work.'

A psychotic episode may indeed, for some individuals, represent a 'second chance' to gather projected aspects of themselves and thus recover some emotional capacities which would further their previously arrested capacity for mentalization (Bateman and Fonagy 2010), emotional growth and creativity. Laing (1967) considered that, for some individuals, psychotic states of mind may be considered as creating an enforced journey into the inner world, where inner and outer realities are confused, but which, if successfully negotiated, can ultimately be seen as a healing process.

Rey (1994: 14–15) suggested that a frankly psychotic episode might be necessary to return to the point of bifurcation between normal and abnormal development – a regressive dissociation of parts that have become assembled in a faulty way. At this point, the growth of a paralysed affectivity, previously enslaved and rigidly controlled, may be resumed and the edifice reconstructed. This process chiefly depends on the capacity of the patient's mental apparatus for symbolic transformation and whether or not the patient has developed the capacity to integrate some of his loving and hostile feelings in such a way that he can have concern regarding another's well-being and take responsibility for aggression which may cause damage to 'the other'. This is what is described as depressive concern for the other.

What if?...

It is possible to speculate that at the early depressive stage of his illness Nash might have been accessible to experienced psychoanalytic psychotherapy if it had been available. Successful psychotherapy would have involved the working-through of the dangerous underlying pathogenic conflicts in the safe containment of a therapeutic transference, a major undertaking that would require great skill and experience. A less ideal outcome would be a less intensive involvement that might have led to the reduction of the severity of the pathogenic psychopathology and the modification of the persecutory superego that was causing him such suffering. Such an outcome would have recaptured the opportunity that he subsequently regretted having lost, at the onset of his illness, when he discharged himself from McLean Hospital.

Recovery and after

Whatever human problems remain for him, it is clear that Nash has emerged from his long ordeal with important new insights and with new stability. It is impressive to see how he has described the residue of his intra-psychic upheavals. Nash feels fairly certain that he won't suffer a relapse because he has experienced profound changes in his mental processes. He indicates:

> it's like a continuous process rather than just waking up from a dream ... when I dream ... it sometimes happens that I go back to the system of delusions that's typical of how I was ... and then I wake, and then I'm rational again.
>
> (Nasar 1998: 389)

The implication of this type of experience is that Nash has acquired a working channel of communication with his unconscious phantasy life and has found what seems to be a new capacity to express his preoccupations in symbolic form in his dream life. Nevertheless, he still shows inner vulnerability when he describes how the system of delusions visit him in his dream life.

Some interdisciplinary and social implications

When asked his views about the evaluation of recovery from mental illness Nash remarked that there was a great tendency to accept rather low standards for recovery. He felt that generally accepted criteria for recovery may have an essentially economic basis:

> If the 'case' becomes inexpensive for society and/or the family to manage then it is classed as a recovery even though any special abilities or talents of the individual may have been lost and the lifestyle of the person may have become transformed to a more limited form, for example like the pattern of life of a monk or a nun.
>
> (Nash 1996)

It is of interest at this point to note that an eminent colleague has considered Nash's work subsequent to his breakdown to be far more rich and important than his earlier economic-political work, which the colleague considers to be an ingenious, but not surprising, application of well-known methods (Milnor 1998).

Psychoanalytic theories of psychosis and treatment approaches have advanced greatly since the time of Freud's early groundbreaking formulations. Psychoanalytically based psychotherapy with the right therapist, in the right situation for a selected person suffering from a psychotic disorder, can be highly effective (Oldham and Russakoff 1987; Robbins 1993; Lotterman 1996 and 2015 (in press); Jackson and Williams 1994). An individual who is in a severely regressed psychotic state requires the availability of specialized hospital resources or community-based psychiatric care in which psychological and biological factors and treatment requirements can be carefully assessed and appropriate interventions rationally planned. Some very promising contemporary approaches provide psychoanalytically informed 'need-adapted' treatment strategies, incorporating an option of individual psychotherapy and psychotherapeutic support for families (Pylkkanen 1989; Alanen 1997; Seikkula *et al.* 2011; Martindale *et al.* 2000; Cullberg 2002). Current socio-economic pressures prioritize brief therapies, but research shows that longer term effectiveness comes through longer term approaches (Leichsenring 2011).

The exposure of the psychotic core in the course of psychotherapy brings risks, as does medication, which is why the skill of the individual therapist and the quality of the psychiatric supporting network is so vital. However, under appropriate conditions at least some individuals suffering from psychotic states can safely work through conflicts in either intensive psychotherapy or psychoanalysis.

Conclusion

This essay might well be considered as an unwarranted intrusion into the private life of a highly respected public figure. Although some less admirable aspects of his personality have been brought to public view by his biographer, this essay speculates about deeper aspects of Nash's life, both external and internal, as portrayed in books and film. However much John Nash's actual experience may diverge from the foregoing speculative pathways, his achievement of a major remission is not in doubt.

The chapter has been an attempt to illustrate the ways that psychoanalysis can add depth and meaning to the conventional psychiatric understanding of psychotic illness. Whether or not the conclusions reached about the fictional Nash are relevant for the person of the real John Forbes Nash, they are certainly relevant to many people suffering from psychosis.

Note

This is the original essay by Murray Jackson which was previously extended and edited by Paul Williams and printed in Williams, P. (2010) *Invasive Objects: Minds Under Siege*. New York: Routledge, pp. 107–145. Paul Williams has given permission for the re-publication of the original essay.

Figure 2 Vaslav Nijinsky.

2

VASLAV NIJINSKY
Living for the eyes of the other

Murray Jackson

Prologue

Vaslav Nijinsky is widely acknowledged as one of the greatest male ballet dancers of all time. Between the ages of 18 and 28 he enjoyed a spectacularly colourful and successful career as principal dancer in the Ballets Russes, which had been recently founded by the impresario Serge Diaghilev. During these ten years he achieved world fame as a dancer and choreographer, introducing an original system of choreography and composing several ballets. The first ballets, *Jeux* and *Afternoon of a Faun* (to the music of Debussy) and *The Rite of Spring* (to Stravinsky's music), were so foreign to tradition that they caused uproar when first performed, and Debussy and Stravinsky at first thoroughly disliked them. Dancers, trained in the traditional academic style, found it hard to adapt to his spectacular innovations, which often required them to dance in an aggressive, even violent and erotic manner. Their task was made even more difficult by Nijinsky's obvious lack of empathy and poor communication skills. Ever since his adolescence he had shown traits of extreme introspectiveness, aloofness and instability of mood.

In 1917, at the age of 28, following a remarkably precipitate marriage, the rupture of his relationship with Diaghilev and the disastrous failure of a tour of North America under his direction, Nijinsky's spectacular career was cut short dramatically by the onset of a severe psychotic illness. This was a terrible catastrophe, which disabled him for the rest of his life. Treatment brought only temporary improvements and, despite periods of apparent social adjustment, relative calm and moments of happiness, he never fully recovered.

Shakespearean in its drama and emotional depth, Vaslav Nijinsky's life encompassed the extremes of ecstatic success and the horrors of a psychotic illness of a severity rarely, if ever, seen today. This chapter will describe Nijinsky's creative activities as a dancer, his personal relationships and his psychotic illness. In particular, there will be a discussion regarding the nature of Nijinsky's mental illness, the factors that precipitated it and the likely reasons for his failure to recover. His illness was rooted in emotionally traumatic experiences in his early life, which led to a pathological disturbance of personality, a predisposition to a future breakdown and a tendency to inexplicable, often bizarre and violent jealous rages. A psychoanalytic perspective on the regressive and creative moments in Nijinsky's will form part of the narrative.

Writings on Nijinsky

Since his death, the story of Nijinsky's astonishing success has been exhaustively documented by innumerable writers, but the first serious psychological study of his madness was made during his lifetime when, in 1946, the Jungian analyst Karl Abenheimer made a detailed examination of Nijinsky's diary. But the first, and last, comprehensive study after Nijinsky's death in 1950 was made by psychiatrist Peter Ostwald in 1991. His book *Vaslav Nijinsky: A Leap into Madness* is a monumental work, a detailed biography of his life from birth to death, an authoritative and painstaking psychiatric commentary which provides a convincing psychoanalytic explanation of the illness.

Helped by cooperative efforts of Nijinsky's family and friends and the nurses who looked after Nijinsky, Ostwald researched his subject in a remarkably comprehensive way. He was also able to search the detailed medical records of Nijinsky's 30-year illness. Ostwald almost seemed to have left nothing more for any future psycho-biographer to add. However, it seems important to reconsider some of his views in the light of the subsequent publication of Nijinsky's uncensored diary, to which Ostwald did not have access, and advances in contemporary psychoanalytic theory. Personal access to Nijinsky's family also provides the opportunity for this chapter to present a slightly different perspective to some of Ostwald's conclusions.

There are two versions of Nijinsky's diary, the first, *The Diary of Vaslav Nijinsky*, produced by his wife, Romola, in 1936, was followed by a revised English translation from the Russian by Kyril Fitz Lyon, edited by the psychologist and dance critic Joan Acocella in 1999. The first version was a great success and helped Romola promote the legend of 'Nijinsky the God' but Romola had deleted almost half of Nijinsky's writing and presented an idealized and highly sanitized account both of their relationship and of his psychosis. The 1999 Acocella version of Nijinsky's diary was unabridged and provided detailed information about the onset and course of Nijinsky's psychosis, some of which would have been unknown at the publication of Ostwald's book (1999). My other important sources of information are personal discussions with the daughter, Tamara Nijinsky, and the granddaughter, Kinga Nijinsky Gaspers. Relevant books by Romola and his sister Bronislava also form a background to this chapter.

PART 1 NIJINSKY: A BIOGRAPHICAL SKETCH

Nijinsky's early life

Nijinsky was of Russian nationality, born in Kiev on 28 February 1889. He considered himself to be Polish, for he was the second son of Polish parents who, as very successful professional dancers, were touring in Russia with their own ballet company. Nijinsky's father, Thomas, was renowned for his ability as a dancer and, in particular, he was known for his capacity to make great leaps on the stage. Thomas bullied Nijinsky's mother, Eleonore, until she was forced into an unloving marriage with him. Her own mother had married in similar circumstances. Eleonore, like her husband, was a gifted dancer, but her devotion to her three children limited her professional development. Nijinsky's father's demanding behaviour and violent outbursts of temper provoked great fear and misery in both Nijinsky's mother and her children.

Eleonore had already had a tumultuous life for, when she was around seven, Nijinsky's maternal grandmother, in a state of pathological mourning for her husband, starved herself to death. Being deprived of parents must have contributed to Eleonore's emotional fragility and incapacities as a mother. She experienced tendencies towards helpless depression or explosive rage. Because artistic directors of dance companies were reluctant to engage dancers encumbered by children, Eleonore, on several occasions tried to abort her children and/or kill herself by jumping from high places. This may have enhanced her depression and despair and contributed to her guilt. Despite all this, Eleonore bore three children within five years and managed to maintain her dancing career.

The three Nijinsky children were subject to both parents' extreme tempers and emotional neglect. The eldest son was Stanislav, followed two years later by Vaslav, and four years later by his beloved sister, Bronislava. At the age of four, Stanislav, a hyperactive child like his brother, fell through an open window and sustained severe brain damage. This accident, which led to Stanislav's frequent outbursts of rage, affected the whole family profoundly. When Vaslav, Stanislav's younger brother, won a scholarship to the school of the Imperial Theatres, Stanislav became even more violent. He was furious with his mother and frequently screamed in a jealous fury at his brother and sister when they were playing together. His violence became so serious that, on the advice of a psychiatrist, he was sent to live with his father. While staying with his father, Stanislav was left in the care of a couple, who apparently treated him badly. His reaction to this was so uncontrollably violent that he had to be admitted first to a sanatorium, and shortly afterwards to a Russian mental asylum. It seems that while in the mental asylum Stanislav was a placid, rather backward child who lived happily enough with his peers. It will never be known whether Stanislav, with his postulated brain damage playing a contributory part, had suffered from a psychotic illness similar to that of his brother, Vaslav. Stanislav remained in the mental hospital until, during the 1917 Russian revolution, he died, at age 30.

The sister, Bronislava, known as Nijinska, two years younger than Vaslav and deeply attached to him, eventually found fame in her own right both as a dancer in the Ballets Russes and as a choreographer. She had the stability, verbal fluency, capacity to do well academically at school and the organizational ability that Vaslav lacked. She was probably the only woman, apart from his mother, whom he could truly love. We shall later consider how the likely unconscious dissociation of inevitable negative feelings of sibling rivalry, allowed this highly creative 'twinship' to flourish.

His parents' instability and his intra-generational traumatic family history, which included his grandmother's pathological mourning and suicide by starvation, may have promoted Vaslav's similar tendencies towards instability as well as his phantasies of starvation and death. All three children were natural dancers and took to dancing as soon as they could walk. However, all three were handicapped to some extent in their social and emotional development by growing up in a family in which neither parent was able to provide a stable, trustworthy emotional base, a loving environment or an atmosphere where intimate family ties were established. The requirement to be on stage as a dancer and please the public always came first. Although creating a stable family life often seemed secondary, Bronislava stated that the siblings were happy together and loved their dancing.

Early stages of Nijinsky's dance career

When Vaslav was four years old, he began his professional career, dancing in his parents' company, which was always moving from one town to another. When Vaslav was seven, his father, an unfaithful womanizer, fell in love with another dancer in his troupe. When she became pregnant, the father abandoned his family, leaving them with no means of support. Vaslav was deeply affected by the loss of his admired and loved father, whom he also hated and feared. Vaslav's father was particularly important to him for he had inspired him to dance and taught him so much.

Eleonore's plight as a single parent of three led her to a considerable emotional, as well as financial, dependency on Vaslav. Although she earned a precarious living by managing a boarding house in St Petersburg, the family lived a very hard life. At the age of nine, Vaslav was accepted at the Russian Imperial Ballet School, where his exceptional talent combined with his poor capacity for empathic communication led him to be bullied by his envious fellow students. On one occasion they tricked him into a dangerous test of his dancing capacities, which caused him to fall heavily. As a result he sustained severe abdominal injuries, was detained in hospital for several days and did not return to school for several months. He made a complete recovery, narrowly escaping the fate of his brother, Stanislav, whose accidental injury had caused permanent brain damage.

From the beginning of his training, Nijinsky's brilliance was noticed and fostered by some outstanding teachers who gave him special attention. Through their tutelage his dancing capacity for mimicry and emotional expressiveness was enhanced. In the spring of 1906, at age 17, Nijinsky graduated from the Imperial Ballet School in St Petersburg. At this time his poverty came to an end as he began performing solo roles as the leading dancer with a tenured contract with the Marinsky theatre.

Approved and supported by the Tsar, at that time ballet was flourishing. Movement from the formal 'Apollonian' to a 'Dionysiac' approach to dancing was stirring: tutus and pointes were replaced by focus on bodily movement, exposure of flesh and passion. Isadora Duncan was the pioneer of this revolution and the influence of eurhythmics and the acting methods of Konstantin Stanislavsky were spreading. The time was ripe for Nijinsky's experiments.

The following year he was noticed by a wealthy aristocrat, Prince Pavel Lvov, with whom he began a homosexual affair. Lvov treated Vaslav and his family with kindness and generosity, and at first exercised a benign paternal influence on his protégé. This form of conduct among wealthy bisexual and homosexual balletomanes was considered quite acceptable at the time, and many homosexual and heterosexual performers had their lives and careers fostered by such wealthy patronage.

Lvov's kindness was a godsend to Nijinsky's mother who saw Lvov as the father her son had never had. For a long time she had been worried that he would turn into a womanizer like his father and, prophetically, she repeatedly warned him not to get involved with 'loose' women because of the danger of acquiring venereal disease. When Nijinsky declared his love for a young ballerina his mother was convinced that if it led to marriage it would simply repeat the misery of her own disastrous one. Feeling that a homosexual relationship with the Prince was much to be preferred, Nijinsky's mother quickly put a stop to Nijinsky's budding relationship with the ballerina.

The relationship with Lvov, which lasted almost a year, helped Nijinsky to begin to grow into a more mature and stable personality. Lvov introduced him to high society, helping him overcome his shyness, dress stylishly and become more self-confident. Nijinsky later recorded that he loved Lvov because he knew that Lvov loved him. But Lvov soon tired of him as a lover and passed him on to his friends who introduced him to the underworld of prostitution and gambling in St Petersburg. Nijinsky, now bisexual, became infected with gonorrhoea, which lasted several months. Later he felt disgust at his homosexual activities. Lvov treated him with his habitual kindness, behaviour that led Bronislava to remark that Lvov behaved like a loving parent to them all. In this sense Lvov was extremely helpful, representing the good father that Nijinsky and his family had lacked. On the other hand, in abandoning Nijinsky to a shallow and degenerate world, Lvov proved to be a negative influence. This abandonment must have wounded Nijinsky deeply, reviving the traumatic memory of his father's desertion. The inability to bear the hurt and depression linked with this and other losses seemed to promote Nijinsky's excited, manic states of mind.

By this time Nijinsky had already come to the attention of Serge Diaghilev who, recognizing his prodigious talent, engaged him in the Ballets Russes, and began their ten-year homosexual relationship with fateful consequences. Diaghilev was a brilliant impresario, a cultured and artistically sensitive man, often regarded as arrogant but selflessly committed to the creation of beautiful works of art. His mother had died when he was three months old from infection consequent to his difficult birth. When Diaghilev was two his father remarried a highly intelligent and cultured woman who encouraged his artistic development. Upon his father's remarriage, Diaghilev had little contact with his father, a cavalry officer whose extreme incompetence and lack of interest in the great estate led to bankruptcy and impoverishment of the family. When Diaghilev was 18 he was left with the financial responsibility for the whole family, including his two younger step-brothers. A small inheritance left him by his mother allowed him to continue at university and to begin to earn his living as an art critic. He shared Nijinsky's experience of an inadequate father.

In the first two years of his relationship with Diaghilev, Nijinsky was reported to have been ill on several occasions, once being hospitalized with an attack of typhoid fever, from which he had already suffered in his childhood. However, it is not clear to what extent other disturbances, which earned him his first psychiatric diagnosis – acute cerebrospinal neurasthenia (Ostwald 1991: 41) – were stress-related, neurotic or excuses for being clandestinely with Diaghilev. The directors of the Imperial Theatres regarded Nijinsky's frequent absences from rehearsals as truancy. His insistence on appearing in *Giselle* in what they regarded as an indecent costume was the last straw, and they dismissed him in January 1911. Knowing that he would fare better with Diaghilev, Nijinsky accepted the dismissal and resigned. This debacle suited Diaghilev very well, and he exploited it by announcing the formation of the Ballets Russes as an independent company, at first rehearsing, and sometimes premiering, in Monte Carlo.

Nijinsky thoroughly enjoyed the high life, which brought him great public admiration and the identity of unique unrivalled star, which he craved. His personal feelings about Diaghilev were complex, and it is not clear whether he felt any sexual enjoyment, love or gratitude towards his benefactor. With the onset of his breakdown Nijinsky kept a notebook, which we shall later consider, in which he wrote that he felt increasing fear and hatred towards Diaghilev and only acquiesced to his sexual requirements to save his mother from starvation. Although Diaghilev had, as did Lvov, a benign paternal influence on Nijinsky, the relationship was to prove very much more complicated. Diaghilev was much more deeply committed to Nijinsky both sexually and emotionally than Lvov, and he remained so for over ten years.

The golden years of 'Nijinsky the God'

Under Diaghilev's masterly and imaginative direction, and Nijinsky's brilliantly daring and original innovations, the years 1909 to 1919 were to see an amazing flowering of creativity. The Ballets Russes became known as the world's leading dance company, a position it retained until it was disbanded when Diaghilev died in Venice in 1929.

Nijinsky's self-confidence increased as he continued to receive rapturous acclaim in the roles that made him world famous. In Michel Fokine's great exotic ballet *Schéhérazade*, set to the music of Rimsky-Korsakov, Nijinsky played the erotic role of the Golden Slave with such a passion and conviction that the costume designer Alexandre Benoit was moved to pronounce it as 'fiendishly agile, feminine and wholly terrifying' (Buckle 1975: 160), while an enraptured Marcel Proust declared, 'I never saw anything so beautiful' (Eksteins 2000: 26). It was Nijinsky's performance in this and Fokine's other masterpiece, *Le Carnaval*, that established his worldwide fame.

Developing his own innovativeness

As his self-confidence grew, Nijinsky began to create his own ballets. His first ballet, *Jeux*, was not well received and did not survive for long. Because the theme of the flirtations between three young men in the 'game' of sex was considered to be too frankly homoerotic for the audience of the day, its meaning was camouflaged by two of the male roles being danced by women while the third 'boy' was to be danced by Nijinsky. He later described it as a commentary on Diaghilev's preference for sex with two boys at the same time.

The unconcealed eroticism involving masturbation in his second ballet, *Afternoon of a Faun*, shocked and disgusted the audience. Even more of a disaster was the *Rite of Spring*, premiered exactly a year later, whose primitive violence and sexuality astonishingly provoked the first-night audience to riot until they were calmed by the intervention of the police. After a few performances in Paris and London, Diaghilev withdrew it. Whether he welcomed the publicity, as Stravinsky believed, or was alarmed by the violent public response, Diaghilev continued to support Nijinsky and appointed him chief choreographer. When Nijinsky was appointed, his elder, Michel Fokine resigned from the Ballets Russes in a rage.

Diaghilev soon realized that Nijinsky's impatience and inability to empathize with his dancers was putting great strain on them, and so Diaghilev engaged Marie Rambert to work with him. She found that the dancers were finding it very difficult and painful to adapt to the new postures that Nijinsky was forcing them to adopt. The dancers had to unlearn years of classical training. Nijinsky's moodiness, overbearing manner and childish temper tantrums were also causing discord in the ballet. Nijinsky's promotion to ballet master when Fokine defected had given Nijinsky more responsibility than he could manage. He experienced enormous personal strain as he found himself unable to exercise a calm, containing authority over the whole company of dancers.

Around this time Nijinsky turned against Diaghilev's various sexual practices, including having sex with two boys at once, which had begun to disgust him, and to arouse feelings of shame about himself. Finding sufficient courage, Nijinsky decided to lock the door between their adjoining rooms, hired rooms in a small Paris hotel, began to seek out prostitutes and became increasingly aggressive towards his master. Nijinsky writes:

> I began to hate him quite openly, and once I pushed him in a street in Paris. I pushed him because I wanted to show him I was not afraid of him. Diaghilev hit me with his cane because I wanted to leave him.
> (Nijinsky 1999: 110)

Infuriated, Diaghilev complained to Bronislava: 'This is the end. I must part with Nijinsky! ... Me, Diaghilev, to be insulted by this young man. He is no longer a boy!' (Nijinsky 1981: 472).

Search for an independent self

In abandoning his passivity towards Diaghilev and opposing him with such aggressiveness Nijinsky may have been unconsciously motivated by the search for a strong father whom he could oppose, a father who could understand him and his right to be properly treated while at the same time containing his adolescent son's aggressive behaviour

In July 1913, Diaghilev's patience was exhausted, and fearing Nijinsky's reaction he asked Bronislava to inform him that he was reinstating Fokine who would take over the choreography of Nijinsky's future ballets. Nijinsky received the news that he would be replaced by his discarded father figure, Fokine, with rage and utter bewilderment. His sister realized the seriousness of the situation and Nijinsky accepted his sister's advice to apologize to Diaghilev for insulting him.

The first tour to South America

Diaghilev accepted Nijinsky's apology and put him in charge of the choreography of the Ballet's first overseas tour, a two-month engagement in South America. Diaghilev decided not to join Nijinsky on the tour and did not even come to see the boat off when it sailed, in August 1913. He would come to regret his decision deeply because Nijinsky, escaping from his watchful eye, made a sudden impulsive marriage, which was to change the whole course of his life.

Romola, Nijinsky's future wife

Romola Pulszky, a beautiful Hungarian socialite, was the younger of two daughters of wealthy and cultured parents. Her mother, Emilia, was Hungary's most famous actress, a glamorous star of the Budapest theatre, and her father, an eminent politician, was the director of the Hungarian National Gallery of Art. Favoured by both parents over her sister, Tessa, who was eight years her elder, Romola adored her father, who spoiled and pampered her. Her parents' marriage was an unhappy one and came to a tragic ending. When Romola was five, her father, Charles Pulszky, was arrested on suspicion of embezzling government funds when in London buying paintings for the Gallery. Seeking to avoid further scandal he moved to London, where he had been educated. His wife refused to join him and he vanished, leaving his family and wealth behind him. Three years later he wrote two letters from Australia, the first announced his state of bankruptcy and deep depression. This was followed by a suicide note, saying farewell to his family, apologizing for his failures, and declaring his intention to commit suicide. He shot himself with a revolver allegedly given to him at the time of his disgrace in Budapest by friends who had encouraged him to do the honourable thing.

This tragic event must have inflicted a huge emotional trauma on his adoring daughter, Romola, with damaging effects on her developing personality. She later came to hate her stepfather and to envy her glamorous mother and her vivacious, musically talented sister Tessa. Romola only developed some grudging sense of gratitude towards Tessa when later she supported Romola in her adult life. As an adolescent Romola coped with her hostility by adopting a façade of cold and unapproachable beauty. Her unhappy restlessness led to her being sent abroad to improve her education. She spent time in England, France and Germany, becoming fluent in all three languages. At the age of 20, drawn by the prospect of wealth and the prestige of marrying into the nobility, she became engaged to a social-climbing Baron, whom she discovered was both homosexual and deceitful.

When Romola first saw Nijinsky dance in Budapest she instantly fell in love, with the same intense adoration that she had felt for her father, and she resolved to marry him. She broke her engagement to the Baron and began a determined pursuit. With no talent for dancing, Romola took lessons to make herself more acceptable to Nijinsky, who initially dismissed her as a dilettante. This did not impede Romola, for she insidiously attached herself to the Ballet, eventually joining them on their voyage to South America.

Having lost the unconditional love and support of Diaghilev, Nijinsky was in a very vulnerable emotional state, and must have hoped that Romola would provide the infantile adoration he craved, and without which he could not function. As he later stated in his diary in 1919, 'I am the God who dies when he is not loved!' (Nijinsky 2006: 152).

Romola set about seducing him, and succeeded with spectacular effect. Nijinsky responded with a declaration of his love and, despite Diaghilev's cables imploring him to stop, the couple were married in Buenos Aires soon after their arrival. The ballet company was both dismayed and astonished. Only Bronislava approved, hoping that it would encourage Nijinsky to behave in a heterosexual way and finally lead him to forgive her for provoking his jealousy. Heartbroken, enraged and humiliated, Diaghilev swore vengeance.

Nijinsky quickly realized that he had made a disastrous mistake in his choice of wife. He knew that Romola could never become the dancer he had wanted her to be, nor could she ever love him the way he wished. In the first place, she could not speak Polish or Russian and they could only communicate by body language, pantomime or with his rudimentary and halting French. Both were emotionally immature and driven by their own self-centredness. Nijinsky was searching for the infantile adoration he had lost, while Romola was looking for someone as glamorous as her mother, an imposing ornament with which she could repair her fragile self-esteem by making her feel more important and valuable. She also wished to find a partner who was more reliable than her father. Disappointed in his wife, Nijinsky withdrew emotionally and sexually, only recovering some sense of warmth when he learned that Romola was pregnant. Shocked by this entirely unwanted pregnancy, Romola prevailed on her mother to arrange an abortion; however, Nijinsky, showing uncharacteristic solicitude, halted this plan.

In December 1913 the tour ended and shortly before the final performances of *Carnaval* in which he was to star in the part of the harlequin, Nijinsky insisted on taking a day off as he was worried about pregnant Romola, who was feeling very unwell. Despite the fact that there was no understudy for the part he refused to waiver in his resolve to have the day off work. This involved a conflictual power struggle with the distraught manager. For Diaghilev this was the last straw, an act of high treason. Consequently, in December 1913, Nijinsky received Diaghilev's telegram from Paris announcing his instant dismissal. At first bewildered and incredulous, he appealed in vain to Stravinsky for help, saying that if Diaghilev was really refusing to work with him then everything was lost.

Nijinsky discovered that his dismissal from the company was final when he returned to Europe to find that Diaghilev had persuaded Fokine to return and replace him. Nijinsky experienced being outcast from the Ballet Company as an unqualified disaster for both him and his wife, Romola. Romola was also extremely distraught since she saw her hopes for a glittering social career dashed. Her husband was thrown into the position of having to find work at a time of imminent war and few opportunities for employment. With the help of his sister, Nijinsky accepted a two-month engagement in vaudeville at a music hall in London, something he had previously sworn never to do. Despite the fact that this sort of work was acceptable to many dancers, including his occasional dancing partner, the great Anna Pavlova, for Nijinsky it represented serious humiliation. Vaudeville provoked his sense of failure in losing both a prime position in the Ballets Russes and another father-figure, Diaghilev, who was the promoter of his success as a dancer and choreographer.

Working in vaudeville proved to be an ignominious disaster. After the first two weeks in the music hall Nijinsky was so anxious that he responded to others' demands with hysterical temper tantrums. He raged against his sister, almost came to blows with his supporting male dancer and insulted the owner of the music hall. When a stage-hand made a harmless flirtatious gesture towards Romola, Nijinsky attacked him violently, knocking him down. Nijinsky recovered some thoughtfulness briefly and, in a panic, he confessed to Marie Rambert that he had nearly killed the man. His dancing lost its spark, and his restrictive eating habits changed dramatically. He developed a ravenous appetite, voraciously eating and greedily drinking too much wine. He suddenly became incredibly weak and it was three days before he could resume his dancing. On his return Nijinsky was summarily dismissed by the exasperated owner on the grounds of breach of contract. This calamity was a serious financial blow. Nijinsky disbanded his troupe. Being very concerned about her brother Bronislava talked to Diaghilev and arranged for Nijinsky to resume working with him in Russia.

The doctor who was summoned considered Nijinsky's state as a 'nervous breakdown', the result of overwork, and suggested, like the previous doctor, that Nijinsky had cerebrospinal neurasthenia. Nijinsky's symptoms of anxiety, fatigue, depression and preoccupation with disturbing bodily sensations, were usually labelled as hypochondria or hysteria during Freud's time. Freud suggested that such symptoms were sometimes caused by unconscious aggressive and sexual impulses blocked by moral considerations. Later in the chapter there will be a consideration of how Nijinsky's physical and psychological regression suggested a vulnerability to much more serious psychological problems.

Despite his depressive mood, Nijinsky accepted an invitation to dance in Madrid in the presence of the King and Queen of Spain. When his performance was reported to have been very successful his depressive mood temporarily lifted. Then, hoping to see Diaghilev he attended a performance in Paris, only to learn that Diaghilev was absent. Nijinsky also heard a rumour that Diaghilev had mocked his downfall.

The birth of a daughter, Kyra

While searching for work, in May 1914 Nijinsky was offered a contract with the Paris Opéra, but he felt too anxious and depressed to accept it. Soon afterwards his wife went into labour and, to his bitter disappointment gave birth to a girl, Kyra, rather than the boy they were confidently anticipating. There then followed a dramatic scene on the obstetric ward. Romola, who had begun to resent her mother's preference for her sister Tessa, refused to allow her mother to hold the baby. When her stepfather objected to Romola's refusal, Nijinsky once more lost control of himself and attacked him.

Shortly afterwards Nijinsky realized that the baby, now named, was unusually attractive. Suddenly his bitterness about his life was transformed by his adoration of Kyra. Romola later observed that the baby had a striking resemblance to her father and that 'before long they were so closely attached to each other that the child seemed like an extension of the father. The father lost himself in the child ... the world ceased to exist for him' (Ostwald 1991: 126).

Enchanted by his daughter, Nijinsky accompanied her everywhere, watched over her in her sleep, helped the wet nurse with the feeding, and when the nurse left he completely took over the bottle feeding, an arrangement that suited Romola well for she seemed to be a cold, remote and indifferent mother much of the time.

It seems that in the adoration of the baby, Kyra, Nijinsky had at last found someone whom he could truly love, in the way he had always wished to be loved himself. However, his capacity to give love and feel love could only last as long as he did not have to share loving or being loved with a third person. Sharing would often confront him with the conflictual triangulation, which he had been unable to negotiate in either his conscious or unconscious life. Nijinsky's possessive love had already been shown in his strange desire that no one should look at his wife's pregnant body. Later his extremely possessive love for Kyra in her adolescence, made it very difficult for them to separate, for he expected her to mother him.

Nijinsky had long been plagued by guilt about his masturbation and sexual phantasies. From time to time he became obsessed by the belief that eating meat brought about sexual lust and drove him to masturbation. He watched over Kyra suspiciously and when he saw Kyra eating meat, crossing her legs or moving in manner that he experienced as suggestive, Nijinsky's separation between the internalized good nurturing mother and bad sexual mother briefly broke down. In these moments eating and sexual activity seemed to become equated in his mind prompting Nijinsky to punish his daughter brutally. For example, when he saw Kyra eating meat he threw it on the floor or out of the window (Ostwald 1991: 173).

Being a prisoner of war

Hostilities broke out in Europe in August 1914 while the Nijinskys were staying with Romola's mother in Budapest. Being a Russian citizen, Nijinsky found himself a prisoner of war, obliged to report weekly to the authorities and forced to remain in the country. Although horrified by reports of the scale of the slaughter, his mood gradually improved and over the next year he became closer to his wife, sharing companionable walks and literary interests. While in Budapest, Romola studied Russian and Nijinsky attempted to create a system of notation for future ballets. Apart from these activities it was an unhappy time because Romola's hatred of her mother led to constant feuding with her and Nijinsky felt distressed by this as he was fond of his mother-in-law.

Meanwhile, back in Paris, Diaghilev was having second thoughts about his dismissal of Nijinsky because the decision had brought him widespread criticism and had diminished the Ballet's lustre. When Fokine decided to pass the war in St Petersburg, Diaghilev found himself without a sufficiently inspiring substitute and tried to persuade Nijinsky to return, only to be coldly rebuffed. Diaghilev soon realized that it would soften Nijinsky's intransigence if he could bring about Nijinsky's release from captivity. By dint of exerting his influence with the highest authorities, Diaghilev eventually achieved his goal, and in January 1916 Nijinsky and Romola were able to move to Vienna, where Nijinsky's fame was recognized once again.

While in Vienna Nijinsky found himself able to practise dancing and he enjoyed the acquaintance of such celebrities as the painter Oskar Kokoschka and the composer Arnold Schoenberg. He also met Richard Strauss with whom he discussed his ideas of a ballet based on the story of *Till Eulenspiegel* (Hauptmann 1927). Now accepted again by Diaghilev and welcomed by the audiences, Nijinsky felt full of creative thoughts and plans. He was gradually recovering from his depression and, although his creativity was still permeated with a manic quality, his family was greatly relieved. Romola was delighted to find that her glittering social career had not been lost after all and she went on a huge shopping spree in Paris, on the promise of the money that was to come.

The first US tour

Diaghilev had brought the Ballets Russes to North America in January 1916, and in March Nijinsky and Romola left to join them. Diaghilev was in severe difficulties because the public, filled with great eagerness to see Nijinsky, were sorely disappointed when he did not appear in Diaghilev's first 16 performances in cities throughout the USA. The dancers often played to near-empty houses and the press dramatized Diaghilev's break with Nijinsky, the star. Being aware of this, Romola, using her good negotiating skills, secured an enormous fee for Nijinsky's services and would not let him begin until he was paid money owing from the past.

After a fraught week and a cold reception from Diaghilev, on 12 April 1916, Nijinsky's American debut brought great rhapsodic applause and an enthusiastic welcome from the press. However, there were many critics in the press who considered Nijinsky's dancing in *Spectre of the Rose* as unmanly and his refined gestures as effeminate. His sensitive portrayal of the beautiful youth in *Narcisse* was greeted with giggles and his virile performance of the black man in *Schéhérazade* so enraged one critic that he had to restrain his impulse to jump on the stage and thrash Nijinsky.

Despite the depressing effect of this encounter with hatred of black people and with homophobia, Nijinsky was undeterred. Eagerly expecting to perform in his own ballets *Till Eulenspiegel* and *Mephisto Waltz*, he became indignant when Diaghilev, already feeling exploited by Romola's bargaining, resisted his wish on the grounds that too much extra rehearsal time would be necessary. Diaghilev also did not defer to Nijinsky's insistence on including *Faune*, a version of a ballet in which Diaghilev's current lover, Léonide Massine, had been performing in Europe.

However, in dancing his familiar roles Nijinsky won tremendous applause, quickly regaining his status as superstar. Nijinsky seemed thrilled in New York as he danced privately for socialites and made the acquaintance of many famous artists of the day. He realized that motion pictures' potential could be used in recording the work of dancers, but he was unable to convince Diaghilev, with the result that only one short film was ever made. So successful was the spring tour that Diaghilev wanted to repeat it later in the year. The Metropolitan Opera offered Diaghilev a six-month contract, beginning at the end of October, on condition that Nijinsky was included. Nijinsky made it known that he would only come on condition that he could be in complete charge of the company. Diaghilev had serious misgivings about this proposal but, realizing that the tour would be more profitable and safer than in war-torn Europe, Diaghilev accepted these conditions and arrangements for the tour began.

The second US tour

The tour proved successful despite the strains on the company caused by Nijinsky's administrative incompetence. His dancing was as brilliant as ever, but his instability of mood worried Romola. Nijinsky fluctuated from being excited to being depressed. He frequently withdrew from Romola, preferring the company of two disciples of Tolstoy with whom he discussed matters of religion and philosophy.

This led Nijinsky to tell Romola that he was planning to give up dancing, live in Russia as a peasant and nature-lover like Tolstoy, become celibate and renounce the eating of meat, which he felt provoked sexual excitement. In wishing to imitate Tolstoy, to live intimately with Mother Russia, Nijinsky was seeking the symbiotic love that he craved.

When he made an unprovoked assault on her, Romola left him for some days and consulted a lawyer who advised her to leave Nijinsky. Upon her return, Romola gave Nijinsky an ultimatum that she would leave him if he continued his behaviour and the pursuance of his Tolstoyan phantasies. Her threat quickly restored Nijinsky's sense of reality, but his suppressed notions resurfaced later.

Madrid and the second tour to South America

Diaghilev accepted a second engagement involving Nijinsky in South America. While he was preparing for his tour Nijinsky, on learning from his brother-in-law that his sister Bronislava was pregnant, suddenly attacked him with great violence. Although this outburst was attributed, no doubt correctly, to Nijinsky's frustration that her pregnancy would prevent her from joining the tour, it seems likely that he also felt jealous of the baby's intrusion into his relationship with his beloved sister.

Subsequently, Diaghilev wanted Nijinsky to stay with the company and dance in Spain, where he had earlier met with great success. Nijinsky accepted this offer despite his awareness that he was needed mainly as a money-maker. He was also disappointed in that he knew that his wish to design new ballets would not be supported because the choreography would be in the hands of Diaghilev's current lover, Massine, a talented choreographer and brilliant dancer.

In Madrid the Nijinskys had an enjoyable vacation for two months while awaiting Diaghilev's arrival, but when Diaghilev finally appeared he proved so amiable that Romola suspected he would be as erratic in his payments as he had been previously. Her intuition was right for Nijinsky and Diaghilev had a violent confrontation which ended only when Nijinsky threatened to leave the company. Realizing that Diaghilev was in a weak bargaining position, Romola, with her customary skill, negotiated a contract that protected both parties against the possibility that Nijinsky might repeat the defection that had caused his dismissal in South America. Diaghilev overcame his misgivings and accepted Romola's terms. This costly deal left Diaghilev with the bitter feeling that he had been manipulated, and put an end to any further friendly encounters between him and Romola.

Nijinsky danced with his usual brilliance, but it was clear that he was becoming increasingly disturbed. He began to believe that his life was in danger, either from plotters or from falling to his death through the stage trap door. Romola, infected by his panic, hired detectives to protect him. Needing the money, Nijinsky kept on dancing and it was not long before the whole company became alarmed by his bizarre behaviour. The South American tour ended in confusion and in October 1917 Nijinsky returned with Romola to Europe.

Reunion with his beloved daughter, Kyra

Rested by the sea voyage, Nijinsky landed in Europe in a much calmer state. He was delighted to be reunited with his daughter Kyra. Romola recounted how Nijinsky and Kyra were both ecstatic with mutual adoration when he entered the room. She added: 'it was as though they had been one person split apart, and constantly wishing to be reunited, like mother and baby' (Ostwald 1991: 165).

Suddenly Romola felt uncomfortable in her role of mother, experiencing herself 'intruding on the couple'.

Moving to St Moritz

Since the war was still raging in Europe, the Nijinskys elected to live in neutral Switzerland, and in December 1917 they rented a house in St Moritz. Nijinsky had reservations about this location, declaring that he hated mountains because 'they hide the view. I want to see far, I do not want to be shut in' (Ostwald 1991: 166).

During the busy St Moritz social season Nijinsky was fairly stable and happy. The couple were joined by Romola's sister, her husband and a young doctor, Dr Hans Frenkel, who practised in the town. Frenkel was interested in psychiatry and had attended lectures given in Zurich by both Eugen Bleuler and Carl Jung. Later Frenkel was to prove important in the lives of both Romola and Vaslav. In 1918, with the coming of spring, St Moritz was practically deserted and Nijinsky, missing the busy social life and the adulation he had received everywhere, began to feel isolated. During the winter of 1918–19 he was often remote and disturbed. He frequently spent his time composing and drawing strange circular and elliptical forms. These designs depicted watching eyes, mouths and perhaps female genitals. Nijinsky talked of his wish to design a circular theatre, like an 'all-seeing eye'. Looking in the mirror he said that he had a single eye in the middle of his forehead. Subsequently, he began to compose a ballet about prostitution.

As the year of 1918 passed, Nijinsky's behaviour became increasingly bizarre, fluctuating from depression to sudden outbursts of excitement and aggression. He had days of being lucid while at other times he began hallucinating (one auditory hallucination he reported was, 'God said to me, Go home and tell your wife that you are mad' (Moore 2013: 200)). His phantasies of living as a peasant in Russia surfaced again and along with these came his recurring preoccupation with the dangers of eating meat. He lectured on the topic and felt compelled to throw food that displeased him around the room. On one occasion he tried to strangle the nanny, Marta Grant, who then fled the Nijinsky household (Moore 2013: 200). Sometimes Nijinsky would be calmer as he busily occupied himself in creating dance notations and ideas for new ballets, but his erratic and eccentric behaviour was beginning to alarm his friends and to frighten his wife.

Later in the year news came from Russia that Nijinsky's mother and sister had survived the revolution, but that in 1917 his brother Stanislav had died in a fire in the mental hospital. Nijinsky received this news with calm resignation and a strange smile, just as he had done in 1912 when his father died. Soon afterwards he announced that he was going to compose a ballet about lunacy, 'a dance for life against death'. He indicated he would play the part of a 'lunatic' who would fiercely reproach the public for sending young men to their death.

Breakdown

As Nijinsky began to prepare for this ballet he became increasingly disturbed. He returned to his plans to lead the life of a celibate religious peasant in Russia. He also entered into frequent manic phases in which he indulged in a manic orgy of shopping, became wildly excited, rushed around the village, preached religion in the street, accosted people, telling them to go to church and proclaiming the evil consequences of eating meat. He also made sudden physical attacks on Romola and had several near-fatal accidents. 'Driven by a mysterious force' (Nijinsky 1999) he climbed a cliff where he contemplated leaping down into the village, explaining this as a response to the voice of God commanding him to jump. He was beset by hallucinations and manic ideation that prompted others to fear for his safety and their own.

Terrified and desperate, Romola turned for help to Dr Frenkel, who felt Nijinsky was suffering from 'a state of acute exhaustion, the result of dancing sixteen hours a day for several months' (Ostwald 1991: 175). This was a mis-diagnosis, perhaps influenced by knowledge of previous psychiatric diagnoses which Nijinsky had been given. Frenkel administered large doses of chloral hydrate, a powerful sedative in routine use by psychiatry of the day, and assigned a male nurse, posing as a masseur, to supervise him day and night and keep him in bed. Under this regime Nijinsky gradually became calmer and after ten days his behaviour had changed dramatically. He explained to visitors that the behaviour that had terrified both his wife and Frenkel was simply play-acting; he declared that he had been missing the stage so, as part of a six-week experiment, he had played the part of a lunatic; and the family, the villagers and even his physician had believed that he was indeed mad. Nijinsky seemed to be very pleased with himself about this event, and may perhaps have had in mind the 'merry pranks' of his ballet *Till Eulenspiegel* which had been a great success in the United States in 1916.

Restored to a calmer state by the regime, Nijinsky returned to composing the ballet about lunacy and the war and made plans to perform it. Relieved by his apparent return to normality Frenkel and Romola found a suitable venue for his performance in the ballroom of an elegant hotel, Suvretta House, on the outskirts of St Moritz. The January 1919 performance was a disaster. Clad in black and white Nijinsky stood at the head of a cross made of black and white fabric. After half an hour of immobile silence he launched into a diatribe lecturing the audience saying, 'I will dance you the war with its suffering, with its destruction, with its death. The war which you did not prevent and so you are responsible for' (Moore 2013: 203). Then with a face ravaged by fright and horror he danced the devastation to humans caused by the war. At the reception that followed he behaved in an equally bizarre manner, which increased his wife's alarm even further. This was Nijinsky's last public performance. At this moment he also stopped creating his unusual drawings.

Commencement of psychotherapy

Nijinsky's behaviour continued to deteriorate and a week after the Suvretta debacle, at Romola's request, Frenkel, having a great interest in psychoanalysis, but no training, attempted to engage Nijinsky in daily psychoanalytically based psychotherapy. Frenkel's attempts to persuade Nijinsky to talk about his past and present life were met with puzzled incomprehension by Nijinsky, who continued to behave in a bizarre, frequently violent way. It should be added that it was purported that Frenkel and Romola were having an affair during this time (Moore 2013: 200).

After a month Frenkel realized that his treatment was not helping and he turned for help to his old mentor, Eugen Bleuler, who agreed to see Nijinsky. When Nijinsky learned of the impending consultation, he began to record his thoughts and feelings in his now well-known diary (Nijinsky 1936). For six months he wrote at a frantic pace while waiting for his appointment with Bleuler.

On March 6, 1919, accompanied by Romola, his in-laws and Dr Frenkel, Nijinsky made the four-hour journey to Zurich where the group settled into a fashionable hotel. Two days later Romola went to the Burgholzli Hospital where she told Bleuler about her husband's strange behaviour and his unpredictable outbursts of violence against her. Bleuler considered that Nijinsky's recent ballet performances had become obscene and that he seemed to be trying to communicate some of his feelings through mimicry in a way that no one could understand.

The next day he interviewed Nijinsky, who explained that he acted insane in front of his wife in order to see how she would react, a claim that could make it difficult to decide whether he was simulating madness or was truly experiencing psychotic states. He talked in an excited way but was not forthcoming about what he was experiencing. Bleuler recorded that although very intelligent in the past he now was experiencing 'schizophrenia including manic tendencies' (Ostwald 1991: 196). Bleuler invented the term 'schizophrenia' to replace the previous classification made by the great pioneer Emil Kraepelin of 'dementia praecox' (precocious insanity), which he considered to be a progressive and incurable organic disease distinct from the more benign manic-depressive psychosis. Bleuler, being in close communication with both Jung and Freud, believed that a person suffering from psychotic states could respond to psychotherapy and various rehabilitation measures.

According to Romola, Bleuler said that Nijinsky should not be hospitalized in the Burgholzli hospital but rather should go discreetly to the Bellevue sanatorium, a private psychiatric hospital directed by his close colleague Ludwig Binswanger. Binswanger had been trained by Bleuler and Jung and he was subsequently Freud's colleague. Under Binswanger's direction, the Bellevue Sanatorium had become famous for its humanitarian approach, orientation to psychotherapy, moderate use of drugs, minimum use of mechanical restraint, intensive nursing care, and its methods of individual and group therapy and rehabilitation, principles which were to be followed later by the Chestnut Lodge hospital in the United States. Both institutions have made extremely important contributions to the understanding and treatment of people suffering from psychotic illnesses.

Romola was also advised by Bleuler to divorce Nijinsky but she was horrified by this prospect and rejected Bleuler's suggestions. It is during this time that Romola was purported to be having an affair with Frenkel and upon returning to the hotel Romola decided to sleep in another room. When Nijinsky tried to enter it, he found the door locked and flew into a rage, ostentatiously showing his relatives a big knife that he had bought. He claimed the knife was for sharpening pencils, and shut himself in his room, refusing to come out. After 24 hours Romola and her parents, fearing that this homicidal behaviour was the real thing and not just an act, called the police, who broke down the door. They called Bleuler who sent his colleague Emil Oberholzer to assess the situation.

After calming the haughtily indignant Nijinsky, who was insisting that he loved his wife and did not wish to hurt her, Oberholzer repeated Bleuler's opinion that they must be separated. That afternoon Oberholzer took Nijinsky back to the psychiatric clinic, where he was observed to be calm, cooperative and in high spirits. At that moment he ended his diary.

Psychiatric assessment and admission into hospital

During the 48-hour assessment period Nijinsky lay in bed, insisting that he was not mentally ill. He behaved in a remarkably passive way, at times sitting or lying immobile and mute for long periods, a condition known as catatonia. The doctors studied his diary and decided that some of his thinking was delusional and grandiose. They also indicated that Nijinsky's repeated insistence that he loved his wife and wanted peace for the whole world suggested that he might be sheltering her from his violently aggressive feelings.

Nijinsky left the psychiatric clinic with a diagnosis of catatonic schizophrenia. Catatonia is rarely encountered nowadays, and when it is it usually responds quickly to treatment with tranquillizing drugs. It is widely understood as a psychogenic reaction to extreme anxiety, the immobility serving as a partially successful attempt to withdraw from reality and to control underlying aggressive impulses. Bleuler concluded that it would be most unwise for Nijinsky to return to the hotel, and in March 1919 Dr Frenkel brought him directly to Binswanger's care at the Bellevue Sanatorium in Kreuzlingen, Switzerland.

Final separation

Binswanger decided that the catatonic symptoms were a form of play-acting at which, understandably, Nijinsky was extremely skilled. For this reason Binswanger decided that it would be a good idea to allow Nijinsky to spend the weekend with

Romola. The Nijinskys, accompanied by Dr Frenkel, travelled to a nearby mountain village. At first all seemed well, but Nijinsky's apparent placidity was broken by outbursts of jealous rage against Frenkel. On 5 April 1919 Dr Binswanger was summoned to persuade Nijinsky to return to Bellevue Sanatorium. With deep feeling, Nijinsky declared his everlasting love to Romola, saying that only God could separate them. Because Nijinsky sometimes used God as a voice dictating his own actions, it may be that his thinking was designed to control his aggressive feelings towards his wife.

Romola was deeply distressed, but she had reached the conclusion that they needed to separate. When the moment of parting came, Nijinsky relapsed into his state of catatonic withdrawal, but on the way back to hospital he became increasingly accessible and when they arrived he was in good humour, behaving as if nothing had happened. Nijinsky must have realized that he had lost Romola emotionally to Frenkel, in a final and fateful triangulation. Romola had left Nijinsky for periods in the past and had threatened divorce, but this particular separation was pivotal. Although Romola never cut off completely from Nijinsky (nor actually divorced him), she did now leave him for years at a time, in conditions where he was severely neglected. In his final years, when he was reduced to a quasi-lobotomized state with a very small emotional capacity, they seem to have shared a certain amount of happiness and congenial companionship.

Psychotherapy attempted for a second time

Believing that Nijinsky might respond to psychotherapy, Binswanger transferred him to his nephew Kurt Binswanger, who had more experience of psychotherapy than Frenkel. Nijinsky became very involved in the treatment and with the psychiatric nurses who were assigned to provide intensive care for him.

With the beginning of psychotherapy Nijinsky became more disturbed. The next two months saw deterioration in his behaviour, with violent mood swings fluctuating between mania and depression, sudden outbursts of rage, attacks on his carers and on himself, and terrifying hallucinatory experiences in which he lost his sense of identity and felt his body was being invaded by some alien person.

Binswanger noted that Nijinsky's behaviour had changed dramatically after leaving Romola and entering hospital. He was no longer depressed or terrified but had become more aggressive, and seemed to have cast off any need for restraint of his jealous violence towards Romola and Frenkel, whom he perhaps rightly suspected of having an affair. His attacks on his nurses increased and he was considered so dangerous that he had to be put in an isolation room or given repeated warm baths to calm him down.

Later in the year his mother and his sister, Bronislava, managed to escape from Russia and they visited him. Bronislava was able to elicit some brief signs of interest in her continuing work as a dancer, and after the visit she rejoined the Ballets Russes, enlivening it with her dancing and brilliant choreography. In this respect she replaced her brother and set out on a highly successful career.

The end of the 'talking' treatment – but why?

Kurt Binswanger had not given up hope, but it was clear that the psychotherapy was becoming increasingly disturbing to Nijinsky. An inevitable increase of sedative and potentially hallucinogenic drugs were given to calm Nijinsky. With hindsight it can be argued that Nijinsky had developed a violent and dependent infantile transference to Binswanger, which Binswanger was not skilled enough to understand and contain through intuitive use of his countertransference. It appears that initially, when separated from Binswanger, Nijinsky split-off his hostility to his therapist and redirected his hostility to the devoted nurse. Later the splitting between the 'bad-nurse' and the 'good-therapist' lessened and everyone turned bad in his mind. At this point Nijinsky's paranoia and accompanying violence were uncontainable. Even today, well-intentioned psychotherapeutic interventions by unskilled practitioners, particularly those who are unaware of patients' possessive jealousy and hostile reactions during separation, can have similar consequences, with damage to the reputation of psychoanalytic treatment and to the hopes of a significant number of psychotic people who might benefit from a well-trained psychotherapist's understanding.

In July 1919 Romola, alarmed by the deterioration in Nijinsky's behaviour, called a halt to the psychotherapy, removing him from hospital against medical advice and confining him to a room in a villa in St Moritz where sedative medication was prescribed by Dr Frenkel. In the villa there was no psychiatric supervision and the nursing attendants were incompetent. After two months Romola became pregnant, hoping that it would be the son for which Nijinsky longed, and mistakenly assuming that a new baby son might restore her husband to health.

When in a cheerful mood Nijinsky would play contentedly with his five-year old daughter Kyra, but when depressed he would cry silently, and complain pitifully about his confusion. These shifting moods would be interrupted by fits of rage; Nijinsky would scream incoherently and threaten to assault anyone who came near him for he was having hallucinations which led him to experience himself as being attacked by demons. When one of the attendants left he was replaced by another with more nursing experience. Being shocked by Nijinsky's state, this more experienced nurse informed the police that Nijinsky was extremely dangerous and not being supervised properly. The police were summoned and in October 1919 Nijinsky was returned to the Bellevue Sanatorium in Kreuzlingen, Switzerland under a court order.

Romola's removal of Nijinsky from Binswanger marked the end of any systematic psychotherapy. Although she may have had good reason to be alarmed at his deterioration, and to believe, perhaps correctly, that the psychotherapy was causing the deterioration in his behaviour, it appears to have been Romola's need to control the violence that led her to oppose the medical care. Although Kurt Binswanger was apparently out of his depth with a patient who had replaced reflective thought by action, he had nevertheless retained some rational hope. When such violence is aroused in psychotherapy it can often be found to stem from the basic problem that needs understanding and working through in the therapeutic transference. It seems likely that this was happening in the psychotherapy, and that the encapsulated therapeutic transference relation was being displaced onto the trustworthy nurse.

For some reason Kurt Binswanger did not have possession of Nijinsky's diary or the facts about his brother, Stanislav. Binswanger also lacked an adequate understanding of the crucial processes of transference and countertransference with psychotic patients, for such theoretical understanding was not yet developed as part of the equipment for psychoanalysts.

In February 1920, Romola again removed Nijinsky from Binswanger's care because she wanted to give birth to her second child in the same clinic as her first. The Nijinsky family all moved to Vienna and Nijinsky was transferred to a psychiatric clinic there. Hoping that psychoanalysis might help him, Romola consulted the psychoanalysts Sándor Ferenczi and Sigmund Freud, who politely declined to become involved. At this time Freud, unlike some psychoanalysts of today, considered psychotic states as being unresponsive to formal psychoanalysis.

The arrival of the second child, Tamara

The birth of the second child, Tamara, occurred in June 1920. It was rumoured that this was Frenkel's child and Romola's feelings for the baby were complex. Romola had hoped that the baby's birth might help cure Nijinsky, who wanted a boy, and when the baby was a girl, Romola showed little affection for her. Their unhappy relationship resulted in Tamara being adopted by her maternal grandmother when she was eight. It was not until Tamara's adult life that she and her mother grew close. At the time of the birth, Romola, running short of money, decided to take up residence with her mother and step-father in the Pulzsky mansion in Budapest. In July 1922 she then moved to Paris hoping to go into business and establish herself independently. Even though all of Romola's enterprises failed and she was constantly on the verge of bankruptcy, her determination and her remarkable capacity for eliciting financial support from others helped Romola maintain a comfortable lifestyle.

Freud, Adler and others

At one point Romola took Nijinsky to Lourdes to be cured. She was so desperate to rehabilitate Nijinsky she consulted 'all the eminent French psychiatrists' (Ostwald 1991: 265) as well as the Americans, Alfred Adler and Frieda von Reichmann (a psychoanalyst who made fundamental contributions to the psychotherapy of psychosis at Chestnut Lodge Hospital). Admission to specialist clinics in the United States was considered. When Adler made an attempt to interview Nijinsky, he did not speak and was completely uncooperative. Two years later Romola invited Adler to write a preface for the *Diary*. Based on what he had learned from her and the staff, Adler wrote that Nijinsky had had a stressful childhood and a deficient education. He added that this had left Nijinsky with an inferiority complex, which made him prone to feeling slighted. Adler suggested that Nijinsky's despising of rational thinking was a vain attempt to support his notion of superiority.

Romola, refusing to have the notion of inferiority attached to her 'God of the Dance', judged it 'completely erroneous' (Ostwald 1991: 290), and she wrote her own preface. In this she described her husband as 'a seeker after truth whose only aim in life was to help, to share, to love' (Nijinsky 1936: xii) and indicated that he was a heroic humanitarian brought low by 'an uncanny, invisible power – a ghastly force' (Nijinsky 1936: xi). His devoted daughter, Tamara, described him as a gentle and kindly man, a loving judgement which was no doubt true in terms of their relationship. However, this admirable side of Nijinsky's character co-existed with a dissociated infantile self, suffused with violence, which exerted its 'uncanny, invisible power' unconsciously, with destructive consequences for Nijinsky and others. Psychoanalysis has replaced the idea of a single self by the concept of separate, often conflicting selves, in one individual.

Although no doubt there were moments when Romola did understand Nijinsky better than the doctors, her insistence that she knew what was best for him repeatedly interrupted his treatment. Adler's view of Nijinsky was also true of Romola, for whom, as we have already seen, a deeply unhappy childhood had created a striving to outdo her envied siblings, and had given her the arrogance and sense of entitlement which sometimes led her to pursue her goal in a ruthless fashion.

Family members' separation

In 1924 Diaghilev, who had not given up hope for Nijinsky's recovery, invited him to see Anton Dolin rehearse, but throughout the rehearsal, much to the distress of the company, Nijinsky remained withdrawn. Romola, now desperate for money, sent her children to stay with their grandmother. Tamara, aged four, settled down happily with her grandmother and lived with her until adulthood. Kyra, now ten years old, was showing symptoms of psychological stress for which Bleuler was consulted. As a result, Kyra was returned to her mother in Paris where Romola enrolled her in ballet classes at the Opéra; she showed great talent, made rapid progress, then went to boarding school and was soon performing professionally. In 1926 Romola, hoping to find work in Hollywood, moved to the United States, where she stayed until 1929, leaving Nijinsky in the care of her sister Tessa.

Tessa's care of Nijinsky quickly broke down when two attendants arrived to find Nijinsky shut in a cell-like room, looking neglected, raving incomprehensibly and smearing faeces on the walls. Romola persuaded Binswanger to re-admit Nijinsky to Bellevue Sanatorium, in Switzerland. They brought him there with much difficulty. After a month's observation he was assigned to psychotherapist Dr Marta Wenger, who was to look after him for the next three years.

She observed him very closely and made determined attempts at engaging him in psychotherapy and rehabilitation, none of which aroused him from his state of mutism. On the other hand he was very fond of Bellevue's excellent pastry, which had a distinct tranquillizing effect on him. Much of the time, however, Nijinsky seemed to be lost in another world, talking to himself and, regressing to an infantile rage, smearing his room with excrement and urinating on the carpet.

When Romola visited Nijinsky for the first time in three years he became increasingly disturbed, and in 1930 she returned to the United States. Here she remained until 1934, forming two passionate lesbian relationships both of which ended in the death of her partner: the first, Lya de Putti, in a drunken incident when she choked on a chicken bone, and the next, Frederika Dezantje, by pulmonary tuberculosis. Consumed by grief, Romola began to pine for her daughters and, with substantial financial support from her many friends, she returned to London. In 1935 she occupied herself in editing Nijinsky's diary and occasionally visiting him in Bellevue Hospital, getting him to sign autographs, and sometimes taking him for car journeys.

Insulin shock treatment

When the 'talking treatment' failed, Romola sought the opinion of numerous specialists throughout Europe. In 1937, she heard about the new insulin shock treatment for psychotic states which had been developed by Manfred Sakel. Sakel believed that the destruction of brain tissue was essential for treating people with psychotic states. Romola invited Sakel to administer the 'insulin cure' to Nijinsky, to which Binswanger, with considerable misgivings, agreed. In July 1938, the 'insulin cure' was finally started. Insulin treatment was a dangerous intervention, with a significant mortality rate. In fact, Sakel's insulin-based treatment was subsequently discounted by the medical profession. Sakel was not a psychiatrist and his best results were found with people in their first six months of illness, which was too early for a reliable diagnosis to have been established.

When, after daily treatments Nijinsky showed some improvement, Romola was delighted and announced to the world's press that he had recovered and would shortly resume dancing. This combination of wishful thinking and propaganda seems to have been characteristic of Romola who fostered the legend of Nijinsky in the hope, perhaps, of gaining some reflected glory. Without Binswanger's consent she invited the press to the hospital to meet him. When Serge Lifar danced for him Nijinsky showed some interest, but when Nijinsky executed some clumsy steps himself, Lifar was dismayed to see neurological signs of twitching, grunting and severe lack of co-ordination. Nonetheless, Romola judged the event a success and a foundation was set up by wealthy admirers to finance continuation of the treatment for as long as she considered necessary.

However, after some initial improvement Nijinsky returned to his previous state of mute withdrawal and unpredictable excited aggressiveness. After some 40 treatments Binswanger called a halt, but Romola insisted on continuing the insulin treatment, so Nijinsky was transferred to a State hospital directed by Dr Max Muller. Under further relentless pressure from Romola the treatment was resumed and continued for a total of 228 sessions over seven months. In retrospect it could be seen that this cerebral insult had probably caused brain damage similar to that which was later to be deliberately inflicted for therapeutic purposes by lobotomy.

When the insulin treatment finally ended in August 1939 Nijinsky was sufficiently calm for Romola to take him to stay in a nearby hotel. Shortly afterwards he again became disturbed and she was forced to return him to hospital where Dr Muller offered to keep him in safety until the end of the war. Romola declined Muller's offer and moved with Nijinsky to her mother's house in Budapest. By August 1941 Nijinsky had become so disturbed that he had to be taken, restrained in a strait jacket, to the Hungarian State Mental Hospital. Romola managed to borrow a substantial amount of money and in the harsh winter of 1941–42 Nijinsky was moved to a private clinic. With the defeat at Stalingrad in 1942 the occupying German military began to round up Jews and the mentally ill population of mental hospitals. In fact, the hospital in which Nijinsky was staying on and off was ordered to exterminate all the mentally ill people residing there. Romola and Nijinsky narrowly escaped the round-up by hiding in the underground passages of a Carmelite convent.

When the Russian troops finally arrived, they welcomed Nijinsky as a national idol and he joined them in their dancing and singing, sharing his pleasure with this congenial and admiring company. With the ending of the war Romola returned with Nijinsky to Vienna, taking up residence in a castle occupied by the American military. Still helpless, explosive and inarticulate, Nijinsky was able to recognize works of art, to behave with dignity much of the time and to find some measure of contentment.

In London – Nijinsky's final years and his death

In November 1947 the Nijinskys returned to Switzerland for health checks, and then in 1948 to London where, being treated with great respect and kindness, Nijinsky's behaviour greatly improved. The couple stayed at first in Great Fosters, a luxury country house near Heathrow, which was provided for them by Romola's friend, the Hungarian film director Alexander Korda. There they passed the winter of 1947–48 accompanied by a wealthy admirer of Romola. In the spring of 1948 a well-wisher offered them residence in a very pleasant house near Windsor Great Park. Romola continued her quest to go to America in the hope of continuing the insulin treatment with Manfred Sakel, but this proved impossible. In March of 1949 an exhibition of Nijinsky's work was held at the Harold Rubin Art Gallery in London to which Romola invited all the important people she could think of, including Queen Mary, who politely declined. One of Romola's American friends again discussed the possibility of treatment at Chestnut Lodge with Frieda Fromm-Reichmann, but this plan came to nothing.

Towards the end of 1949 Nijinsky began to show symptoms of renal failure and on 5 April 1950 he was admitted to the London Clinic in a coma. After a brief return to consciousness, he died suddenly on 8 April 1950. He was 60. A mass was held the following week at the Church of St James in Spanish Place, Marylebone,

London with over 500 people from all over the world attending. The pallbearers included Serge Lifar, Anton Dolin and the critics Richard Buckle and Cyril Beaumont. Nijinsky was buried in St Marylebone Cemetery in the Finchley Road in London. Three years later his teacher and rival, Serge Lifar, had Nijinsky's body exhumed and re-interred in Paris in the cemetery of Montmartre alongside the tomb of the legendary dancer August Vestris. In Paris, a Russian Orthodox funeral service attended by a great crowd of mourners was also conducted.

PART 2 NIJINSKY AND THE TREATMENT OF PSYCHOSIS

Psychoanalytic treatment of psychotic states: then and now

Since the time of Bleuler and Kurt Binswanger there have been great advances in the understanding of people suffering from psychotic disorders. Developments in psychoanalytic theories of psychosis have clarified how emotional development in early childhood influences both good and poor mental health, and these theories have shown how both genes and early childhood relationships establish a vulnerability to later psychotic disorders.

At the time of Nijinsky's breakdown 'schizophrenia', which was the name given to his illness at that time, was widely considered by psychiatrists to be a disease of the brain for which medical treatment alone was required. Nijinsky's symptoms included hallucinations, delusions of many kinds, distracted thoughts, disorganized language and behaviour, a loosening of connections and associations and he had a bi-polar disorder. During his life, treatment resources were largely limited to custodial care, sedative drugs and attempts at rehabilitation. On some occasions a psychotherapeutic approach was employed, usually with only short-term success. Nijinsky's main psychiatrists were the most advanced practitioners of their time and although they did employ group and individual psychotherapy with people suffering from psychotic states, they were unable to find a way of relating to Nijinsky. It was only in the 1950s, with the development of psychoactive drugs and advanced psychoanalytically based knowledge, that deeper understanding and more effective psychotherapy became possible.

People suffering from different types of psychotic illnesses have in common a seriously disturbed sense of reality, with both psychological and biological factors in their constitution. In more enlightened services there is a more sophisticated approach involving a bio-psycho-social model of assessment and the stress-vulnerability approach to understanding and treatment of each unique individual. Modern techniques of brain imaging are throwing light on certain neurological anomalies in some people suffering from psychotic states, but whether or not these are of causal significance, or are linked with trauma both external and internal, has yet to be established. The psychoanalytic view is that emotionally traumatic experiences in infancy have a great influence, alongside genetic factors, on severe mental disorders. In some psychiatric settings this still remains a controversial notion.

A person suffering from psychotic states exists with a sane part often present and more like us than we think (Sullivan 1962). Psychotic states of mind often make sense when considered in the context of the individual's life history. The individual's communications have a meaning which needs to be understood. People suffering from psychotic states can often be greatly helped by modern techniques of psychotherapy, very frequently in association with psychoactive drugs, and with group and family therapy. It is the task of the therapist to enter into the person's world and to work alongside the sane part of the individual's mind to identify his feelings, to understand his anxieties and to help him find better ways of understanding himself, containing his emotions and dealing with his conflicts.

When an individual is functioning in a psychotic state of mind, his mental state is akin to that of dream life, where thoughts may be felt to be things, ideas find expression in symbolic terms, phantasies replace reality, and the capacity to distinguish between concept and percept, past and present, inner and outer reality is lost. This perceptualization (or desymbolization) of thinking results in a state where memories belonging to the past may be experienced as happening in the immediate present. Some expressions of psychotic thinking resemble those of infancy and childhood in the period before higher levels of abstract thinking are achieved. The capacity for comprehension of symbol and metaphor, not yet sufficiently acquired in early development, is lost to a variable extent in psychotic states of mind. It is in this sense that portions of an adult's psychotic thinking can be regarded as regressive, a return to developmentally earlier, 'primitive', 'infantile' modes of expression.

The origins and evolution of psychotic disorders

The current approach of psychoanalysis to the understanding of psychotic states of mind rests on the view that the basis for future mental health and ill health depends on the quality of the relationship of the mother and father to their baby from birth throughout the early years of life. It is the interaction of this process with constitutional and genetic elements in the young child that determines the degree of mental stability or vulnerability to stress, external or internal, where the seeds of mental illness (Akhtar 1997) are sown. Such stresses may be social, such as poverty or malnutrition, and/or psychological, such as abuse (physical, sexual or emotional), or specific types of inner and familial emotional conflict, as exemplified in this book.

Genetic influences

The role of genetic factors remains unclear and complex. Whatever their role, the environment, especially disturbed relationships, interacts with constitution and temperament. It is important to note that genetic research in mental illness seems to confirm that genes can be modified or switched on and off, and that a healthy early environment in infancy or, in certain cases, successful treatment with psychotherapy, can annul whatever malign influence may be inherited. Thus, a flawed genotype can be converted to a healthy phenotype (Tienari 1992).

All three Nijinsky children were different: Vaslav and Stanislav were both volatile in mood, hyperactive and prone to risk-taking behaviour, while Bronislava was stable and reflective. Vaslav was to develop into an adolescent with poor verbal communication skills and a tendency to emotional withdrawal, features which might be regarded as schizoid tendencies. All three were innately endowed with exceptional kinaesthetic capacities. With the interests of their parents and their highly developed sense of balance and movement in space they found dancing easy and enjoyable.

The early environment

Babies differ widely in their excitability and capacity to tolerate discomfort. The roots of mental health derive from the quality of attunement between the parents and their baby (Stern 1985) and the siblings' relationship to the baby (Cooper and Magagna 2004). A mother who is depressed, unstable, rejecting, emotionally overwhelmed because of her own earlier experiences, or unsupported by the father, may not be able to bear the brunt of her infant's intense anxieties, to help him regulate his emotional state and to know and understand his feelings. In the absence of parents who compassionately contain the baby's physical and emotional experiences, the baby, such as Nijinsky, already extremely sensitive and easily frustrated, may resort to immature methods of protecting himself from anxiety. Such protections which can arise in infancy may involve dissociative splitting and projection. These processes bring about a deep sense of isolation within the baby, for he loses contact with part of his emotional experience and then becomes unable to interact appropriately with his parents and to introject their love and understanding, enabling him to separate from his parents and develop in a normal way.

The mother, Eleonore Nijinsky, had an episodically disturbed relationship with her ill-tempered husband, and from their earliest years the children were exposed to the traumatic experience of violent marital quarrels. This emotional neglect contributed to adverse consequences for their development. Nijinsky's mother could not create a secure home base because of her stormy relationship with her husband, who frequently had affairs. Wishing to pursue her dancing, she attempted to abort at least her first child but had three children in five years. Nijinsky's older brother, Stanislav, although loved by both parents and greatly encouraged in his dancing by his father, thus had a very insecure beginning. Stanislav also suffered brain damage through an accident involving falling out of a window. Still, it is puzzling to understand how Bronislava escaped with simply a sense of insecurity, which she was eventually able to overcome.

Factors contributing to Nijinsky's vulnerability to later psychosis

Nijinsky's disturbed childhood deprived him of the strength of personality required of an emotionally mature and responsible adult. His sense of personal identity and self-esteem were fragile and the limitations of his relationship with his idealized mother and his beloved, but terrifying father, often left him with the inability to express any conscious aggressiveness towards anyone towards whom he might feel love and dependence. He seemed to have an unconscious assumption that his possessive love was destructive (Fairbairn 1952). It was this belief that led the infant Nijinsky to dissociate the mental representation of his 'bad', frustrating mother, whom he hated, from that of the 'good' feeding mother whom he loved. Outwardly, much of the time with his mother he seemed to be gentle, passive and obedient.

Once this splitting is consolidated, any form of aggression towards any figure of dependency will arouse extreme anxiety and must be avoided at all costs. This splitting creates the image of an idealized, ever-loving mother who is felt to be wholly in the infant's control – an infantile, symbiotic relation, that was henceforth the only type of love that Nijinsky could imagine and which he pursued unsuccessfully all his life. He could not imagine sharing the mother and giving the mother freedom to have 'a life with the father' or 'the other children' (Meltzer 1967).

Nijinsky was deprived by his failure to develop a mature loving relationship with his parents and to internalize an emotionally containing parental couple. Such failures in development deprived him of the capacity to integrate his feelings of love and hostility, which would foster the security, self-assertiveness and personality growth necessary to master the demands of adult life. There was not a sufficiently good relationship with his abandoning father to make a positive identification with him, work through his Oedipal difficulties and develop a safe, secure base from which he could separate from his mother. More contemporary psychological research in child development based on the work of such pioneers as Bowlby (1969, 1973, 1980), Mahler *et al.* (1975), Klein (1935), Fairbairn (1952), Stern (1985), Brazelton (2006), Main (1991) and Bateman and Fonagy (2006) have elaborated theories of attachment, empathy, mentalizing and separation/individuation which help to explain the consequences of success or failure of the infant and child's development. The significant role of the father in a child's development has recently been given more of the attention it deserves through books such as *The Importance of Fathers* (Etchegoyen and Trowell 2002).

For Nijinsky, sharing his mother's loving attention with his father or siblings was impossible. Also, he may simply have not internalized a sufficiently good mother and father to be able to be generous to his siblings and bear the many rejections that he felt. To accept the inevitable loss of his mother's exclusive attention that growth requires would undo the dissociative splitting: his 'good' mother image would instantly become 'bad' while his jealous rage would threaten to destroy her and himself. This belief condemned him to the unconscious conviction that he could only love someone who filled the role of an idealized mother figure or idealized father figure (here the term 'unconscious' is being used in a descriptive fashion, meaning 'unbeknownst to himself', implying a knowledge that has not yet been consciously thought).

When his wish to possess 'the other' was frustrated, typically within triangular relationships, Nijinsky was likely to respond with a temper tantrum, or at the worst, a fit of homicidal rage. As a small boy Nijinsky could not confront his erratically violent father because to do so would bring the fear of lethal retaliation. It was not until he was a muscular adolescent that he was able to confront his father physically and eject him from the family home. However, this achievement in outer reality did not serve to mitigate Nijinsky's hatred, nor did it reassure him. He retained a fear of lethal consequences at the hands of his inner world's imagined murderous father. This fear of the 'violent man', whose violence was augmented by projections of Nijinsky's hatred, weakened him and provoked a deep passivity. Such paranoid fears were only revealed when Nijinsky was emotionally overwhelmed by a series of extreme stresses, both in his inner and outer world. The precise nature of his paranoid anxiety was discovered only when it found symbolic expression in Nijinsky's diary. There he described variations on the theme of cruel and dangerous men killing helpless creatures. This was probably a theme linked with both his experiences with his father, but also with his Imperial Theatre School boarding experiences where he was ordered about, sneered at, teased for dancing as well as a girl and generally bullied in various ways.

The encapsulation complex

Nijinsky's pathological relationship with his sometimes violent father was filled with hatred. This was perhaps not in itself enough to predispose Nijinsky to experiencing psychotic states. It might rather have predisposed him to subsequent neurotic or dissocial traits of character. Perhaps it was in the relationship to his violent father combined with the difficulties present in his earlier relationship to his mother that his predisposition to psychotic anxieties was to be found. In the presence of such a fragile, easily depressed mother, hostile and dangerous inner phantasies may be denied from consciousness and reside split off in the unconscious. This split-off unconscious infantile part of the self can remain as an encapsulated psychotic part of the self (Klein 1980). Such encapsulation leads the self to harbour a chronic inner abscess that impedes development.

Regressive episodes and murderous rage

The influence of these unconscious phantasies may simply take the form of eccentricities of character and only reveal their pathological nature if the vulnerable person is aroused by a specific set of conflicts producing outer and inner stresses that are more than his limited mental defensive strategies can manage. Under these circumstances the defences collapse and hidden aggressive feelings find expression in sudden regressive behaviour: the infantile psychotic self briefly erupts, the abscess breaks open and aggression erupts (Williams 1998: 40). Such events may be only brief, or recurring, when they can be regarded as moments of regression – as in Nijinsky's case. The increasing frequency of Nijinsky's violence suggested they were premonitory symptoms of a more prevailing psychotic state of mind.

The first time that the homicidal quality of Nijinsky's jealous rage became clear was on the occasion in London when he saw a stagehand flirting with his wife and made a murderous attack on him. Afterwards he became acutely anxious and confessed to Marie Rambert that he had almost killed the rival. From time to time other events aroused his latent violent jealousy, such as the episode in South America when his brother-in-law told him of Bronislava's pregnancy, or another occasion, when his wife Romola was at the top of a flight of stairs holding his baby daughter Kyra and Nijinsky suddenly attacked them both by pushing them down the stairs. Suspicions about the relationship between Romola and Dr Frenkel were also a trigger, as when, feeling fury at being shut out of Romola's room, Nijinsky brandished a knife in an out-of-control state of rage with Romola.

Some of these events are recorded in Nijinsky's diary, which we will now examine, and attempt to understand.

The diary

Nijinsky's diary provides a unique record of the struggle between the sane and psychotic parts of a personality in great detail. He shows how his sanity is being successfully undermined by destructive internal forces. The diary consists of four notebooks, collected under the headings 'on life' and 'on death', and a collection of 16 letters, never to be posted, of which 14 are addressed to various friends and notables, and probably not sent, the fifteenth 'to Mankind' and the sixteenth 'to Jesus'. Nijinsky's entries record thoughts and feelings at a time when his sense of reality and personal identity – always vulnerable since childhood – were disintegrating under the impact of the huge emotional stresses that were overwhelming him.

Early entries show how his rational, even shrewd, comments about the important people in his life and everyday events are being infiltrated by the psychotic process. The cause and effect present in rational logic is being undermined by the reversal of cause and effect through using psychotic (symmetrical) logic. Here are two examples of such logic: 'He [a violinist] is poor because he plays at night' (Nijinsky 1999: 6) and 'The audience did not like me, because they wanted to leave' (Nijinsky 1999: 6).

Also, Nijinsky shows in the diary how he reaches conclusions instantly. He dismisses any need for reflective thought by the repeated use of such connecting words as 'because' and 'therefore'. One example of this is that 'because' or 'therefore' are found 20 times in two pages – not always illogically, but always attempting to demonstrate to the reader that Nijinsky is completely in command of the logic of his thinking and is not in the least confused.

One also sees that Nijinsky writes in the diary with a surprising lack of inhibition about his bodily processes. He says that he exposes himself to public gaze with such frankness in order to punish himself. He shares his feelings about eating meat, how it provokes lust, how he hears the cries of the animals being slaughtered, what he feels about his wife's behaviour and that of politicians. His litany of observations show omnipotent certitude, with no room for doubt about his conclusions. This gives the impression that he is repeatedly trying to convince doubting readers that their perceptions are mistaken.

Because the dairy's logical parts become increasingly undermined by psychotic thinking, the reader may find the diary progressively confusing, unreadable and boring. Nijinsky's fragile attempts to keep to the point eventually begin to give way to his interest in the words that he is using. Bleuler (1978) describes this as a 'loosening of associations' in which there is an attraction to the sounds of the words (sonic) or the meaning that he gives to them (semantic), rather than their logical associations. Verbal associations may also be both semantic and sonic at the same time. An example of this is when a person in a manic state, being restrained by a nurse, screamed at her 'sister blister wrister twister!', conveying both a message and a triumphant alliteration.

As the diary proceeds, Nijinsky begins to show evidence of manic excitement, making puns and playing on words. His letters become increasingly incomprehensible, taking the form of blank verse. The ninth letter, a criticism of Diaghilev, is fascinating in the logical coherence – and the sanity – of some of his thoughts, but the thoughts are embedded in manic associations. Thereafter Nijinsky writes in French, and fragments of a coherent theme can sometimes be detected. He shows that he is writing with awareness of the existence of both his reader and of himself, in the form of 'I am' and 'you are'.

Here is one illustration in verse form:

I want to write. I want to say to say.

I want to say to say

I want to say, I want to write to write

Why can one not talk in rhyme when one can talk in rhyme.

I am rhyme rhyme rif. I want rifa narif. You are narif and I am tarif. We are rif. You are rif we are rif. You are He and I am he. We are we you are they

(Nijinsky 2006: 122–123)

It should be pointed out that the word 'rif' is the first syllable of the Russian word for rhyme, 'rifma', and that 'rifa', 'narif' and 'tarif' are meaningless neologisms created for the sake of the rhythm.

Later Nijinsky writes:

> I want to say that you want to sleep and sleep.
>
> I want to write and sleep.
>
> You cannot sleep and write.
>
> I write write write.
>
> You write write write
>
> (Nijinsky 2006: 123)

Then he goes on: 'We are you and you are in me' (Nijinsky 2006: 124).

These comments seem like a desperate attempt to bring his mind back under his control, to address his sense of self-identity and to differentiate his mind from others, whom he is using as containers of his projections, bringing severe confusion, altering their identity and weakening his own. The result is an excited repetitive babble in which he seems to have finally abandoned the attempt to communicate with the reader, or with himself, and is completely preoccupied with sonic associations in a manic fashion. Nijinsky eventually gives the impression of struggling desperately to fill his mind so completely that there will be no room for sane reflective thought. Awareness of his madness is left safely projected into the mind of others whom he experiences as being in the process of taking control of his life.

Nijinsky's motives for writing must have been complex. Terrified that Bleuler would confirm his wife's belief that he was insane, and that he was about to be confined to a mental asylum where he would meet the same fate as his brother, Nijinsky appeared to be trying to understand what was happening to him. Perhaps in a desperate attempt to gain control of a world that was disintegrating, he was writing to convince himself and others that he was not mad. He was locked in the throes of a desperate struggle to escape the thinking that would make him realize that his self-control was breaking down, that he was 'losing his mind'.

His infantile rage, long slumbering in his unconscious mind, was breaking through its encapsulation. There was a breaking down of the primitive splitting mechanisms that protected his love for his good mother from the hatred towards his bad mother. Because there was more hatred than love, the hostility threatened to destroy the good mother and his own existence. In figurative language, the leaking abscess was bursting, the infantile psychotic and aggressive phantasies were erupting from their encapsulated state.

Nijinsky's infantile reaction to triangular situations had emerged several times in the past. He had not been able to develop a satisfactory relationship with his mother which would enable him to face sharing her with others. As a result, he was not emotionally mature enough to tolerate three-person relationships. Instead, he needed to possess and control the other with a symbiotic infantile love. It was only in the period of mutual adoration that developed between little Kyra and himself that he had moments of pure joyful happiness. As a result of this discovery of a new-found happiness with Kyra, somehow Nijinsky generally managed to regain control of himself and continue with his dancing – the dancing which provided him with a permanent source of reassuring adulation. He must have had some awareness of what dancing and its rewards meant to him, for he said, 'I am the God who dies when he is not loved' (Nijinsky 2006: 152).

The diary is replete with examples of Nijinsky's use of projective and manic defences against his overwhelming anxiety and depression. For example, he says,

> I danced frightening things. They were frightened of me and therefore thought that I wanted to kill them. I do not want to kill anyone. I loved everyone, but no one loved me, and therefore I became nervous ... I felt God throughout the evening ... I told my wife that today was the day of my marriage with God.
>
> (Moore 2013: 204)

Increasingly as the diary proceeds, Nijinsky proclaims that he is God. At other times he insists that his own destructive actions have been commanded by God.

Another illustration of his omnipotent certitude followed when Nijinsky had a disagreement with his wife. He was walking in the snow when he saw what he perceived to be blood. Immediately he felt 'sure somebody had been killed' (Nijinsky 2006: 15). Although somehow he realized that the stains were not blood, but urine, the illusion and belief continued. He then felt that he should jump to his death from a precipice. This was the occasion when he also heard God tell him to go home and tell his wife that he was insane. Nijinsky obeyed the hallucinatory voice and went home where he told his wife that on his way he had met a man whom he believed had murdered his own wife.

This episode illustrates several important characteristics of psychotic thinking. It shows how there is often a conflict between the sane and psychotic parts of the personality. Usually an island of sane thinking can be found by the psychotherapist. In this case Nijinsky's psychotic thinking was protecting him from awareness of his dissociated murderous wishes towards his wife (representing his 'bad' mother). He did this by displacing onto a passer-by his feared lethal destructiveness (symbolized by urine) and symbolizing its consequence (blood). His underlying guilt then pressed him to destroy himself, but he had sufficient sanity to be able to resist the command hallucination and to impute to God the belief that he was insane.

This process can be considered as a moment of regression to infantile forms of thinking. In the course of psychotherapy this can sometimes be seen as a therapeutic regression and thus as an opportunity to return to the point where development went wrong. The perception of that particular situation at that particular moment as constituting a therapeutic transference to the therapist can be beneficially used in therapy. Hallucinations can be discussed with a person at those times when the sane self is sufficiently strong to help understand the meaning of his confusion of love and hate, depression and persecution.

Nijinsky's unconscious phantasy seems to have been that any aggression towards or act of independence from his 'breast-mother' would not only upset her, but would also destroy her, leave his internal mother damaged and thus lead to annihilation of himself. His psychotic thinking involved this persistent unconscious phantasy in his inner world becoming an external reality. His sane thinking was increasingly infiltrated by his psychotic thinking.

Even shrewd observations about the people involved in his situation were filled with Nijinsky's expressions of infantile omnipotent thinking and a severe confusion between outer reality and the inner reality of unconscious phantasy. Nijinsky seems to have lost the capacity to think in terms of 'as if', 'like' or 'resemble'. At times, the servants who looked after Nijinsky, Kyra and the family may have been experienced as nourishing mother figures of his infancy and at other times may have been experienced as potentially dangerous retaliating figures who would starve him. In this 'symbolic equation' the symbolized thing or situation is experienced as having the same reality and emotional quality as would a real event or person.

Many examples of Nijinsky's loss of appreciation of symbol and metaphor are to be found. Here is one of them: when writing about his luncheon he declares – 'I do not want to upset my servants. If they are upset, I will die of hunger' (Nijinsky 2006: xxix).

He explained this apparently concrete thinking by suggesting that his servants did not want to leave his wife by herself. The doctors didn't want him to go to his wife. He knew that if the servants separated him from his wife he would starve. If one follows his thinking it makes sense that he feared that if he upset the servants by disobeying the doctors' orders he would be starved of being with his wife (Nijinsky 2006: xxvii).

Nijinsky's struggle to keep murderous wishes at bay can be detected in his repeated declaration of the purity of his love: 'I love everybody, I don't want war ... I want to love, to love, I am love and not bestiality. I am not a blood-thirsty animal. I am a man' (Ostwald 1991: 192).

He also asserts, 'I am a madman who loves people' (Nijinsky 2006: 32).

The tragedy is that these noble sentiments, although genuine, could only feel real to him by denying (dissociating) himself from the other side of his personality in which he feels exactly the opposite. The diary is full of such assertions of Nijinsky's innocence, love and harmless lack of dangerous aggression.

> I love her and will pray that she [Romola] may remain with me ... I have explained everything to my wife about the revolver. She is no longer afraid, but she still has a nasty feeling ...
>
> (Ostwald 1991: 194)

The significance of red roses

Nijinsky did not like red roses. The colour red reminded him of blood and provoked feelings that would be appropriate to witnessing blood as the consequence of hatred and destructive cruelty. Red roses therefore had the opposite significance for Nijinsky to white roses. This and other utterances show that he felt that loving brings hatred, violence, destruction and death. In fact, a very possessive, symbiotic love did arouse violent feelings inside him.

But a red rose would not frighten a normal man because he knows that the red of the rose is merely representing, or symbolizing, blood, while Nijinsky has feelings about the rose that would be appropriate to feelings about blood. Simultaneously, in the sane part of his mind he may have known this to be an illusion for without this sane realization he would have been too frightened to enter a florist's shop. A similar mental process can be seen in the religious ceremony of mass where the participant is asked to believe that the bread wafer is the body of Christ. This is a special form of belief, a symbolic statement that frees the ritual from its literal cannibalistic connotations.

Repeatedly throughout the diary, Nijinsky reassures himself – in the person of the future reader of his diary – of his innocence. For instance, taken to a bullfight by Stravinsky, he realized that he was going to a cruel and bloody spectacle. At the entrance he turned pale and became acutely anxious. In a process of projection he then reinforced his denial of murderousness by attributing it to the bullfighters. On other occasions too Nijinsky focused on an evil humanity external to himself, saying 'The Germans commissioned Zeppelin to produce many zeppelins. They thought they would get chickens, but they got dead people' (Nijinsky 2006: 220); 'Lloyd George does not like people who are in his way and has them murdered' (Nijinsky 2006: 37); 'Aeroplanes destroy birds' (Nijinsky 2006: 34). The infantile origins of these preoccupations are clarified by his additional comment that 'Eagles must not prevent small birds from carrying on with their lives, and therefore they must be given things to eat that will destroy their predatory intentions' (Nijinsky 2006: 37). He also referred to Lloyd George and Diaghilev as 'eagles' who 'prevent small birds from living' (Nijinsky 2006: xxiii). He even went so far as to write a letter (which he did not send) to Diaghilev saying, 'Your feeling is evil. My feeling is good. You want to destroy me. I want to save you. I like you' (Nijinsky 2006: 255).

These phantasies make it clear that in his confused unconscious phantasy he was the hungry infant who mustn't upset the mother/servants or the terrible father who destroys little birds/children. But elsewhere the good father appeared as he described how an aeroplane can express goodwill. A comparable process of having predominant in his mind just a good, idealized relationship or a bad, hostile relationship filled with murderous wishes can be detected in his repeated declaration of the purity of his love for his idealized 'good' mother and her symbolic representatives. He said he loved his mother immensely and wrote to her every day.

Searching for someone who could tolerate and understand his aggressiveness, Nijinsky found an inanimate mother figure, which he could not harm. He wrote about how he hugged a tree for the tree understood him. In saying this he has found a symbolic representative of the ideal mother, strong enough to understand and withstand his aggression.

Poignantly, he remarked 'I am a man in God ... I love everyone equally' (Nijinsky 2006: 225).

And he suggested the only way to avoid the awareness: 'I do not think therefore will not lose my head' (Nijinsky 2006: 24).

If Nijinsky were to think, he would realize that he was mad and had, to a degree, lost control of his mind, so he would only feel and never think reflectively.

The murderous internal father

As we have seen, the image of a murderously dangerous male has its origin in Nijinsky's childhood experience of his father, who terrified his children. Just before the father abandoned the family he sought to teach his six-year-old son to swim by throwing him into a nearby river. In the diary Nijinsky recorded how he escaped drowning through his own Herculean efforts, implying that his father was leaving him to drown. Projection of his own infantile aggression turned the actually aggressive father into the inner phantasy of a dangerous murderer. This process deprives the developing boy of the self-assertive aggressiveness that he needed to establish his independence and free him from his infantile tie to his mother. The consequence was that his ill-tempered father was changed into a murderer, in whose presence he was absolutely helpless. Of course, his father was *actually* neglectful in throwing his son in the river when he couldn't swim! Nijinsky's response of appearing not to mind the experience of being thrown in may have been a precursor of the peculiar trait of lack of emotionality such as was present on the separate occasions when he heard of both his brother's and his father's deaths.

If the father's masculinity was six-year-old Nijinsky's role model, it is not surprising that he had no hope of becoming a normal assertive male, for this would have meant being violently abusive. Less malevolence towards his internalized father could have developed if Nijinsky had later been sufficiently influenced by a benign external father figure. Such a benign father would have helped him to tolerate and contain his Oedipal violence. Such a transformation of an internal mother and/or internal father can occur in successful psychotherapy. The fact that Diaghilev did not fulfil this benign paternal role for Nijinsky attests both to the complexity of their relationship and to Diaghilev's own lack of a suitable paternal influence in his childhood. Although Diaghilev exerted a paternal role in guiding his protégé into society and the world, he also rejected Nijinsky in many ways and, like Nijinsky's mother, attempted to keep him away from any move towards independence.

Guilt and the death of Stanislav: 'the strange smile'

Guilt probably played an important part in determining Nijinsky's personality. It is likely that guilt towards his father also contributed to Nijinsky's vulnerability. He loved and needed his father, and was grief-stricken by his abandonment. More importantly, Nijinsky also hated his father both as an Oedipal competitor and for his ill treatment towards both the children in the family and his mother, whom Nijinsky loved, needed and wished to protect. Persecutory guilt prompting fear of attack then followed.

The death of his brother, Stanislav, was followed by a series of changes in Nijinsky, which suggested that his already present persecutory guilt was exacerbated. When he learned of his brother Stanislav's death in the asylum fire during the Revolution of 1917, and some years earlier, of his father's death, Nijinsky's response was of calm resignation, accompanied by a strange smile (Ostwald 1991: 273). This style of reacting with a strange smile might suggest that Nijinsky had strange, and conflicting, feelings when hearing news of their deaths. It is possible that in some way the smile could have some connection with parricidal and fratricidal phantasies.

Stanislav's fate must have contributed to Nijinsky's long preoccupation with death and his dread that he would finally share his brother's fate. In the diary Nijinsky wrote that, having visited Stanislav, he understood lunatics well.

Factors precipitating the breakdown – triggers on a loaded gun

Possibly the sight of heavily medicated people in hospital with choreiform movements, may have contributed to the striking convolutions that characterized some of Nijinsky's dancing. Soon after learning of his brother's death, Nijinsky began to compose a ballet about lunacy. Vaslav's 'acting the lunatic', by putting himself in the place of the dead Stanislav, served the purpose of unconsciously bringing him to life in his own person, thus achieving a massive act of manic reparation and at the same time absolving himself from guilt. This kind of reparation actually repaired nothing internally, because it did not involve Nijinsky in becoming aware of his jealous phantasies, the damage resulting and the nature of what needed repair. At the scheduled dance performance Nijinsky blamed the audience for permitting people to be killed in the war, thus projecting his own sense of unconscious guilt for his own aggressive phantasies.

It was the loss of his brother Stanislav that triggered the eruption of Nijinsky's psychosis. The loss of Diaghilev's patronage and parental indulgence, a disaster which effectively excluded him from ever dancing independently again, had set the scene for the final trigger of guilt. Nijinsky's futile attempts at separation and independence from Diaghilev's control and the Ballets Russes, had brought disaster and shame in the London music hall. The ending of the adulation as a superstar provoked a deep sense of loss in Nijinsky. Also, the absence of dancing roles which contained a displacement of his aggressiveness (the fuel for many of dazzling performances), compounded his sense of despair. Nijinsky had a profound sense that the audience's appreciative look and applause was the love he needed as an artist. Perhaps a manageable degree of emotional stability was achieved through balancing this love with his hatred, which could be given expression through his dancing.

Separation and jealousy

There was another event which some have considered to have precipitated Nijinsky's psychotic states. As we have seen, Romola's close relationship with Frenkel had become the subject of gossip, which included the following details. It was said that Frenkel fell madly in love with her, and that they had a passionate affair but Romola refused to leave Nijinsky, even when he was confined to the asylum. Being rejected, Frenkel plunged into a deep depression, became drug-addicted and attempted to kill himself. To conceal the disgrace Frenkel's family changed their name. Frenkel subsequently returned to his wife.

At certain moments Nijinsky suspected that Romola and Frenkel were secretly having an affair. Perhaps this is what Nijinsky felt when he exploded with rage at the time Romola closed her bedroom door on him. In addition, Nijinsky's conflicted feelings find considerable expression in the diary, where he declares his hatred and jealousy of Romola while at other times also affirming his love.

Despite his resentment of Frenkel for thinking that he was mad, Nijinsky had good reason to feel grateful to him for his determined attempts to help him. Although subsequent doubts were raised about Tamara's legitimacy as Nijinsky's daughter there is no serious evidence to support the gossip; however, only Kyra was mentioned as his daughter in the obituaries.

Epilogue

One question remains as to whether Tamara was correct in her opinion that Romola's influence on her husband and her search for reflected glory ruined Nijinsky's life. It was certainly a tragedy for both Nijinsky and his wife that their grossly mismatched marriage made Kyra the main victim of the impossible requirement that he and she exist in an idealized mother–baby relationship. At an unconscious level, Nijinsky was looking for a symbiotic parent–child union in his relationships with many people. At times this wish was temporarily gratified by his little daughter Kyra, into whom he projected his loveable baby-self while he fulfilled the role of the loving parent.

Unfortunately Nijinsky's real moments of joy and happiness were conditional on the joy not being interrupted by the inevitable triangularities which provoked his response to a 'bad mother' who shares her affections, as on an occasion when he attacked Kyra's nursemaid when she was feeding the child. However, even the most mature of women would not have had the capacity to tolerate and live with Nijinsky's possessive infantile transference. Possibly only a very knowledgeable, experienced and compassionate psychotherapist could have understood Nijinsky and helped him recover from the intensity of his psychotic preoccupations.

The worst things

It should be remembered that the information to be found in Nijinsky's diary, unique in illustrating the way that psychotic states of mind infiltrate sanity, is not necessarily telling us about his actual experience. Perhaps Nijinsky's babble was designed to avoid the pain of knowing his mind was losing its coherence. To understand more of Nijinsky's distress, Ostwald (1991) looked at the original medical notes from the various institutions where Nijinsky was treated.

When Nijinsky was in the hands of Kurt Binswanger he was assigned devoted and observant nurses who recorded his experiences in detail. Here we see clearly how, as the psychotic process advanced, Nijinsky lost the capacity to use and recognize symbolic thinking. Thoughts were experienced as things – word-presentations were replaced by thing-presentations – the attributes of symbolic thinking (such as 'like', 'resembles', 'analogous') were disabled, and symbolic equivalents became symbolic equations. This perceptualization of the conceptual replaced abstract thinking with concrete thinking.

It was said about Nijinsky:

> Today he saw a picture of Christ in a magazine, and it seemed to him as though he were Christ. He cannot explain such ideas to himself at all. He says that his thoughts are sick and that his poor head is sick. He also has the feeling that someone else may be inside his body. When he moves his arm he feels that it is someone else's arm, which does not belong to him.
>
> (Ostwald 1991: 237)

Nijinsky repeatedly begged his doctors to do something about his disturbing thoughts, which he recognized were delusional, and he tried to negate the thoughts by engaging in various behavioural stratagems (compulsive behaviour, mannerisms and rituals). The earlier excerpts provide a perfect example of the survival of a sane part of the self in a mind that is succumbing to the encroachment of the psychotic process. Also, it would have been interesting to hear more about why the attempts at therapy with Nijinsky were felt to have failed.

One likely explanation of Nijinsky's proneness to such an alarming regression lies in his basic weakness of self-identity, his low self-esteem, his tendency to infantile omnipotent thinking and the projective defences. Rosenfeld (1965: 72) suggests that 'When a schizophrenic approaches his object in love or hate he immediately becomes confused with the object' (Rosenfeld 1965: 72). Rey's (1994) explanation for this is that such fusion and confusion with the object is linked with excessive fears regarding attachment and separation. It is conceivable that Nijinsky projected aspects of himself into the therapist and in the transference relationship to the therapist separation and separateness became unbearable between the therapeutic sessions. It may have been one of the phenomena, not well understood at the time, which led to his persecutory fears and his becoming violent between sessions.

Nijinsky felt unloved, unable to dance, unable to choreograph and now he was losing his mind. Living for him was working, and not working felt like death. He wrote, 'I feel so much pain in my soul that I am afraid for myself. I feel pain. My soul is sick' (Moore 2013: 200). As Nijinsky's incarceration in hospital continued he suffered even more terrifying experiences in which he wept and wept, screamed uncontrollably and showed infantile expressions of rage in the form of urinating on the carpet and smearing surfaces with faeces. He masturbated in public, harmed himself and begged for permission to kill himself. His regressed psychotic state of mind can perhaps best be compared with being inflicted by a nightmare in which one is losing one's mind and filled with unbearable terror of death of the Self.

Nowadays the worst of these psychotic states can be contained with psychoactive drugs used skilfully in moderate quantities. With such medication a patient can bring psychotic states of mind within the influence of psychotherapeutic understanding and while being cared for in a therapeutic group milieu. Unfortunately, in Nijinsky's lifetime these helpful psychoactive drugs and sophisticated therapeutic milieus had not been adequately developed. He, unlike Nash, van Gogh and Saramago, did not have a supportive family helping him during much of his life. He was abandoned by Romola for years on end – left to his hallucinations, delusions of persecution, grandeur, control, distorted thoughts, disorganized language and lack of connection of his thoughts. At times though, he poignantly revealed important, valid insights about people and his view of reality.

In ending, one recalls those moments when Nijinsky danced. 'There have been certain moments on the stage – four or five times – when I have suddenly felt a feeling of "I am"' (Moore 2013: 210). These were exceptionally transcendent moments of creativity for which he will be remembered forever.

Figure 3 José Saramago.

3

JOSÉ SARAMAGO

Sanity and the overcoming of adversity

Murray Jackson

Saramago, the world-famous Portuguese novelist, wrote a story, *Blindness* (Saramago, 1997) of extreme violence which won him fame and a Nobel Prize. All his novels are a journey into the past of his country, his childhood, his own mind, and his conscious and unconscious phantasies, both destructive and creative. His depiction of human cruelty portrays the destructiveness that threatens the future of civilization (Barrosso, 1998). Its profound impact derives in part from the echoes that it arouses in the introspective reader.

In this chapter there will be an exploration of various themes, including the way that creative artists may very often derive their inspiration from the interplay between conscious and unconscious sources, in which destructive and creative forces interact. Particular attention will be paid to acknowledging the reality of both conscious and unconscious processes in the inner world. As with the lives of the other artists mentioned in this book, there will be an exploration of the way that loss and emotionally traumatic experiences, particularly in early childhood, may play a part in promoting the artist's creativity.

Early history

In both his 1998 Nobel Prize acceptance lecture entitled *How Characters Became the Masters and the Author Their Apprentice* (Saramago 1998) and in *Small Memories* (Saramago 2009) Saramago presented a memoir of his life, character, personal growth and development. These two publications have made it possible to attempt a psychoanalytic reconstruction of his life, bearing in mind that he is dead and not able to pass judgement on its reliability.

Small Memories (Saramago 2009) is a remarkably frank and moving account of Saramago's childhood from birth to adolescence. It recounts in intimate detail experiences both good and bad, and joys and terrors that have found indirect expression in many of his works, shaped his personality and contributed to his strength of character and his brilliance as a storyteller.

José Saramago was born on 16 November 1922 to a policeman father and a mother who scrubbed floors for the neighbours to supplement their extremely frugal income. The family moved many times from apartment to apartment, sharing the rooms with other families. Sometimes they were so poor they had to rely on charity. On at least one occasion, Saramago's father beat him severely and he also beat his wife who, because of this, temporarily left her husband when Saramago was 18 months old.

When Saramago was two and a half years old his only sibling, Francisco, aged four, died of diphtheria. Immediately after describing this in *Small Memories* (Saramago 2009) Saramago remembers being left alone by his mother who was probably scrubbing the adjoining neighbour's floors. His almost four-year-old brother was climbing up a chest of drawers and 18 month old Saramago, with dummy in his mouth, was watching him, knowing he could not save his brother if he fell.

In Saramago's next memory there is a description of himself at age two or three. He was alone in the street and a group of three or four older boys grabbed him and threw him into a heap of rubble, removed his clothes, and while others held his arms and legs, one of them began to insert a piece of wire into his urethra. He screamed and kicked as the wire penetrated deeper and blood gushed out. No one was there to help him as he wandered in his street. After some time his mother began searching for him, and found Saramago in that wretched state (Saramago 2009: 144–145).

As just witnessed in the earlier passages, after he recalls his childhood memories regarding the possibilities that his brother might injure himself and the story of his brother's death, Saramago's next association is the horrific tale of the neighbourhood boys' sexual assault. This sequential train of thought makes it possible to imagine that Saramago's nightmares were associated with persecutory guilt in which he should be punished for unconscious hostile feelings towards his brother resulting in thoughts about his brother's death. It is that intermingling between internal hostile feelings and external threatening events which could conceivably have propelled Saramago's repetitive and cumulatively traumatic nightmares. The terrifying nightmares began after he saw a horror film at the local cinema and lasted throughout much of his childhood. Night terrors and a recurrent nightmare occurred at night while he had hallucinations by day. A sensitive and imaginative child, Saramago was also, for a time, subject to vomiting attacks brought on by unpleasant smells.

Saramago very much looked forward to visiting his grandparents each summer. He tells of his grandparents taking the piglets under their bedcovers at night to prevent them from dying in extremely cold weather, partially out of concern for the piglets, but also to protect the family's sustenance. Saramago worked hard on the land, assisting his grandfather, a swineherd, whom he loved dearly. He had many memories of his grandfather telling him stories of fights and adventures as they lay together under the fig tree with the stars shining through its branches (Saramago 2009). His grandparents were illiterate but Saramago described his grandfather, who was abandoned from childhood, as the wisest man he had ever met. Saramago seems to have retained the grandparents, rather than his parents, as images of 'the good parents' with whom he identified. Perhaps his father's violence contributed to Saramago's turning to his grandparents as the source of good memories.

Saramago was a bright boy, achieving good grades at school. Almost immediately after learning the basics of reading, without being able to fully understand, he moved himself onto the regular study of *Diário de Notícias*, a newspaper which his father was given daily by a friend. This seemed to foster his interest in politics. Saramago's vivid and rich imagination was obviously stimulated by his grandfather's storytelling, but it was also fired by posters of unaffordable movies at the local cinemas. In *Small Memories* he described how:

> From those eight or ten images I would concoct a complete story, with beginning, middle and end ... Slightly envious, my companions would listen attentively, asking the occasional question ... and I would heap lie upon lie, almost believing that I really had seen what I was merely inventing ...
> (Saramago 2009: 132–133)

Saramago mentioned that in the Liceu Gil Vincente, which he attended for two years:

> I became the biggest liar I've had the misfortune to meet. I would lie for no reason. I lied right, left and centre ... Once I told a classmate my father had bought a copy of Antonio Ferro's book *Salazar* [1939].
> (Saramago 2009: 101)

Saramago's compulsive interest in lying seemed motivated by the wish to create a public image of being from a more educated and wealthier family than his own very poor, unsophisticated one. From the time he was a teenager, imaginative lies infiltrated his dramatic storytelling.

Because his family's poverty made it impossible to pay the school fees, Saramago went to a vocational school in Lisbon where he learned to be a mechanic and metal worker.

Childhood's end – the final scene of the memoirs

Saramago's memoir ends with the 16-year-old Saramago surprising a couple who have just had sexual intercourse in the fields. He turned away and sat on a wall, where a few days before he had seen a large green lizard. The woman hurried away and the man came over and sat beside him on the wall.

> 'Nice woman' he said. I didn't respond. The woman kept appearing and disappearing among the trunks of the olive tree, moving further off all the time.

'She said you know her and would tell her husband.' I still did not respond. The man lit a cigarette, blew the smoke out twice, then let himself slide off the wall and said goodbye. 'Goodbye,' I said. The woman had finally disappeared from view. I never saw the green lizard again.

(Saramago 2009: 181)

This scene seems an apt portrayal of the combination of curiosity regarding the beginnings of adult genital sexuality, the psychoanalytic 'primal scene' of his parents' sexual relationship and the end of the green years of childhood.

Saramago was a self-educated man. When he completed his schooling, he worked as a mechanic and for many years worked by day, and at night read library books to satisfy his passion for language, literature and politics. Later he worked as a translator, a journalist, a newspaper editor and director of the *Diário de Notícias*, the newspaper he had read as a child, before writing poetry, short stories and novels.

Saramago married Ilda Reis at 22, had a daughter, Violante, when he was 25, and divorced at 48. He remarried at 66. His second wife Pilar del Rio, 30 years his junior, is a Spanish journalist who translated his books into Spanish. Saramago spoke about Pilar with gratefulness and fondness, dedicating his autobiographical book, *Small Memories* (2009) to her, saying she 'took so long to arrive'. He lived with Pilar for 21 years until he died.

Memories return – 'From times past comes an image'

In *Small Memories* Saramago recounts a deeply moving experience that emerged involuntarily at a moment when:

The rain is pouring down, the wind is shaking the leafless trees, and from times past comes an image, that of a tall, thin man, an old man, I realise, now that he draws nearer along the sodden track.

(Saramago 1997: 154)

As the old man approaches he discovers that it is his grandfather, long dead. This image, arriving with hallucinatory vividness, releases vivid recollections of happy memories of Saramago's childhood relationship with this remarkable, beloved father-figure:

He looks weary. He bears on his back seventy years of a hard life, full of privations and ignorance. And yet he is a wise man, taciturn, one who only opens his mouth to speak when necessary ... I can hear him talking about the life he's led ... about the livestock he reared, about stories and legends from his remote childhood.

(Saramago 2009: 154)

And with these memories of past happiness comes grief and pain:

> But the image I can't shake off at this melancholy hour is of that old man advancing beneath the rain, stubborn, silent, like someone fulfilling a destiny nothing can change, except death. This old man, whom I can almost touch with my hand, doesn't know how he will die. He doesn't yet know that a few days before his final day, he will have a presentiment that the end has come and will go from tree to tree in his garden, embracing their trunks and saying goodbye to them, to their friendly shade, to the fruits he will never eat again. Because the great shadow will have arrived, until memory brings him back to life and finds him walking along that sodden path, or lying beneath the dome of the sky and the eternally questioning stars. What word will he utter then?
> (Saramago 2009: 155)

Saramago follows this poignant tale of love, gratitude, loss and mourning through a memory, voluntarily recalled, of his grandmother:

> There you were, grandma, sitting on the sill outside your house, open to the vast, starry, night, to the sky of which you knew nothing and through which you would never travel, to the silence of the fields and the shadowy trees, and you said, with all the serenity of your ninety years and the fire of an adolescent never lost: 'The world is so beautiful, it makes me sad to think that I have to die.' In those exact words. I was there.
> (Saramago 2009: 156)

Here we see how Saramago remembers, restores and mourns the lost valued relationships with his grandparents in his inner world. It seems they may have helped him become resilient and survive the turbulence of life with a predominance of loving concern for himself and others, and that in these 'small' memories may lie the explanation of why Saramago writes so much and so compellingly about death, life and searching for the truth about the past. They also provide an answer to the question: where does the artist get his material and by what art does he acquire the power to evoke in us feelings we may not even know we had?

On *Blindness*

Perhaps his most well-known book, *Blindness* (Saramago 1997), is an enigmatic and mysterious story of catastrophe, violence, destructiveness and ultimate recovery. It was made into a film of the same name in 2008. *Blindness* appears to be quite out of character with all Saramago's previous work. Reflection on the content of the book suggested its interesting similarity to nightmare and psychosis. It is clear that Saramago wrote political allegories through describing the lives of unassuming characters. He had been living under Salazar's reactionary 'new state' dictatorship for many years and until the very end of his life he wrote about the dehumanizing logic of dictatorships. One conjecture considered is that in *Blindness* Saramago portrays his consideration of the interaction between Salazar's dictatorship in which he lived and the internalized traumas of his childhood.

Blindness (1997) begins with a taxi-driver waiting at traffic lights and, without warning, going blind. A good Samaritan takes pity on the taxi-driver and drives him home to his wife. That same night the blind man dreamt that he was blind. The next morning, the wife takes her husband to see an optician, who is baffled. Then, that very same afternoon, his wife goes blind! So does the Samaritan. The following morning, the optician goes blind. Later that day, one by one, each of the optician's patients go blind, perceiving not a black, but a white visual screen.

The contagion of blindness spreads throughout the city. Panicked by this infection of 'White Blindness', the Government sets up internment camps and rounds up the blind people. The camps are undermanned and under-provisioned; thereafter, the situation deteriorates. The Government panics, abandons the victims to their fate and fills a mental hospital to overflowing. In the remainder of *Blindness* people make a dramatic entry into a nightmarish experience. Corpses lie rotting, torn and eaten by dogs gone wild and excrement covers the ground. Victims of blindness who are imprisoned in the mental hospital are revealed as both good and bad. In this terrifying situation, where one expects people to band together, there are criminal, brutal and sadistic men, who rape and in one case tear apart a girl with their nails, bite her in a sexual frenzy and leave her with her belly torn open to die.

Starvation within the mental hospital becomes life-threatening. Life is only made tolerable for the central characters, comprised of a group of seven people encompassing each stage of life. They are somehow safeguarded by the doctor's wife, who has concealed the fact that she is the only one with intact sight remaining. The doctor's wife's compassionate behaviour ultimately saves everyone's lives. When the main source of food is destroyed by fire, the doctor's wife collapses in tears of despair, but she soon revives. At this point recovery begins. A sudden rainstorm arrives and washes clean the filthy victims. Everyone's sight returns! The first thing that they see in the church, where they have gathered for sanctuary, are religious statues blindfolded with white bandages. They presume that this mysterious phenomenon is the work of a disaffected priest, condemning God for allowing such suffering.

The story ends with the doctor's wife giving her opinion of the reason for the ordeal. With this dénouement Saramago leaves the reader with the revelation that the story is an allegorical one, as was heralded in the epigraph of the book:

> If you can see, look.
> If you can look, observe.
>
> (Saramago 1997: ix)

Saramago the writer

The chapters of *Blindness* (Saramago 1997) are neither numbered nor titled and there is no paragraphing and few full stops. One feels as though one is listening to someone telling a story. All this adds to the timeless, dreamlike atmosphere of the drama as the reader reaches the moving and enlightening finale in which the group finds its way to the doctor's house, where the story began.

Saramago writes in the style of 'magical realism' typical of such Latin-American authors as Borges, Marquez and Allende, and his unusually complex style of writing has generated a large amount of critical evaluation by specialists. This idiosyncratic style of writing, which may deter some readers, neglects the ordinary rules of punctuation, and confronts the reader with the challenge of persevering with sentences of extraordinary length, peppered with apparently random asides, associations of a near obsessional nature, instructive homilies, analogies and various kinds of information. Despite, or perhaps because of this, Saramago's use of symbolic expression, of dream, allegory, metaphor and analogy offers remarkable wisdom, humour and subtle wit. He emerges as a master storyteller, political satirist and humanist. Saramago was a profoundly introspective and cultured person, devoted to words and meanings, and acquainted with psychoanalytic thinking.

At the time of publication most established critics pronounced *Blindness* (1997) to be Saramago's greatest work, a masterpiece, worthy of the Nobel Prize. Some saw it simply as science fiction, a replica of such classics as *The Day of the Triffids* (Wyndham 1951). Most regarded it simply as a political allegory, the blind leading the blind through the barbarism underlying civilized society. The namelessness of the cast of seven deeply embeds them in the narrative, since the reader may find himself repeatedly needing to recapitulate the drama in order to re-locate the individual in space and time. Their ages and anonymity suggest that the author, using the analogy of the seven ages of man, is asserting that this is a morality tale for Everyman.

Psychoanalytic reflections on *Blindness*

It is widely believed that the work of great artists and scientists is often inspired by emotional conflict, that it is therefore more or less consciously or consciously autobiographical and that such artists are often unstable personalities, prone to experiencing psychotic states. The possible association of genius with psychotic states of mind has been shown for example in Jamison's (1993, 1995) description of her own bipolar disorder.

Freud's discovery of the reality of unconscious phantasy life and of symbolic representation made it possible to attempt a deeper understanding of dreams and of works of art. Freud's (1910) book on Leonardo da Vinci was the prototype of such endeavours, addressing the question of how the artist comes by his material, and what it is that makes him able to arouse both positive and negative emotions of which people may not consider themselves capable.

Although the film *Blindness* (Meirelles 2008) was praised by many, it is possible that severe criticism of it arose from disgust at the content, and from the disturbing effect of the primitive, psychotic quality of the narrative. To the psychoanalytic eye, the content in *Blindness* impresses one as mysterious and much more profound than might at first appear. The story is emotionally disturbing, and for some readers it is likely to be judged as a terrifying nightmare, a response which is common to the familiar genre of horror stories and movies. This horrific quality raises Freud's question, mentioned above, of how the artist comes by his material, and what is it that makes him able to arouse such extreme emotions in the reader? One can ask: What can be discovered about of the nature of the contact that Saramago has with such material? How could such a cultured, benevolent and humanitarian individual write such a horrific story? Moreover, where did he find the motivation to write the story and portray the narrative within it? Segal (1952) implies that, in order to move us deeply, the artist must have embodied in his work some deep experience of his own. This is most likely true of Saramago's work and there will be a consideration in this chapter of what profound experiences of Saramago's may have been present, first in the story, *Blindness* (Saramago 1997), and in some of his other stories, covering both internal experiences and family and social events. This will include consideration of how Saramago has embedded his wisdom and humanitarian philosophy and the acquisition of the capacity to think about the self and the inner world. In *Blindness* (1997) there are various scenes which illustrate the interplay of the forces of destructive violence and compassionate creativeness, love and courage.

Sin and guilt

Guilt is an anguished state of mind arising when one feels that one has wrongly done harm. There can be guilt which is normally appropriate to the situation or guilt which is pathologically persecutory, implying the predominance of 'the law of talion', 'an eye for an eye' morality. Persecutory guilt involves a phantasy that punishment will occur and it will be precisely equivalent to those injuries and damages which had been inflicted upon the victim (Klein 1927). Persecutory guilt involves fear of a dangerous reprisal from the other and thus a fear for the survival of the self, which feels under severe threat (Hinshelwood 1989: 201).

Psychoanalytic theory describes 'depressive' guilt as an achievement during the maturation of personality in which one realizes that one has harmed one's loved objects and there is concern for the other rather than concern solely for the safety of the self (Klein 1940). From early infancy onwards these two opposing attitudes, that of persecutory guilt and depressive guilt, alternate and interact. In the more emotionally mature individual the depressive anxieties involving concern for harm done to the loved other tend to be more prevalent than the persecutory anxieties regarding fears for one's own safety. Depressive moods or depressive illness can co-exist with this 'stage of concern' for others. Depressive illness involves a sense that all one's loved ones within are dead and destroyed and all that is left is utter desolation (Bott-Spillius *et al.* 2011: 312).

In *Blindness* (1997), after the 'good Samaritan' has helped the blinded taxi-driver at the traffic light, he steals the taxi-driver's car and is immediately thrown into a moral conflict of opposing wishes: on the one hand he was obeying those feelings of generosity and altruism and on the other hand, after helping the taxi-driver home, he stole his car (Saramago 1997: 17).

But the balance of good and evil is a delicate one. In other circumstances, perhaps a sense of moral responsibility might have inhibited the criminal temptation and permitted more noble sentiments, found in even the most depraved souls, to emerge (Saramago 1997: 18).

The narrator now begins to reflect on the acquisition of insight and the development of a moral conscience, which can at times become severely persecutory:

> With the passing of time, as well as the social evolution and genetic exchange, we ended up putting our conscience in the colour of blood and in the salt of tears, and, as if that were not enough, we made our eyes into a kind of mirror turned inwards, with the result that they often show without reserve what we were verbally trying to deny. ... the remorse caused by committing some evil act often becomes confused with ancestral fears of every kind, and the result will be that the punishment of the prevaricator ends up being, without mercy or pity, twice what he deserved.
>
> (Saramago 1997: 18)

This passage describes persecutory guilt dominated by 'the law of talion' of the cruel superego. One can liken this to John Nash's 'merciless superego' from which he desired relief (see Chapter 1).

Saramago demonstrates how persecutory guilt might be relieved if the individual achieves sufficient emotional growth to mobilize his latent capacity for empathy, which brings fear, then remorse and regret. The thief was sitting at the steering wheel when he imagined himself in the place of his victim who had been struck blind. At this point a sense of fear arose within him, but it was then followed by remorse as he viewed the image of the blind man saying he needed further help from the car-thief while at the same time being blind. At this point the car-thief, in order to prevent such terrifying thoughts from occupying his mind, focused fully on the traffic (Saramago 1997: 18–19).

These thoughts are terrifying because they bring the fear that he will suffer the identical fate of his victim, and be suddenly struck blind. The 'law of talion' which dictates that punishment identically match the crime (Klein 1927) dominates the car-thief's thinking.

Much later, when the car-thief has become blind and is incarcerated in the mental hospital, he makes a sexual advance to the prostitute, the dark glasses girl, who lashes out, injuring his leg with the stiletto heel of her shoe, inflicting a wound that will eventually prove fatal. Immediately she defends herself against anticipated criticism: 'I couldn't help it, repeated the girl before blurting out in exasperation, The bastard was touching me up, what sort of woman does he think I am' (Saramago 1997: 48).

In extreme pain, the car-thief has a moment of regret and pleads for the girl's forgiveness. This suggests another kind of guilt, which is depressive guilt.

Later the first blind man tells his wife that he has recognized that one of the internees is the scoundrel who went off with the car. Now he had a badly injured leg and so the blind man concludes that he had been injured enough (Saramago 1997: 58–59).

Then follows an awful ordeal that finally ends in the car-thief's death. As his wound becomes infected and agonizingly painful he decides to go to the gate in the hope that the sentries will take pity on him and find him some medication. Trying to find a way to get there he plans to hold on to the guiding rope and crawl on all fours. As he is doing this, the car-thief's conscience accuses him for stealing the car of a blind man, saying that the blind man was sacred. The car-thief thought in reply that technically he didn't rob him, but his conscience suggests that he should forget the sophisms and proceed on his way (Saramago 1997: 70).

This moral conflict proves to be his last, because the soldiers obediently open fire when ordered to kill the car-thief and others.

The drama continues as hell breaks loose. As new victims are forced into the already crowded space of the mental hospital's wards, a criminal element takes charge of the food supplies and commit rapes and murders. The doctor's wife, the only sighted person, herself gang-raped, kills a rapist to save others from being raped and suffers a crisis of severe guilt. Starvation becomes life-threatening, and it is only made tolerable for the group that forms the central characters of the drama by the only one left with intact sight, the wife of the doctor. When the main source of food is destroyed by fire, the seeing wife collapses in tears of despair, but eventually revives and helps the others to survive.

Redemption and transformation of the personality

When the doctor's wife recovers, she weeps long and sorrowfully and responds to the reassurances of her husband. Her weeping could express many different emotional states linked with this situation in which she finds herself: 'tears are often our salvation, there are times when we would die if we did not weep' (Saramago 1997: 93).

In this process of recovery, the doctor's wife begins to lose her belief of having been unpardonably destructive and falls asleep.

Here, as elsewhere, the doctor's wife is accompanied by a dog who has renounced the instinctive aggressiveness of the pack. This 'dog of tears' becomes her faithful and compassionate companion, comforting her in moments of distress by licking dry her tears.

There is a question regarding the nature of the wife's destructiveness. 'If they were to come in with their shoes covered in mud and excrement, paradise would in a flash become hell' (Saramago 1997: 256).

But this filth does not compare with the putrefaction that they have left. The doctor's wife begins to understand something of the significance of their experience. She told herself that they shouldn't forget that all of them went down the steps of indignity and degradation. Previously they had maintained the excuse that degradation belonged to someone else but:

> not now, now we are all equal, regarding good and evil ... forgive this moralising speech, you do not know, you cannot know, what it means to have eyes in a world in which everyone else is blind ...
>
> (Saramago 1997: 260)

The others begin to understand her new awareness – bodily dirt is not psychological destructiveness – the dirt of the soul:

> ... the doctor simply said if I ever regain my eyesight, I shall look carefully into the eyes of others, as if I were looking into their souls, Their soul, asked the old man with the eye-patch, Or their minds, the name does not matter, it was then that, surprisingly, if we consider that we are dealing with a person without much education, the girl with the dark glasses said, Inside us there is something that has no name, that something is what we are.
>
> (Saramago 1997: 261)

The group are emerging from the depths of terror and despair towards a new and deep self-awareness. They begin to recover their capacity to experience dreams in their mind:

> All this still seems like a dream, the wife of the first blind man said, it is as if I were dreaming that I'm blind, When I was at home, waiting for you, I also thought so, said her husband.
>
> (Saramago 1997: 272)

Back in the doctor's waiting room the girl with the dark glasses, confused and perplexed, reminisces:

> the dream continues, but I don't know what dream it is, whether it was the dream of dreaming which I experienced that day when I dreamt that I was going blind, or the dream of having always been blind and coming, still dreaming, to the surgery in order to be cured of an inflammation of the eyes in which there was no danger of becoming blind, The quarantine was no dream, said the doctor's wife, Certainly not, nor was it a dream that we were raped, Nor that I stabbed a man
>
> (Saramago 1997: 280)

Love begins to bloom, idealizations recede, weeping of despair gives way to sorrow and relief, and happiness. They drink for the first time from fresh water:

> When they had put their glasses back on the table the girl with the dark glasses and the old man with the eye-patch were crying. ... the dreams went from sleeper to sleeper, they lingered there, they brought with them new memories, new secrets, new desires that is why the sleepers sighed and murmured, This dream is not mine, they said, but the dream replied, You do not yet know your dreams, ...
>
> As dawn broke it began to rain. The wind beating fiercely against the windows sounded like the cracking of a thousand whiplashes
>
> (Saramago 1997: 262–263)

The noise awakens the doctor's wife. She tries to go to sleep but she awakened hearing the rain suggest to her that she should get up. This led her to wonder what the rain required of her:

> Don't let it stop, she murmured as she searched in the kitchen for soap and detergent, scrubbing brushes, anything that might be used to clean a little, at least a little, of this unbearable filth of the soul. Of the body, she said, as if to correct this metaphysical thought, then she added, It's all the same.
>
> (Saramago 1997: 263–264)

With the acquisition of new insight, normal actual sight returns to the group. The wife is the first to understand the meaning of their ordeal. As the story ends she gives her opinion of the reason for the ordeal: 'I don't think we did go blind, I think we are blind, Blind but seeing, Blind people who can see, but who do not see' (Saramago 1997: 309).

With this dénouement, Saramago leaves the reader with the revelation that the story is an allegorical one, which, as we have already seen, was heralded in the epigraph of the book:

> If you can see, look.
> If you can look, observe.
>
> (Saramago 1997: ix)

This truly archetypal theme appears in endless forms: in classic mythology, as in the hero's voluntary journey into the underworld, returning 'a sadder and wiser man' (Coleridge 1797). Numerous comparisons can be found in religion and psychoanalysis: Balint (1968) talks about a new beginning and, in clinical practice, Rey (1994: 15) speaks of a return to where psychological development goes astray, which brings the possibility of re-growth in a deeply searching psychoanalysis.

The story illustrates great courage and the psychoanalytic concept of growth, from a drama of crime and punishment to the transformative potential of compassion and mercy in the depressive position. This is shown most clearly when the dying criminal is overcome by remorse, and when heaven-sent cleansing rain allows the heroic doctor's wife to weep, and frees the victims from their ordeal. This dramatic conclusion seems to be analogous to the powerful religious theme of cleansing of sins.

With the striking metaphor of the merciful and cleansing rainstorm – 'the most beautiful and glorious thing that has happened in the history of the city' – the author echoes the wisdom of earlier writers, none more explicit than Coleridge's *The Rime of the Ancient Mariner* (1798). A psychoanalytic reading of this powerful poem suggests that after an act of wanton cruelty toward the albatross, symbolizing the beautiful breast-mother, the mariner enters into a state of psychotic depression, a depression accompanied by an inner world of destroyed, dead shipmates existing in the rotting sea with its slimy creatures representing despicable objects of disgust. These represent the destroyed internal objects by which he is claustrophobically surrounded. He tries to escape, but some evil thought prevents it:

> I looked to heaven and tried to pray;
> But or ever a prayer had gusht,
> A wicked whisper came, and made
> My heart as dry as dust.

But the mariner's ordeal, like that of the victims of *Blindness* (Saramago 1997), begins to come to an end with the beginning of love which transforms his contemptuous view of the sea creatures. His benevolent emotions of love, concern and pity have allowed a transformation and reparation of the creatures who have been damaged by hostile feelings. Through his love for them they become beautiful:

> O happy living things! no tongue
> Their beauty might declare:
> A spring of love gushed from my heart,
> And I blessed them unaware:
> Sure my kind saint took pity on me,
> And I blessed them unaware.
>
> The self-same moment I could pray;
> And from my neck so free
> The Albatross fell off, and sank
> Like lead into the sea.
>
> The silly buckets on the deck
> That had so long remained,
> I dreamt that they were filled with dew;
> and when I awoke, it rained.

Here, after killing the albatross, it is the mariner's compassion which releases him from his inferno.

Mourning and creativity

Psychoanalysts consider that it is the work of mourning that installs a lost past and its 'objects' in the inner world, thereby enriching it. This capacity is a measure of emotional maturity acquired in the course of psychological development, when the infant comes to realize that his ambivalent feelings of love and hatred, originally for the nurturing mother, concern a whole person, rather than a 'good'-loved person and a 'bad'-hated person. This depressive concern for damage done through hate to a loved person (Klein 1940) brings guilt and the pain of loss, but also remorse for damage felt to have been done – and that which may still be being done – and the wish to protect and spare or repair the mother, and her later 'significant' equivalent figures. It is this reparative drive that many psychoanalysts see as a most important source of mental growth and creativity (Segal 1991). When depressive concern for damage done to the loved one is not sufficiently developed within an individual, there is the risk of future severe paranoid anxieties arising. The more fully a person's own destructiveness can be recognized, whatever the kind and degree, from envy and small cruelties to murder, the greater is the possibility of reparative wishes being mobilized.

As an experienced translator from the French, Saramago must surely have been well acquainted with Proust's work. It was Marcel Proust's (1989) opinion that the artist is compelled to create by his need to recapture his lost past, in an emotional, not simply intellectual, way, bringing life to the dead and to the emotionally dead living. All artistic creation, he believed, is really a re-creation, the revival of lost memories of once-loved individuals and of a lost past life. Proust revived the term *involuntary memory*, to describe the involuntary recovery of memory by chance associations to experiences such as the taste of a cake, the smell of a public lavatory. Saramago's hallucination of his dead grandfather is a perfect example. Through his descriptions of his grandfather, grandmother and his brother one sees how Saramago recovers, through memory, lost objects in internal reality. He takes a personal journey through mourning of loved ones whom he has lost externally but recovers internally through memory.

Dreams and nightmares – real and fictional – meanings

On the night of his becoming blind at the traffic light, the first blind man dreamt that he was blind. In dreaming of what he knew, the blindness had suddenly become a fact. The dreaming man is thus forced to face a truth that he wishes to deny. In the last line of the book's opening chapter, the author invites the reader to consider that there are two realities, the outer reality of observable facts and the inner reality of dream and phantasy. At that moment they are presented as identical. This paradox is only resolved in the last sentence of the book, when the experience has finally been recognized as a dream. However, the paradox remains, since the sighted doctor's wife has registered the event as being like a dream, but has carried the bodily scars of violent abuse as a reality.

Dreams can be considered as the transcription into symbolic language, by way of the 'primary processes' of thinking, of forbidden wishes, and of unresolved conflicts, conscious and unconscious. Primary process thinking involves visual, instinctual logic of the unconscious. Dreaming serves as the symbolic expression of emotionally charged issues and may sometimes serve such purposes as finding psychological solutions, which analysts describe as 'working-through' conflicts, drawing the dreamer's attention to important matters not represented in consciousness, and the 'adaptive' function of preserving the memory by transferring it to the long-term memory bank. Dreams may express multiple levels of meanings, and are subject to 'secondary revision' by the dreamer on waking; in this remarkable process incoherent fragments may be integrated into a coherent story, the dreamer acting as scriptwriter and casting director. Interpreting dreams is usually an important part of psychodynamic conflict-resolving psychotherapies.

The 'nightmarish' quality of the story of *Blindness* (Saramago 1997) provokes the question of whether the story that Saramago has invented resembles a real nightmare and, if so, in what way. The 'White Blindness' deprives the victims of all perception of day and night, replacing this with a white perceptual screen, within which the story unfolds. This 'White Blindness' seems similar to the invisible white screen that psychoanalysts sometimes refer to as the place where the action of the dream takes place. The people are left with only the faculties of hearing, touch and smell.

In both the fictional and the real dream, these events can perhaps be best described in metaphorical language. Thus, the doctor's wife begins, upon her recovery, to 'realise' that outer reality has been substituted for inner reality, that their 'blindness' has been not lack of sight but lack of insight.

This question of what it all means can occur to the dreamer who awakens from a real nightmare, and it may require a higher level of self-awareness, curiosity and knowledge to succeed in finding answers. To extend the analogy into real life, to the case of a terrifying psychotic episode, a person recovering from a psychotic experience may not believe that answers might be found to understand his experience, may not wish to understand and may not have access to the specialist help that might make the quest possible. The sudden blinding arrest of the motorist at the traffic light is a symbolic theme sometimes found in dreams. It may represent an inner communication expressing the thought that a familiar mode of transport, in life and thinking, can no longer continue, or it may imply an injunction from an internal superego figure to the dreamer that he must stop carrying on in his usual way, whatever that might be.

In the 'primary process' thinking of dreams and psychosis involving visual, instinctual logic of the unconscious, the conventional rules of time and space may be lost. Then thoughts, ideas, memories, wishes and fears may be experienced as events happening in the immediate present. Saramago's fictional dream has enough of the qualities of a real dream to consider that it might be interesting to examine it in the same way as a psychotherapist would work with the material of its genuine counterpart. It may be therefore be reasonable to suggest, by analogy, that the drama evolving in front of the white screen is not only an allegory of human instinctive destructiveness, but is also a symbolic tale of states of guilt, in which paranoid and depressive thoughts and feelings are finding expression as events and actions in the containing space of the wards of the mental hospital where the blind people are interned. The mental hospital may be representative of both the external political dictatorship of Saramago's world and interactions present in his internal world holding the figures, once loved or hated, now installed in the internal world as internalized objects.

These internalized objects can be damaged and transformed substantially by destructive wishes or aggressive behaviour in outer or inner reality and taken care of and repaired by love, which involves the creative activity of reparation. It is also possible that these real or imagined internalized figures may be felt to have been killed or damaged beyond repair, as in the case of a psychotic depressive illness. On the other hand, these damaged objects may be felt to have become persecuting to the dreamer or to the victim of a paranoid illness (Jackson and Williams 1994). In this situation a person may live with a frequent sense of terror, persecution and/or dread (Meltzer 1968).

Siblings in the unconscious

In Saramago's book *Small Memories* (2009) there is a photograph of his brother Francisco taken early in Francisco's second year, with the caption:

> This is Francisco, the brother whose image I didn't dare to steal. He lived for such a short time, but who knows what he might have become. Sometimes I think that by living, I have tried to give him life.
> (Saramago 2009: 184)

Referring to once having been tempted to claim that the photograph was of himself since there was no picture of him at that age, Saramago reflects:

> I still have a baby photo of Francisco, the brother, in December 1924. I have occasionally thought that I could claim it as a photo of myself and thus enrich my personal iconography, but I never have. And it would be the easiest thing in the world to do given that, with my parents dead there would be no one to gainsay me, but stealing the image of someone who had already lost his life always seemed to me to show an unforgivable lack of respect, to be an inexcusable indignity. Render unto Caesar what is Caesar's, and to Francisco what could only belong to Francisco.
> (Saramago 2009: 72)

A great deal is known about the reaction of children to the death of a sibling. For some the loss can bring adverse consequences, not least the loss of a vital supporting presence; for others, capable of sublimation and mourning, the loss of a sibling can have a creative outcome. When he was about two years old, Freud himself had personal experience, losing his brother Julius who was aged about six months. Among the memories Freud recovered during his mid-life transition was how he had greeted his one-year younger brother with hostile wishes and real childhood jealousy and how Julius's death had left him with 'the germ' of self-reproach (Newton 1995).

Being freed from such competition led Goethe to consider that he was a 'child of fortune' (Volkan and Akhtar 1997). Freud (1917: 156) observed that 'if a man has been his mother's undisputed darling he retains throughout life the triumphant feeling, the confidence in success, which not seldom brings actual success with it.' However, being regarded as a replacement for a dead sibling can sometimes have adverse consequences, as the case of Vincent van Gogh illustrates so poignantly.

In Saramago's case the impact of his older brother Francisco's death upon him would be related to the nature of their previous relationship, the way in which his brother became represented in his mind, the nature of the unconscious phantasies which Francisco's death provoked in Saramago and the manner in which Francisco's death became sublimated and symbolized in Saramago's subsequent work. What we do know is that at the time of his four-year-old brother's death, his parents living in Lisbon sent Saramago, aged two and a half, temporarily away to live in the country with his grandparents.

At one point Saramago began a search for more information regarding his dead brother. In searching for Francisco's date of death and his burial, Saramago found that, through some administrative error, neither the hospital where his brother Francisco had been admitted, nor the official records had registered his death. Saramago says that for them Francisco was still alive. It was only through the goodwill of friends that Saramago located in the huge archives of the Lisbon cemeteries a record of Francisco's death. His book *All the Names* (Saramago 1999) brings to life the stories of people buried in the cemetery where Francisco was buried. Saramago's search for Francisco and his bringing to life stories of the buried people suggests some attempt by Saramago to restore and bring alive his dead brother internally.

Many dynamic patterns may follow the installation of a dead sibling in the survivor's inner world of unconscious phantasies and they may lead to a wide variety of consequences for him, depending on how much love and hate was present in their relationship. Loss of a sibling accompanied by destructive jealousy of that sibling can bring persecutory guilt which can, in extreme cases, mark the personality for a lifetime. Hatred and jealousy of the sibling, now dead, may create a damaged internal sibling, turning him into a vengeful and persecutory ghost and this may create nightmares and claustrophobic terrors. The survivor may identify with the lost sibling and be left with a disturbance within his personal identity and sense of self.

On the other hand, loss of a sibling who is loved and mourned can bring the wish to repair the damage done through destructive acts or feelings. This love and concern, the depressive form of guilt, can involve installing in the unconscious the lost valued relationship with the dead sibling. The dead sibling may serve as a supporting and guiding internal presence.

Much depends on the circumstances of the bereavement and the effect of the sibling's death on the family dynamics. A mother and/or father may resent the survivor's aliveness, may fall into a state of prolonged mourning or may suffer a permanent unresolved bereavement reaction, as may have been the situation for van Gogh's mother. Intensely ambivalent feelings about the sibling may generate a lasting sense of persecutory guilt in the survivor.

In the memoir of his childhood, Saramago records repeatedly having terrifying nightmares. He describes the claustrophobic terror, in which a balloon-like object slowly expands to fill the triangular space he is occupying and the object threatens to crush him. In his novels, nightmare, claustrophobia, cruelty, terror and guilt find dramatic expression in the experience of his various characters. Very different experiences are also presented, such as remorse, compassion, courage and salvation.

Although matters of life and death, love and hate, form the basis of very many novels, no doubt at least in part autobiographical, Saramago's novels are truly remarkable in their representation of his personal experience, both in external and internal reality. In re-creating his past he brings the dead to life. In *The History of the Siege of Lisbon* (Saramago 1996) he researches recorded history in order to find the truth. At times he creates a different version of accepted history, returning repeatedly to the confusion of identities. This seems connected in some ways to Saramago's wish to steal his brother Francisco's photo and call it his own.

An enigma remains

The 'inferno' of *Blindness* (Saramago 1997) can be considered as representing both a paranoid world of a reactionary dictatorship and an individual's state of mind, populated by damaged, dying and dead objects, for whom reparation is a possibility. As it works to its conclusion we are shown how love, courage and compassion can overcome destructiveness. This is a reflection of what can happen if there is a progressive maturation from the paranoid-schizoid to the depressive position within humanity or within one's internal world. In an interview (Barrosso, 1998) Saramago has stated that *Blindness* is a metaphor for the blindness of human reason. He seems to have a very strong wish to repair human states of mind in which cruelty exists. By way of explanation he describes how part of our blindness is linked with cruelty and questions how, if we are cruel, we can say we are rational beings who think, speak and create. Saramago's reparative drive compelled him to address the question of what it would take to stop humans from doing all the negative and cruel things in which they engage.

The reader is left with many questions. Why was the author content with offering the story simply as a familiar and obvious allegory? One might ask, does

Blindness (Saramago 1997) revive his childhood nightmares, confronting him with personal persecutory guilt arising from the death of his brother and finally finding resolution in his later work, *Cain* (Saramago 2011) in which he exonerates Cain and holds God responsible? Also required was resolution and transformation of Saramago's hate and nightmare-producing trauma (in this chapter and Saramago 2009: 144–145) resulting from what the violent boys had done to him when he was two or three.

As already noted, the tale of *Blindness* is multi-layered and can be considered from different perspectives. As allegory it records depths of human barbarity, the triumph of good over evil, the reparative nature of mercy and compassion, of courage in the face of despair. The quasi-religious reference to the healing power of heaven-sent holy water (the rain) attests to the author's view that a spark of health and sanity can survive in the most destructive of individuals.

We can now consider a possible reason why the story ended in an inconclusive manner, leaving the participants ignorant of whether or not there was a meaning behind their ordeal and, if so, what it was. The same question can be asked of Saramago's sequel, *Seeing* (2006). When we consider Saramago's focus on symbolic representations, the relation of external to internal reality, and on the guilt-ridden conflict that the doctor's wife experienced about her murder of the rapist-criminal accomplished in self-defence, it seems reasonable to conclude that she was referring to the inner destructiveness of the individual, and not only that of society.

The statement regarding 'seeing, but not seeing' presents an interesting construction. The woman realizes that their ordeal has not been an external reality, but we are left wondering what she thinks it actually was. Was it a shared nightmare or a psychotic episode where phantasy is felt to be happening in the present? Fact and phantasy are not differentiated and the reader is left in a state of confusion, perhaps similar to that of the doctor's wife. We are now left with the question of whether this crucial insight that there may have been a failure to differentiate internal from external reality was shared by the others, and what effect, if any, it had on their personalities.

Saramago offered no answer to the inevitable questions – how, why, what does it all mean, how did the afflicted recover their sight, what happened next? This is an omission that has perplexed many readers. It would be nine years before he would return to the topic, in his book *Seeing* (2006), in which he revisits the cast of the seven anonymous principal characters found in *Blindness* (1997) and brings the story to a horrific close.

Seeing as a catastrophic sequel

We can now turn to *Seeing* (2006), published nine years later, to learn more about the group. We discover that the girl with dark glasses has married the man with the eye-patch and that the doctor has returned to his practice. Life seems to be proceeding peacefully, at least for them. The Government is even more despotic than in *Blindness* (1997). When the population registers a pro-democratic wish by returning blank ballot papers in the election, the Government panics and seeks a scapegoat. A relative of one of the victims denounces the doctor's wife as a murderer, and the police search her out as the instigator of the social disaster. The policeman in charge of the investigations is eventually sickened by the paranoid brutality of the Government and sides with the woman. The result is that they are both assassinated by a contract killer in a horrific manner. When, shot twice, the doctor's wife lies dead in her own blood while her companion, the compassionate 'dog of tears' unleashes a terrifying howl. The howl is instantly cut short by another shot. We can now return to the epigraph in *Seeing* – 'Let's howl, said the dog' (Saramago 2006: xi).

And then there comes the realization, which came also in *Blindness*, that both messages have been fulfilled:

> Then a blind man asked, Did you hear something, Three shots, replied another blind man. But there was a dog howling too. It's stopped now, that must have been the third shot. Good, I hate to hear dogs howl.
> (Saramago 2006: 307)

The meaning of *Seeing* (2006) is now clear. In the blind, hearing is intact, but they have neither curiosity nor interest in what is happening. They are deaf to the shots and cries, they hear, but they do not listen. The visual mode of 'blindness' is followed by the auditory one of 'seeing', and we hear its metaphorical implications. This ending presents the reader with complete hopelessness, since all goodness, human and instinctive, has been destroyed and evil has triumphed, whereas *Blindness* ended on a note of enlightenment and hope. In this way Saramago seems to be issuing a warning that democratic values of justice and humanity are still as threatened as ever in today's world.

Reflections

We can now return to considering why Saramago understood himself to be the 'apprentice' to his unconscious knowledge and memories. It was his experiences of nightmares of his childhood, suppressed, forgotten and perhaps recorded in later dreams that appear to have provided the roots, the structure and the violence of *Blindness* (1997). The tale is not the simple recording of a dreamt dream, but a storyteller's elaboration on a nightmare. Insofar as it has a cohesive narrative of good surviving bad, of love, compassion and reason surviving an ordeal of persecution, of destructiveness being overcome by remorse and sorrow, it could represent the author's own emotional maturation and successful mourning.

Saramago's concluding his book *Seeing* (2006) in tragedy, with shocking violence and the end of hope for truth and justice may suggest that his personal journey into his own mind had not ended. In fact, he is still searching for meaning, for, subsequent to the publication of *Seeing*, Saramago wrote among other books: *Death at Intervals* (2008), *The Gospel According to Jesus Christ* (2008), *Small Memories* (2009) and *Cain* (2011).

Psychoanalytically based exploration of Saramago's writings raises several conjectures. First, it seems that experiences of a most benevolent kind contributed to the strength, introspective capacity, humanism and moral character of Saramago's adult personality.

Second, these great benefits seem to have been accompanied by a legacy of traumatic experiences in his family, his country and internally, which have generated unconscious conflicts of both a destructive and constructive nature.

Giving his Nobel Prize acceptance speech, Saramago proclaimed his gratitude towards his forebears as the motivating force of his creative work:

> The day will come when I will tell these things. Nothing of this matters except for me. A Berber grandfather from North Africa, another grandfather a swineherd, a wonderfully beautiful grandmother, serious and handsome parents, a flower in a picture – what other genealogy would I care for, and what better tree would I lean against?
>
> (Saramago 1998)

Before he died in June 2010, Saramago had already announced that he had achieved his purposes, with reservations:

> I wrote these words almost 30 years ago, having no other purpose than to rebuild and register instants of the lives of those people who engendered and were closest to my being, thinking that nothing else would need explaining for people to know where I came from and what materials the person I am was made of, and what I have become little by little. But after all, I was wrong, biology doesn't determine everything and as for genetics, very mysterious must have been its paths to make its voyages so long ... My genealogical tree (you will forgive the presumption in naming it this way, being so diminished in the substance of its sap) lacks not only some of those branches that time and life's successive encounters cause to burst forth but also someone to help its roots penetrate the deepest subterranean layers, someone who could verify the consistency and flavour of its fruit, Someone to strengthen its top to make of it a shelter of birds of passage and a shelter for nests.
>
> (Saramago 1998)

As so often in Saramago's work, his poetic language leaves the reader with uncertainty about his precise meanings, but this expression of profound regret may suggest that having recently had a personal acquaintance with death, reflected through his words his 'diminished sap', he had a need to make a legacy of his creative work. This appeared to him as a matter of urgency. It is conceivable that he had no further need for international acclaim. In fact, before he died, Saramago was considered by Harold Bloom (2005), a doyen of literary criticism, to be the greatest living novelist. *Cain* (Saramago 2011) could possibly attest to unfinished emotional development, but it must be recognized that the possibility of emotional growth only ends with death. Isabel Allende, in *Eva Luna* (1988), also writing in the tradition of storytelling, has a wise grandmother declare: 'There is no death, daughter, no one dies until we forget them' (Allende 1988: 43).

It was in bringing the characters of his past to life and mourning them that Saramago found the necessary spur for his creativity. In reviving emotional memories and in mourning the lost, dead and damaged objects in his internal world, Saramago discovered they were creating and guiding the person he was becoming. In his eighty-sixth year, after he has been ill, Saramago thinks once again of his grandfather, Jeronimo, who in his final hours went to bid farewell to the trees, embracing them and weeping because he knew he wouldn't see them again and Saramago says, 'So I embrace the words I have written, I wish them long life …' (Saramago 2010: 67).

At the risk of straining analogies even further we could wonder why Saramago destined his heroine to further penance in the form of persecution by the monsters of totalitarian government, and to ultimate death, despite the cleansing of her guilt for the murders. In his book *Cain* (Saramago 2011) he brings the tragic remnants of this epic of crime and punishment, remorse and forgiveness, to its final conclusion. These themes of guilt and remorse seem to have an unconscious connection with Saramago's feelings about human destructiveness, his own and that of others, and his feelings of remorse for any lack of love he may have had towards his brother Francisco.

Saramago died, aged 87, on 18 June 2010.

Conclusion

The horror and disgust that *Blindness* aroused launched this attempt to understand and to empathize with the author. As earlier described, at various places in this book there can be found extremes of terror which are similar to those of people experiencing psychotic states of mind. In other chapters there are descriptions of Nash, Nijinsky and van Gogh's psychotic experiences, which had much in common with a nightmare, and could be understood as waking nightmares. In Saramago's case he did not simply use his fertile imagination to tell a science fiction horror story, but rather he seemed to tell a tale which drew its power from his own experiences of childhood nightmares encapsulating fears and feelings about destructiveness which had become embedded in his unconscious mind.

Saramago's novels can be considered as a remarkable work of self-analysis, individuation and emotional growth of a wise and humble man, a tale of love and devotion, dedicated in gratitude to his forebears and, formally, to his wife, Pilar. *Blindness* is an archetypal drama of crime and punishment, illustrating the transformative potential of compassion and mercy. Le Guin (2006) has celebrated Saramago as 'a true elder of our people, a man of tears and a man of wisdom'.

Until the end of his life Saramago was completely dedicated to the opening of eyes, for in *The Notebook* (2010: 269), he is still reminding us:

> Eduardo Lourenco ... explained to us who we are and why we are this way. He opened our eyes, but the light was too strong for us. That was why we decided to shut them again.
>
> (Saramago 2010: 2)

Figure 4 Vincent van Gogh.

4

VINCENT VAN GOGH

Enduring unrequited love

Jeanne Magagna and Murray Jackson

Few artists can have received more praise and critical attention than Vincent van Gogh. The aim of this chapter is to bring a psychological perspective to some of the roots of van Gogh's creative genius. In particular, there will be an emphasis on the importance of his mother in his life and how his complex and often painful relationship with her was a potent influence on his art and writing. It is hoped that through understanding van Gogh more deeply there will be a greater appreciation of his artistic talent, his strength of character and his passionate determination to win his mother's love.

Early years

Vincent was born in Groot-Zundert, Holland on 30 March, 1853. He was the eldest of six children. Little is known about Vincent's early childhood. His father was a preacher with a stern, moralistic attitude. He was preoccupied with his ministry and not very involved in family affairs. Until he stopped sharing his father's Calvinist beliefs, Vincent idealized him. Vincent also felt hurt and very angered by his father's criticisms of his relationships with various women.

At times Vincent also idealized his mother and this view of her may have had considerable expression in his painting, as suggested in his letters, where he unceasingly asserts his genuine love for her. On most occasions he suppresses the other side of all idealized love – hatred. Sometimes, however, he mentioned that his mother really did not understand him at all. For a time he hid his address from her so that for a time they were not corresponding.

Certainly the presence of a depressed mother, whose grief for a lost child detracted from her receptiveness to him, left within Vincent buried memories of unrequited love. Regardless of how much concern and understanding his external parents showed towards him, the state of his internalized parents led Vincent to say that his youth was 'gloomy and cold and sterile'. After being uncontrollably angry with his father for insisting Vincent stop pursuing the cousin whom he loved, Vincent stated, 'father and I are irreconcilable' (van Gogh 1999b: 228). His art was characterized by these contrasting themes: joy and sorrow, isolation and togetherness, anger and gratitude, death and rebirth, darkness and light, earth and heaven – antitheses which were rooted in his intensely ambivalent emotions towards both his mother and his father.

The 'lost loved mother' existed from the time of his birth, for Vincent's mother, although very concerned about him, was encased in a puerperal depression due to the loss of a still-born son who had died on 30 March 1852, exactly one year prior to Vincent's birth. In fact, Vincent had even been given the same name as his dead brother, and throughout his childhood he frequently accompanied his mother to the cemetery to visit his brother's grave. Vincent's mother seems never to have recovered from her depression linked with this bereavement, and as a result Vincent was consigned to the unfortunate role of being 'the replacement child' or 'penumbra baby' (Reid 2013). The 'penumbra baby' is the term used because 'the attachment between the mother and her dead infant often appears to be so strong that it leaves the new baby in an area of obscurity and uncertainty that the mother finds hard to explore' (Reid 2013: 9).

Vincent described his mother as being 'unloving and cruel to him' at times (Lubin 1972: 28). There was a family history of mental illness (Lubin, 1972) and also there were other children with psychological disturbances in Vincent's family (Gedo 1989): Theo had severe attacks of depression and had psychotic episodes near the time of his illness and death, Wilhelmina spent most of the latter part of her life in mental institutions, and some reports suggested that Cornelius died by his own hand in the Boer War (Meissner 1997: 15).

In addition to her unavailability to him, Vincent's mother may simply not have been able to respond to his exceptionally sensitive nature, his explosive anger and his demand for a perfect fit. Vincent's mother had been one of eight children herself and this may have contributed to her difficulties in being sufficiently capable of attuning to her very sensitive son's needs, as well to her difficulties in sharing her love and care for her other five children. The whole truth about his external mother is not known but the image of an 'unloving' mother certainly seemed to be a representation of his internalized mother. It seems the internalized mother was filled with his projections of unconscious hostility towards her for placing some limits on him and sharing her love with the other children, the dead sibling in her mind, and the father. It is important to note that this picture of Vincent's mother was not shared by the family, who saw her as extremely concerned about his emotional state and very loving towards him. Later on, Vincent's parents also made an artist's studio for him and encouraged him to be a painter.

Being a 'replacement child' in his depressed mother's eyes damaged Vincent's attachment. There was some idea that his grieving mother had 'too tender-hearted a way' with him while he had his frequent tempers and self-willed attitude to life (van Gogh-Bonger 1913: xx). Certainly she felt very concerned for her vulnerable, solitary, introspective boy who was easily depressed, distressed and who had temper tantrums which resulted in frequent punishments. At a young age he sometimes ran almost ten kilometres away from home. Hot-tempered hostility to his mother for not meeting his wishes exactly in the manner in which he wished, was a major problem for the family. Vincent felt they had rejected him, perhaps for this reason, when they sent him to boarding school.

His hostility to his parents impeded Vincent's introjection of them as emotionally supportive parents. It is this hostility which led to Vincent having damaged internalized parents and contributed to Vincent's lack of capacity for a healthy separation from both his parents and his brother Theo. Because he could not retain a sense of 'good internal parents' Vincent insisted that Theo, his brother, become 'a parental substitute', a mother, to him as well as a friend. The lack of a 'good internal parent' involved not having a stable psychic structure for containing his feelings through mentalization (Bateman and Fonagy 2010). In addition, lacking good internal parents certainly left Vincent with a fragile sense of self-identity.

Feeling his depressed mother to be in a vulnerable state seemed to promote a splitting of inner images so that he retained an idealized loved mother and also the hated mother. Vincent had an unresolved infantile hatred and grievance toward the limit-setting mother, and he was unable to accept the 'no' which would make her different and separate from him. In fact, intense unconscious and sometimes conscious hostility often affected his relationship with any person who happened to have a differing point of view or put a limit on what he wanted.

On the other hand, as a child Vincent was emotionally receptive to his mother's deep love of nature, her talent for expressing her thoughts through writing and her capacity to draw plants and flowers. She enjoyed sharing her love of art with her children. Being identified with his mother's artistic leanings, Vincent had a sharp, inquisitive way of carefully observing every nuance in nature, of which he was deeply in awe. When outside he caught insects, collected and labelled flowers and stuck them on paper. He loved and was knowledgeable about many flowers and birds, and watched the birds with great interest. Initially, rather than drawing what he saw, Vincent absorbed himself in observing nature and thinking about plant life in its various forms in nearby wheat fields, the heath and pine forest, learning all about them and taking note of everything he saw. At an early age he was noted for his aesthetic appreciation of nature.

In fact, when he was ill later in his life, Vincent visualized these childhood scenes with pleasure as though they represented a good childhood experience which he had internalized. He wrote to Theo:

> During my illness, I would see our house in Zundert ... each path, every plant in the garden, the fields landscape that you could see from the house, the neighbours, the cemetery, the church, our garden at the back – every detail, even a magpie's nest high in an acacia that grew in the graveyard.
> (van Gogh-Bonger 2008: 39)

Vincent first went to school with 200 children and one teacher and, not fitting in, he was then home-schooled for some years. As mentioned previously, from the ages of 11 to 15, Vincent was sent to boarding schools. Being left at school on that first day by his family, Vincent cried and continuously thereafter he experienced an agonizing separation from the family. His longstanding resentment at being sent away from his family was often referred to by him, and unhappiness about being away from his family significantly contributed to his being estranged from all the other students at the schools. His family was struggling financially, and he was forced to leave school at the age of 15 and go to work in his Uncle Cornelius' art dealership, Goupil & Cie, a firm of art dealers in the Hague.

Nevertheless, in 1868, by the time he was 15 years old Vincent had learned French, German and English alongside the Dutch he already knew. He showed a deep curiosity about many subjects and liked to think seriously about the meaning of life. For this reason, throughout most of his life, he voraciously read books which he felt enriched his knowledge and sense of purpose in life.

During the school holidays spent at home, Vincent sometimes invented delightful games for his younger siblings and they once gave him a rosebush to thank him for being so generous in his interest in them. Often though, while his siblings played together, Vincent spent his time alone in the fields.

There remain few drawings from before he was 17, for although he often drew, Vincent generally destroyed his drawings. His mother recognized his ability, saying when he was 23, 'This is a talent that fills me with joy because it can be of great use to him' (van Gogh-Bonger 2008: 44). His brother Theo also was always very encouraging to him, suggesting that he paint. As well as his mother's artistic activities at home, many factors contributed to Vincent's decision to become an artist. Vincent's unusual visual sensitivity led people to say he 'devoured the world', especially nature, with his eyes. He may also have displaced his love and need for being held with aesthetic appreciation by his mother's look by moving his eyes away from his mother to nature.

'Holding on with his eyes' to the tranquillity and the aesthetic beauty of nature may have been a protection against projections from an anxious, depressed mother's eyes. A baby with a depressed mother often averts his eyes from her and looks elsewhere (Stein *et al.* 1991: 46–52). This phenomenon of using his eyes to 'hold onto' the sunlight, as babies do, and holding onto objects in nature as a way of 'holding himself together' emotionally is referred to as adhesive identification by Esther Bick (1968), a British psychoanalyst. This 'holding on with the eyes' as a way of feeling emotionally integrated may have augmented Vincent's already exceptionally heightened sensory sensitivity.

Meltzer (1988) wrote of 'aesthetic reciprocity', when the beauty of the mother overwhelms the baby and the mother responds with a sense of wonder and awe. Vincent's thwarted infantile wish for an aesthetically satisfying communion with his mother could have led first to 'holding on with his eyes' to nature. Then, as he became more developed psychologically, 'holding on with his eyes' could be transformed to visual exploration. Identifying with his mother through communing visually with mother earth and all its beauty may have led to an aesthetic experience which displaced Vincent's wish for his mother's empathic presence. As is characteristic of an exceptional child, he had extremely developed visual capacities as well as an empathic capacity that was impressively wide and deep, as will be shown later.

This empathy, coupled with sufficient sensorimotor intactness, allowed Vincent to express himself movingly through art (Greenacre 1957: 479–504).

With his various languages and deep appreciation of art, he worked very successfully at his uncle's art dealing business for three years, first in the Hague, then Paris and then – after a quarrelsome separation from his family – in London. It was in London that he experienced his first love.

Vincent's first love and its aftermath

In 1873, at age 20, Vincent fell in love with Eugenie Loyer, the daughter of his London landlady, Ursula Loyer. What moved him was the love between Eugenie and her newly widowed mother. 'I never saw or dreamed of anything like the love between her and her mother, he wrote' (Lubin 1972: 34). He was extremely happy living with them. When he fell in love with Eugenie he was afraid to declare his love to her for fear of being rejected and when he finally proposed to her, he discovered to his dismay that she was engaged. He tried to persuade her to give up her fiancé, a man who had boarded with them before, and he remorselessly pursued her after she rebuffed him.

When Vincent, after being rejected, persisted in trying to seduce Eugenie and persuade her to be with him, Eugenie's mother, Ursula, asked him to leave. His stalking of Eugenie seemed to be driven by a state of mind in which Vincent had become so entwined with the 'loved person', Eugenie, that he could not separate from her. When Vincent redirected his unconscious hate towards Eugenie to the people at work, he lost his job.

The lacking of a 'good internal loving mother' led Vincent to search intensely for 'a loving woman', but perhaps it was partly a search for 'a mother'. He stated, 'in order to work and to become an artist one needs love' (van Gogh 1995: 71). Certainly, Vincent's attempts in forming relationships with women failed, causing him immense suffering. One wonders if in his choices of depressed women he was unconsciously re-enacting a scenario of finding a depressed, rejecting mother like his mother. Vincent's 'compulsion to repeat' (Freud 1920) involved him in choosing people who were likely to reject him, reproducing the traumatic experiences of his early childhood (Gedo 1989: 186).

Consciously though, what attracted Vincent to Eugenie, and also later to Kee Vos-Stricker, was experiencing her being in a strikingly loving relationship with a family member. The kind of tender love these two women emanated was what Vincent greatly desired for himself.

Already an outcast in his own family because of his antagonistic behaviour, Eugenie's rejection brought great sorrow and his character changed (van Gogh-Bonger 1913: xxv). Distraught, Vincent became very thin, quiet, depressed and completely withdrawn. He spent much of his time drawing – drawing the window, the front door, the house and an outline of houses seen from his window – and reading the Bible. His profound melancholic sense of depression lasted for years. Vincent wrote:

> It was in this great misery that I felt my energies dissipating and I said to myself, somehow, I'll rebuild myself again, I will pick up the pencil I had left in my dismay, and I will restart to draw, and since then it seems that everything has changed for me, now my pencil has become a little more docile and I am on my way, it seems to want to stay more and more and more each day.
>
> (Bakker *et al.* 2010: 52)

Vincent drew on any paper, anywhere, with whatever he had at hand. He filled three small sketchbooks with drawings which he gave to a friend's little daughter (Meissner 1997: 25). In 1874, when he visited his family, Vincent also drew sketches of the family home and toyed with the idea of becoming an artist. He did not follow this path but instead he began to read voraciously and, in identification with his father, he eventually began working as an evangelist with the miners in the Belgian town of Borinage.

Vincent quoted Ernest Renan saying 'Man is not placed on the earth merely to be happy ... he is here to accomplish great things through society ... to outgrow the vulgarity in which the existence of almost all individuals drags on' (Bakker *et al.* 2010: 14). In this state, Vincent developed an intense identification with a loving Christ. He asserted 'the Bible is my comfort, the staff of my life ... to follow what Jesus taught mankind will be the purpose of my life' (Gorlitz 1890: 596). Vincent also identified with loving parents, and was hoping to be more accepted by them as he worked as a preacher bringing a religious message of compassion and hope to the depressed, impoverished and suffering peasants in Borinage, Belgium. But Vincent's empathy was extended to many people who, from his young adulthood onwards, were known to have appreciated his generous, empathic nature. Although he had little himself, Vincent made sacrifices, giving away clothes, food and money to the poor men on the street, offering compassion and hope to the Borinage peasants and the miners and offering support to the penniless models whom he painted.

In this way he hoped to look after the desolate and hopeless people into whom he projected his own desolation. P. C. Gorlitz, who shared a room with Vincent in his earliest working life, described how much compassion Vincent had for others:

> One Saturday afternoon we went out for a walk; suddenly he saw an emaciated, miserable, deserted street dog, a poor hungry beggar of a dog. He searched his purse and in it found a 'dubbeltje' (two-pence) – it was all the money he had ... Then he bought two rolls for a penny to give to the dog, and stood looking at the animal full of complacency as it devoured the bread in a few swallows.
>
> (Gorlitz 1999: 597)

When he lost his belief in religion, his work as an evangelist failed, but this led Vincent to identify more directly with the desolate oppressed by living with a dirty, coal-covered face, shabby clothing, starving himself and earning no money. These actions not only exemplified his wish to be close to these oppressed people, but also displayed how intensely uncared for and starved of love he felt. In one of his letters to Theo he expressed this powerfully: 'They [the parents] feel the same dread of taking me in the house as they would about taking a big rough dog ... He would be in everybody's way. And he barks so loud' (van Gogh 1999b: 231). Having no good internal parents, Vincent felt incredibly dependent on his external family and at times he felt that they 'owed it to him' to support him financially (van Gogh 1958: 34).

After his difficulties as an evangelist Vincent moved to a miner's home early in 1879 and remained there until August of that year. Feeling miserable, Vincent, aged 27, felt inspired to draw again, depicting the miners and their families. As he explained to his brother Theo, 'I feel inexpressibly melancholic without my work to distract me ... I must forget myself in my work, otherwise it will crush me' (Lubin 1972: 22). He said he wanted to be an artist to bring human suffering to the eyes of others, and in autumn 1880 he moved to Brussels in order to develop his talent as an artist.

Essentially though, he had a need to recreate what he felt in the depth of his internal world (Segal 1996: 86). Vincent, unconsciously and perhaps consciously, drew and painted as a kind of therapy, in order to recover and recreate harmony in his damaged internal world and thus regain his mental balance. Often his painting was based on identification with a loved mother who introduced him to observing and drawing in his early childhood, but at other times it did not succeed in its task of achieving mental equilibrium – sometimes his painting was more manic in its quality, suggesting at times a beginning of hopefulness, but at other times a wish to flee from any idea of internal damage and suffering.

Vincent's second love

Vincent's second love was Kee (Cornelia) Vos-Stricker, a recently widowed first cousin, seven years older than him, the daughter of his mother's sister. He had spent an evening with Kee and her husband in 1877 prior to the husband's death. That evening Vincent had written to Theo:

> When one sees them [Kee and her husband] sitting side by side in the evening, in the kindly lamplight of the little living room quite close to the bedroom of their boy, who wakes up every now and then and asks his mother for something, it is an idyll.
>
> (van Gogh 1958: 110)

What inspired Vincent's love for Kee was seeing how loving she had been with her husband and her son. After Kee's husband died, in 1881, Vincent shared a summer with his family, the widowed Kee and her four-year-old son. Vincent was very fond of children and was very kind to her little boy.

Seeing Kee again in 1881, Vincent wished to have the kind of love she gave her son as well as wanting the love of the wife he had seen her being with her husband. The way in which his love for a woman created a merging sensation with her comes across when he writes to his brother, 'Theo, I love her – her, and no other – her, forever ... and it is as if she and I had stopped being two, and were united forever and forever' (van Gogh 1958: 158).

The way in which Vincent put himself totally into the experience of loving Kee is a reflection of his 'over-strong tendency towards totality of expression' (Rank 1989) which stimulated his creativity; however, once he completely surrendered himself to loving her it was very difficult for him to let go when she rejected him saying 'to her, past and future remained one' (van Gogh 1991: 29). Kee could not let go of her dead husband, feeling she betrayed him if she loved another.

Vincent pleaded desperately and tenaciously in person and through letters for Kee to love him. She did not answer his letters, thus implying she did not return his love. In response, without invitation, Vincent announced that he was going to visit Kee in her parents' Amsterdam home. When Kee heard he was coming she left her family home and went elsewhere. Vincent arrived at the door and Kee's father, Vincent's uncle, Pastor Sticker, ordered him to leave. Vincent felt 'absolutely miserable' (van Gogh 1995: 78) and determinedly begged, while putting his hand in a lamp flame, 'Let me see her for as long as I can keep my hand in the flame' (Art Experts 2013).

This dramatic incident was followed by Vincent having a row with his own father who wanted him to abandon attempts to gain Kee's love. Vincent wrote to Theo saying, 'I do not remember ever having been in such a rage in my life ... Was I too angry, too violent? Maybe ...' (van Gogh 1991: 32). In any case, Vincent's father was terribly angry and upset and asked Vincent to leave the house. Vincent left home the same day. Thereupon a melancholic depression descended. Vincent's depression was linked with the rejection by both Kee and his parents. His violent row with his father seemed to have been exacerbated by Kee's hurtful spurning of him.

It was at this time, following the failed relationship with Kee, and the fiery argument with his father, that the importance of learning to paint with more skill became increasingly vital to Vincent. Once he made his decision to become an artist, Vincent spent hours passionately studying and drawing on his own, in art schools and through talking to artists and asking for advice and critiques of his work. Painting was one way of restoring order, control and meaning into the psychological chaos which Kee's dismissal evoked in him. Vincent concentrated his whole personality on his work, on each detail of expression, however insignificant. The whole of himself was in the art and he expressed himself through it (Rank 1989: 373). Vincent had not actually given up the entirety of religion for he still had some sense of a mystical union with God which influenced his painting. He once wrote that:

> art is something greater and higher than our own adroitness or accomplishments or knowledge; that art is something which ... is not created

by these hands alone, but by something which wells up from a deeper source in our souls ... that reminds me of what in religion may be called self-righteousness.

(Meissner 1997: 126)

In 1881 Vincent formed a supportive friendship with his cousin by marriage, Anton Mauve. Mauve was already a successful artist from the Hague School. He gave Vincent money, clothing, helped him find a place and also gave him his first set of watercolours, but what Vincent experienced as most helpful was Mauve's critique of his paintings.

Following the rebuff by Kee, with Mauve's support, Vincent started painting hard-working, poor peasants. His melancholic state was revealed in his use of sombre colours of grey and black and in the peasants' serious expressions. His paintings from this period included an *Etten-Scheveningen Woman Sewing* (December 1881), showing a woman resignedly sewing a cloth by hand and *Young Man with Broom* (1882) with his face sombrely facing the ground. In this period he also produced a lithograph of *Old Man at Eternity's Gate* (1882) depicting an old man hunched over with his head in his hands facing the inevitability of death. Vincent seemed to be painting his own melancholy. His total immersion in painting was an attempt to repair the hurt and sense of damage, represented by the old man, inside him. Some wish to heal, to bring something better to the impoverished, was again reflected in Vincent's wish to create a studio in which the poor would receive shelter, food and money in return for their posing (Zemel 1997: 48).

After some time Vincent's melancholic paintings changed. Feeling inspired by Mauve who introduced him to painting in oils and then watercolours, Vincent brought colour into his paintings. He often seemed to appreciate his new-found life's work and once said to Theo:

It is like becoming young again. It is a splendid thing to look at something and to admire it; to think about it and then to say: I am going to draw it, and work at it until I have fixed it on paper.

(van Gogh 1995: 100)

Vincent's third attempt to gain love

Still, work was no substitute for love, and Vincent felt extremely despondent about Kee's rejection of his affection. This was obvious as he confessed to Theo: 'I am but a man and a man with passions; I must go to a woman, or otherwise freeze or turn to stone, or am stunned ... that damned wall is too cold for me' (van Gogh 1995: 79).

Vincent was still longing for sympathy, kindness and friendship in an intimate loving relationship with a woman but he could not wait to find a potentially suitable woman. Impatiently he rushed towards prostitutes for sexual soothing, bodily closeness, conversation and friendship. In the process of talking and sexually liaising with prostitutes, in January 1882, Vincent found Sien, a pregnant woman whose full name was Christina Maria Hoornik. Like his mother, she had experienced the grief of losing a child. Sien had lost not one, but two children.

Sien had experienced a sad childhood and been deserted by the man whose child she carried. Penniless, she found herself walking the streets to earn money to pay for her drink problem and food for herself and her five-year-old child. Vincent added, 'she attracted my attention because she looked ill ... I made her take baths and eat as much nourishing food as I could afford' (van Gogh 1991: 33). It seems clear that Vincent put his desolate self in Sien.

Once again, as with Kee who had been mourning for her dead husband, Vincent was attempting concrete reparation of the damaged, depressed mother he carried within himself by looking after this depressed internal mother which he projected into Sien. He said, 'this ugly, faded woman ... I find in her exactly what I want; her life has been rough, and sorrow and adversity have put their marks on her – now I can do something with her' (van Gogh 1991: 34). In an 1876 sermon Vincent had said, 'Sorrow is better than joy ... for by the sadness of the countenance, the heart is made better' (Jethani 2009).

It was in 1882, while living with Sien, that Vincent drew a picture called *Sorrow* (1882). It showed Sien worn, naked and bent over with her head resting on her knees. At the time of this picture Vincent wrote to Theo:

> I want to do drawings which touch some people. *Sorrow* (1882) is a small beginning ... In either figure or landscape I should wish to express, not sentimental melancholy, but serious sorrow ... I want to progress so far that people will say of my work, He feels deeply, he feels tenderly ... This is my ambition, which is in spite of everything, founded less on anger than on love, more on serenity than on passion. It is true that I am often in the greatest misery, but still there is a calm pure harmony and music inside me.
>
> (van Gogh 1991: 36)

Vincent acknowledged that it was not the first time that he felt 'affection and love for those women who are so damned and condemned and despised by the clergymen from the pulpit' (van Gogh 1995: 79). He described women who prostituted themselves saying 'when I walked in the streets quite lonely and forlorn, half ill and in misery, without money in my pocket ... I felt as if those poor girls were my sisters' (van Gogh 1995: 80). Much to the consternation of his family, Vincent took Sien, her five-year-old child and newborn infant to live with him. He cared for Sien and helped her with her illness and miseries. For 18 months they managed to live together amidst volatile scenes and extreme poverty. For the first time in his life, Vincent had managed to be intimate with a woman and, feeling happy with Sien, wanted to marry her. He explained to his brother:

What exists between Sien and me is real ... Look at the result. When you come, you will not find me discouraged or melancholy; you will enter an atmosphere which will appeal to you, at least it will please you ... a new studio, a young home in full swing – a studio with a cradle, a baby's pot – where there is no stagnation, but where everything pushes and urges and stirs to activity.

(van Gogh 1991: 35)

He later poignantly remarks that, 'when the little boy comes creeping towards me on all fours, crowing for joy, I haven't the slightest doubt that everything is all right' (van Gogh 1991: 48).

Vincent's compassion was profound and genuine, but, as in other previously described situations with women including his mother, it concealed the powerful split-off hostile feelings and phantasies belonging to 'the bad mother'. These hostile feelings, linked with a sense of unrequited love, caused further damage to the internal mother. Attempting concrete reparation through rescuing Sien and attempting to make her happy and well within herself did not successfully repair his depressed, damaged, internal mother nor did it succeed in helping Sien to discover ways of healing herself. There were the inevitable financial difficulties and Sien eventually continued drinking and prostituting herself to make ends meet. Her ill treatment of Vincent left him feeling betrayed and abandoned. It was never clear whether Sien loved Vincent or was taking advantage of his wish to look after her.

Reluctantly, in September 1883, when the family discovered Vincent was in such a deplorable state, they enabled Vincent to accept his inability to heal Sien's depression. He gave up the relationship saying 'the fate of the woman and the fate of my poor little boy and the other child cut my heart to shreds' (van Gogh 1991: 53). Interestingly, Sien was a model for Vincent before they lived together and both Vincent and Sien have referred to the new baby as Vincent's, although historians debate this point. With the ending of the relationship with Sien, Vincent suffered many signs of hopelessness and despair both in his psyche and his body: stomach trouble, loss of appetite, dizziness and headaches (Lubin 1972: 59).

Subsequently, while recovering at his parents' home, Vincent, apparently not as keen as he had been with other women, proposed to Margot Begeman, ten years his senior, but her parents opposed the marriage. As a result Margot poisoned herself with strychnine and van Gogh saved her life by taking her to hospital. The relationship wasn't pursued and it seems that she later killed herself.

Despair externalized and mitigated through creative expression

Once again, it was the canvas upon which Vincent portrayed his sense of impoverishment, of being unloved. Vincent relentlessly threw himself into painting and drawing saying, 'my aim in my life is to make pictures and drawings, as many and as well as I can' (van Gogh 1991: 56). Vincent's depressive moods were influenced by his external mother's grieving for her husband and son and his internal damaged and depressed mother. His paintings gave expression to his loneliness subsequent to rebuff by the three significant women he loved in his adult life and his ongoing conflictual relationship with both his mother and father which made it difficult even to visit his family.

A group of pictures expressing his sense of extreme loneliness and isolation included *Landscape with Pollard Willows* (1884) which shows a lonely figure standing in the centre of a large expanse, neither in the immediate world of the viewer, nor in the heavens beyond (Lubin 1972: 5). He also did no fewer than 13 drawings of the *Head of a Peasant Woman in a Black Cap*. All of the women seemed fairly gloomy but the three women in the December 1884, January 1885 and February 1885 drawings were depicted with eyes filled with deep misery and despair. Having the despair, linked with a damaged internal mother, transferred from his inner world to the outer space of the canvas brought some potential for transformation of Vincent's inner state, a state filled with loss of his 18-month relationship with Sien and his frequent despair about the impossibility of establishing and maintaining a good rapport with his parents.

In this letter to Theo, Vincent affirmed how painting was necessary for him survive emotionally:

> I hope to keep courage after all, whatever may happen, and I hope that perhaps a certain frenzy and rage for work may carry me through like a ship is sometimes thrown over a cliff or sandbank by a wave, and can make use of a storm to save herself from wrecking
>
> (van Gogh 1991: 47)

He also comments, 'I work because I must, so as not to suffer mentally' (van Gogh 1995: 361).

When his mother had an accident in January 1884, Vincent went home and nursed her with tender devotion. Then in March 1885 Vincent's father died, and shortly afterwards his mother gave up the family home in Nuen and moved to a different town. Vincent had left paintings at home and, although she appreciated his paintings, his mother gave them to a carpenter who sold them to a scrap metal dealer. The family home which had been Vincent's retreat in desperate moments was gone and so were his paintings.

In the months following his father's death Vincent's paintings were in sombre tones, grey-white opaque watercolours and black chalk. The pictures gave an impression of sadness and of grave diggers even though ostensibly many of the people depicted were simply working on the earth. It seemed Vincent was expressing the van Gogh family's feelings of grief, particularly his own for his father now dead and buried in the ground. These pictures included *The Potato Eaters* (May 1885) showing sad, disconnected people seated at a table; *A Peasant Woman Digging* (July 1885) showing a woman lifting potatoes but with her head bowed to the ground like a grave digger; *The Reaper*

(July–August 1885) and *A Peasant Woman, Kneeling Seen from the Back* (July 1885). *The Reaper*, drawn at least eight times, was considered by Vincent to be an image of death.

However miserable he was feeling, it seems Vincent felt invigorated by the creative act of drawing. As he drew, perhaps his psyche was released from an encapsulating prison within himself and given some expressive form that satisfied him. Vincent indicated that his goal was 'to make someone dream through the unfinished, through suggestion, through free trace, through discontinuities, through emptiness where the sight deepens to dream' (Haziot 2010: 119).

From November 1885 to February 1886 Vincent lived in Antwerp. He was starving, vomiting and had syphilis, but continued his drawing of models in the art academy there. By 1886, as the pain of inner desolation, the loneliness and feeling he was unloved became exacerbated, he was eating little and drinking alcohol excessively to numb the pain. He lamented that 'the only thing to bring ease and distraction is to stun oneself with a lot of drinking or heavy smoking' (van Gogh 1991: 180). He also acknowledged to Theo, that when he left Theo at the station to come south, he, Vincent, was 'very miserable, almost an invalid, and almost a drunkard' (van Gogh 1995: 392).

Simultaneously, as a method of obliterating his longing for 'another' and his wish for loving, sexual intimacy, Vincent engaged with numerous prostitutes. His attempt was to use these women in a rather compulsive way to have bodily comfort and sensuous excitement but also for having the companionship and pleasure of talking to another human being. Around this time, feeling hurt and angered by the contact he had with his mother, Vincent broke off all communication with her and refused to allow his brother Theo to reveal his postal address to her. Vincent later renewed his relationship with his mother, feeling he could 'begin to love dear old Mother more than before' (Meissner 1997: 196). In his letters Vincent suggested that his dependence on Theo was a matter of life and death and at one point he thanked Theo for saving him from suicide.

But throughout, and most importantly, Vincent's almost daily letter-writing to his brother Theo (between the years 1873 and 1890) and his painting provided mental spaces into which Vincent could creatively give symbolic expression to his intense psychological experiences, his pain and joy. In 1878, before deciding he would definitely become a painter, Vincent had written:

> I still can find no better definition for the word art than this: nature, reality, truth; but with a significance, a conception, a character which the artist brings out in it, and to which he gives expression; which he disentangles and makes free and clears up.
>
> (van Gogh 1995: 41)

Vincent also described how 'throwing himself into his work was his salvation' (Lubin 1972: 26).

Vincent's first exhibition

Vincent first exhibited his work in August 1885, six months after his father's death, in an art gallery called Leurs in the Hague, Holland. Then in March 1886 he moved, uninvited, to live until February 1888 with Theo in Paris, where he met many artists. Vincent's sadness depicted in the drawings after his father's death seemed to be somewhat mitigated by his joy in being with Theo. During 1986 he created an exuberant flurry of very colourful, beautiful flower paintings: *Poppies, Cornflowers, Peonies, Chrysanthemums, Roses and Peonies* and *A Vase with Carnations*. Many of the pictures of flowers were sent to his mother, perhaps as a way of expressing his loving concern for her after her husband's death. He also wanted and needed to be loved and to have his art appreciated by her.

Vincent expressed his pleasure in painting in a letter to his brother:

> There is something infinite in painting ... it is so delightful just for expressing one's feelings. There are hidden harmonies or contrasts in colours which involuntarily combine to work together and which could not possibly be used in another way ...
>
> (van Gogh 1991: 38)

Vincent's use of colour had become an independent means of expressing his states of mind and he rapidly developed into a fervent colourist. During their time living together, Theo experienced Vincent as 'gifted, tender and refined' while at the same time being 'egoistic and hard hearted', 'impetuous and violent' (van Gogh 1913: xli). Although Theo and Vincent had a brotherly love and friendship as well as a symbiotic tie which supported Vincent's remarkable creativity, it was impossible for them to live together. After a serious argument Vincent left Theo's place and moved to Arles. The brothers remained confidants and Vincent described how, despite their both having personal difficulties, he felt: 'What makes us work on is our friendship for each other, and love of nature' (Meissner 1997: 75).

Vincent's friendship with Gauguin and his self-harm

Vincent became terribly disappointed in his capacity to form an intimate relationship with a woman. He was still visiting prostitutes, but he apparently tried to limit the visits to once a fortnight. Vincent was intrigued by Gauguin's work. Seeing Gauguin was unhappy and almost penniless after he left his family, Theo decided to try to help Vincent with his plans to establish his Yellow House in Arles as a kind of commune where impressionist painters, particularly Gauguin, would work together, support each other and share his interest in art.

Again Vincent seemed attracted by someone, like Gauguin, into whom he could project his own hopes and despair and look after them in that way. He wrote to Theo, 'I want Gauguin to have the peace and quiet necessary to produce, and be able to breathe freely as an artist ... and the more quickly he has the standing of headship of a studio, the sooner he will get better' (van Gogh 1995: 392). Vincent's letters to and about Gauguin began to emanate immense longing and enthusiasm for Gauguin's presence. Filled with hope and expectation for the living arrangement with Gauguin, Vincent created a pretty room for Gauguin, saying:

> It will be as much as possible like the boudoir of an artistic woman. It will have white walls with the decoration of great yellow sunflowers ... when you open the window you will see the green of the gardens and the rising sun and the road into the town ... I want to make it really an artist's house ... from the chairs to the pictures.
> (van Gogh 1995: 385)

> I want to make a certain impression on Gauguin through my work ... I wish to have a setting worthy of the artist, Gauguin, who is to be at its head.
> (van Gogh 1995: 394)

Filled with joy and expectations for the creative cooperation and friendship he would share with Gauguin, Vincent painted many pictures which included several *Sunflowers* (1888) in bursts of yellow, the colour which Vincent associated with love. He also painted *Night Café* (September 1888) suggesting that colour could express emotions and didn't have to be true to life. He felt that 'red and green portrayed the terrible human passions' (Bakker *et al.* 2010: 95) and described how his particular use of colour expressed how the café is a place where one can ruin oneself, go mad or commit a crime. There was a sense of exuberance as he painted *Starry Sky over the Rhone* (September 1888), *The Sower* (October 1888) making the sky yellow, suggesting new life, and his *House in Arles* (September 1888), the Yellow House in which he hoped Gauguin would live with him and form a little family group of supportive artists. Vincent was particularly appreciative of his own paintings *The Sower* and *Starry Night* and suggested that they conveyed some deep meaning to him, moving him by the presence of 'a greater quiet in them' (van Gogh 1999c: 57). Somehow Vincent was feeling his internal life could be renewed when he was able to share a more personal intimacy with a friend. His hope was that Gauguin would come and share his house with him for a long time.

This hope instigated his exuberance:

> I work even in broad daylight, in the sun, without any shade, in the wheat fields, and I rejoice like a dragon fly (Letter 535) ... Currently I have the lucidity and blindness of a man passionate for his job ... For this environment of colour is totally new to me and it exalts me extraordinarily (Letter 541) ... At moments when nature is so beautiful as these days, I have a terrible lucidity, then I do not recognize myself anymore and the painting comes to me as a dream (Letter 543) ... This is just how I feel

life when I work hard ... I'm in a frenzy of work, since the trees are in bloom and I would like to make an orchard of Provence monstrous with joy (Letter 473).

(Caron *et al*. 2013: 319–347)

Vincent also longingly writes to Theo, 'it would make a tremendous difference to me if Gauguin were here, for the days pass without my speaking to anyone' (van Gogh 1995: 361).

Gauguin on the other hand was rather dangling Vincent on a hook by saying he was coming, but then giving various reasons for not arriving just yet. He said he didn't have the money. He dreaded the journey, but planned to come. He would come, as soon as he sold a painting. Then Gauguin stopped responding to various letters sent by Vincent. In reality, Gauguin was not enamoured by the idea of staying with Vincent. Vincent became worried saying, 'He may have other plans than coming to join me ... We must have loyalty from him' (van Gogh 1995: 377). He also commented, 'I hope he will come for a good long time' (van Gogh 1995: 375). One sees here how completely involved with Gauguin Vincent had become, almost as though Gauguin was arriving as a lover or the master whom he wished to please.

Finally, in October 1888, Gauguin arrived in Arles. Vincent commented with pleasure about their enjoying eating together, their painting and their talking saying:

> We talked a lot about Delacroix and Rembrandt. Our arguments are terribly electric; we come out of them sometimes with our heads as exhausted as an electric battery after it is discharged.
>
> (van Gogh 1991: 91)

One of the main arguments was around whether paintings should be as Gauguin stated, made of 'pure imagination, arbitrary colour, invented compositions' or whether it was better to have them painted as Vincent suggested 'painted by surrendering himself to nature' and 'celebrating the things that exist' (Cook 2013). Vincent had already said that he wanted

> to paint portraits which appear after a century to people living then as apparitions. By which I mean that I do not endeavour to achieve this through photographic resemblance, but by means of our impassioned emotions – that is to say using our knowledge and our modern taste for color as a means of arriving at the expression and the intensification of the character.
>
> (Cleveland Museum of Art 2007: 67)

van Gogh somehow felt they should reach some agreement, whereas Gauguin thought they were incompatible, both in their thinking and in their way of relating. He decided that he didn't want to stay with Vincent. They managed to live together for several months.

The arguments become so fierce that on 23 December 1888 Vincent threw an absinthe drink at Gauguin and also chased after him with an open razor. Distraught and frightened, Gauguin decided to leave Vincent and go to Martinique, vowing never to see Vincent again. In a fit of anger, just as Gauguin was leaving, Vincent cut off his own ear. He was feeling very disappointed by women and now he was terribly thwarted in his wish to have both his artistic thinking supported and his loneliness alleviated by Gauguin. His brother Theo had just become engaged to Jo, and it was Christmas Eve. Vincent may well have felt left without anyone.

His cutting off of his ear could have several meanings. Vincent may have formed such a symbiotic relationship with Gauguin that separation felt to Vincent like losing a part of himself or left him with 'a wounded self'. Also, turning his razor away from Gauguin and putting 'the wound' on his own body involved redirecting his murderous feelings for Gauguin to himself.

More importantly perhaps, Vincent brought his 'wounded cut-off ear' to the lap of Rachel, a friend from the local Arles brothel, with the words 'keep this object carefully' (Art Experts 2013). Perhaps this action reflected his unconscious hope that his 'wounded self' would symbolically receive the love and care that he so intensely desired. Found in his own bed, unconscious and bleeding with a severed artery, Vincent was brought to the Hotel Dieu Hospital in Arles.

While in hospital, Vincent experienced hallucinations, nightmares and paranoid fears that he was being poisoned. It is hard without Vincent's own personal thoughts to understand exactly what precipitated the nightmares and paranoid fears, but it is possible that they were enhanced by both his drinking and his unconscious rage that he had been abandoned yet again by someone whom he very much wished to have as an intimate friend and colleague. Vincent's symptoms were accompanied by a sense of despair which led him to feel there was no point in living. He stated: 'what is the good of getting better' (van Gogh 1991: 195).

Once again, it was painting which served to rescue Vincent from despair. In fact it was while in the San Remy hospital for a year commencing on 8 May 1889, that he painted several of his monumental works, including *Olive Trees in Mountainous Landscape* (1889) and *La Berceuse* (1889). *La Berceuse*, drawn five times between January and March 1889 while he was in hospital, depicted a mother rocking her infant – perhaps a reinstatement or an evocation of Vincent's wish to be held, loved and mothered while he was suffering in despair in the psychiatric institution he had requested to enter. Vincent's sister, Elisabeth, movingly suggested that the following fishermen's saying was relevant to Vincent's repeatedly drawing *La Berceuse*:

> When the storm grows too mighty for his boat and death beckons relentlessly from the sea. Then the fisherman hears from the lips of *La Berceuse* the cradle songs of long ago.
>
> (Du Quesne van Gogh 1913: 48)

Vincent was continually being 'beckoned' by thoughts of death and while in hospital he drank turpentine and paint to harm himself. He felt dying was hard, but easier than living, particularly living with a bipolar disorder in which he fluctuated from states of elation, when he painted furiously, to a melancholic despair which seriously impeded his painting.

Vincent's love for Theo and Vincent's suicide

Vincent corresponded almost continuously with Theo for 18 years, between 1872 and 1890. Writing letters to Theo became another form of self-expression and perhaps these letters represented some of the few moments in the week that Vincent was intimately and lovingly connected to another human being. On one occasion after Theo visited him Vincent wrote:

> I am thankful for your visit. When I saw you again ... I felt more cheerful and alive than I had done for a long time ... Like everyone else I feel the need of relations and friendship, of affection, of friendly intercourse. I am not made of stone or iron, so I cannot miss these things without feeling a void and deep need. I tell you this to let you know how much good your visit has done me.
> (van Gogh 1995: 41)

In 1883, he had also written to Theo saying, 'I have no real friend but you, and when I am low in spirits, I always think of you. I only wish you were here' (van Gogh 1991: 47). Each separation from Theo was a deeply emotional critical event. Once, after Theo departed from a short visit, a very heavy depression overtook Vincent and he stayed in bed, became very worried about his mental state and spoke to a doctor (van Gogh 1995: 59).

The experience of closeness to Theo and subsequent forms of perceived separation created a huge strain on Vincent's mental health. He had earlier remarked that:

> It is a painful thing, it feels like a prison ... Do you know what makes the prison disappear? It is all deep affection ... To be friends, to be brothers, to love, this opens the prison door for sovereign power, with a very powerful charm. But he who does not have that remains in death ...
> (Caron *et al.* 2013: 319–347)

Theo seems to have represented Vincent's last hope of love in this world. In February 1888 Vincent had already been mentioning his hopes that Theo would come, spend his holidays with him and find pleasure in his new little artists' country-house saying, 'I am very keen to arrange it so that you will be pleased with it' (van Gogh 1995: 385). With the new artists' house, to which he was devoting a lot of loving attention, Vincent had become very hopeful:

> I go out at night to paint the stars, and I dream always of a picture like this, of the house with a group of living figures of our own crowd. I

have a lover's clear sight or a lover's blindness. These colours give me extraordinary exaltation ... I have a terrible lucidity at moments when nature is so beautiful; I am not conscious of myself any more, and the pictures come to me as in a dream.

(van Gogh 1995: 391)

It seems that from the time of Theo's engagement until Vincent's death there were serious hints that Vincent was at risk of suicide. Theo's marriage, in April 1889, seems to have put Vincent's loneliness into sharp relief, and it was just a few weeks later, on 8 May 1889, that Vincent, suffering epileptic seizures, had entered the psychiatric hospital of Saint Rémy de Provence for one year. He wrote to Paul Signacin in April 1989 about his brother's marriage saying 'but at times it is not easy for me to take up living again for there remain inner seizures of despair of a pretty large calibre' (van Gogh 1991: 199). In addition to his despairing thoughts there were psychotic episodes which disturbed his creative activity. Near the same time, Vincent also wrote to his sister, Wilhelmina, saying,

Mother will doubtless be pleased with Theo's marriage ... Every day I take the remedy which the incomparable Dickens prescribes against suicide (opium) ... this is the limit to which melancholy will take me: all the same, at some moments – oh dear me ...

(van Gogh 1991:199)

After Theo's marriage to Jo, on 18 April 1889, Vincent had said:

I am struggling with a canvas begun some days before my indisposition, a '*Reaper*'; ... For I see in him the image of death, in the sense that humanity might be the wheat he is reaping ... I do not know if my zeal is anything different from what I said, it is like someone who meant to commit suicide and, finding the water too cold, struggles to regain the bank.

(van Gogh 1991: 205)

Vincent consciously applauded Theo's marriage but he suffered very severely between July and August 1889 when Theo's wife's pregnancy became known. In fact shortly after hearing the news Vincent had both an epileptic seizure and psychotic symptoms. It took three weeks before he was 'reasonable' again. In his maternal transference to Theo, Vincent may have felt unconscious hostility and jealousy towards the about-to-be-born baby who had interrupted his intense symbiotic bond with Theo. Vincent's epilepsy could represent an attack on his body in lieu of mental representation of these unconscious hostile feelings towards his brother, on whom he so greatly depended (Freedman and Adatto 1968: 437–447; Hendrick 1940: 43–52). Of course, one could say that the timing of Vincent's collapse into more severe psychotic crises and the epileptic attacks was simply coincidental. Certainly though it is striking how Vincent's more chronic mental collapse occurred at times when Theo was preoccupied with his own chest disease, a wife and an ill son. These events made Vincent painfully aware that he was 'alone' and no longer the primary focus of Theo's attention. At the end of his stay in hospital Vincent said, 'I need air; I feel overwhelmed with boredom and depression' (van Gogh 1995: 468).

In Auvers-sur-Oise, in May 1890, Vincent suggested that everything but his work as an artist was very secondary, feeling he did not have the gift for relationships, but couldn't help that at all (van Gogh 1995: 470). A good relationship with Theo in which Theo had emotional space to think about him was absolutely central to Vincent's well-being.

This made it all the more disappointing when Vincent met Theo, Jo and their four-month-old son, Vincent, on 8 June 1890. On this occasion Theo complained of the family's ill health and suggested that his business was bad for his heart. Theo, Vincent's main source of money, was also complaining of lack of money now that he had a new family and the business wasn't going as he expected. Vincent felt he was a burden and a drain on his brother. With all these tensions, Theo and Vincent became irritable with one another and Vincent abruptly went back to Auvers (Lubin 1972: 232).

Vincent had made it clear to Theo that his life depended on Theo's help. He felt threatened by the loss of his brother's financial and emotional support and the quarrel which distanced them from one another. At this point Vincent continued to experience psychotic episodes separated by periods of lucidity. At one point he wrote to Theo: 'As for me, I can't go on ... I can't stand any more – I must make a change, even a desperate one' (Meissner 1997: 99).

Just prior to his suicide, Vincent continued to have episodic psychotic attacks which eroded his painting capacities. He repeatedly begged Theo to spend a week of his holidays with him. He also hoped that Theo would consider having a pied-à-terre in the country with him. In June 1890, Theo's son was very ill, unable to feed and crying through many days and nights. On 14 July 1890 Theo was, according to the evidence, ill with syphilis and was also very worried the family might starve because of lack of money. Both Vincent and Theo became very dispirited about the future.

On 13 June 1890 Vincent's *Portrait of Doctor Gachet* (June 1890) showed its subject with a heartbroken expression, something like Gauguin's *Christ in the Garden of Olives*. Vincent saw it as 'an expression of melancholy ... sad but gentle' (Bakker *et al.* 2010: 22). Vincent had described Dr Gachet as his only friend, but as someone as ill as he was. At Doctor Gachet's request, Vincent also made a drawing *Pieta (after Delacroix)* (September 1889), making the dead Christ's red hair and facial expression similar to his own. In his New Testament paintings van Gogh revealed an overt identification with Jesus and certainly the red-haired Christ reflected this identification (Gedo 1989: 118). Melancholic depression had begun to be a predominant theme in Vincent's mind, but he was still able to continue to paint.

At the same time Vincent ominously reported that 'the prospect grows darker, I can see no happy future at all' (van Gogh 1995: 478). After the quarrel with Theo, in the same letter, of 13 June 1890, Vincent acknowledged, 'my life too is threatened at the very root, and my steps too are wavering' (van Gogh 1995: 478). He also described, 'whether in figures or in landscapes, I would like to express not something sentimentally melancholic but deep sorrow' (Bakker *et al.* 2010: 23). In two paintings Vincent gave expression to this feeling through making vast stretches of wheat under troubled skies: *Wheatfield with Crows* (7–10 July 1890) and *Wheatfield under Clouded Sky* (July 1890). One can imagine that the black crows are symbols of death (Schapiro 1956), but it seems not to symbolize resignation to death but rather to suggest a person who is 'confronted with and afraid of being attacked, killed and possibly devoured' by a persecuting death-force (Heimann 1942). It is as though Vincent felt imprisoned by a hovering, sinister suicidal despair. In speaking about the two paintings Vincent said to Theo: 'I did not need to go out of my way to try to express sadness and the extremity of loneliness ... these canvases will tell you what I can't say in words' (van Gogh 1995: 478).

Vincent felt a symbiotic dependence on Theo, a dependence as well as a loving friendship which was crucial for his creativity. Subsequently, feeling quite depressed, Vincent had again asked Theo to cancel his Amsterdam holiday with his wife and son to see Theo's mother. Vincent wanted Theo to stay with him instead in Auvers-sur Oise, 20 miles outside of Paris where Theo lived. Theo refused and went instead from 15 July to 23 July to Amsterdam with his wife and child.

Theo was preoccupied with his physically ill child, his wife and serious financial difficulties. His choice to have a family and to holiday with his own family rather than being unreservedly present for Vincent left Vincent feeling overwhelmingly painfully rejected, lonely and isolated. He felt left out of 'the family'. Vincent had always denied the negative side of his gratitude to his brother Theo, but he had previously declared that if he lost Theo's love he would commit suicide (van Gogh 1958: 328, 242, 588). Vincent's intense pangs of envy and jealousy towards Theo's family were incredibly magnified by Vincent's earlier jealousy of his mother's attachment to her firstborn dead child, Vincent.

On 27 July 1890, while Theo was with his family on the holiday he had chosen to have away from Vincent, Vincent shot himself. He shot himself in those same fields which he had drawn and described to Theo. When Vincent discovered he was still alive in the evening, he tried to find his revolver to shoot himself again.

Vincent's injuries led to a slow death on 29 July 1890, allowing time for Theo, representing his 'good idealized mother' to come to Vincent's bedside. When he arrived, Theo said he would try to save Vincent, but Vincent said he wanted his life to end, suggesting 'I did it for the good of everybody' (Lubin 1972: 135).

As mentioned, in his *Pieta* (1889) painting of Madonna holding her dead son, Vincent painted Christ's face in a striking likeness to his own, thus showing Vincent's identification with the Christ child and the crucifixion story. Vincent killed himself in his mid-30s, an age similar to Christ's crucifixion. The *Pieta* gives expression to one of Vincent's possible phantasies – that death results in being merged with one's mother, a grieving mother who finally loves and accepts him because he is dead, like his beloved dead brother Vincent. Also, Vincent's lifetime identification with Christ as he painted in his search for the divine and his identification with Christ's death, resulting in Christ being held in his mother's arms, may have contributed to Vincent's suicidal act.

He had experienced two fairly contemporaneous rejections: abandonment by Gauguin and the lack of a visit from Theo. After a lifetime 'of pain, of hurt and rejection, of the failure of love and life' (Meissner 1997: 205) death, with the promise of an eternal blissful place as the sole occupant in a loving mother's lap, may have seemed a very attractive prospect to Vincent.

Shortly after Vincent's death Theo, grief-stricken by Vincent's death, collapsed both physically and mentally. Like Vincent, Theo had also been held intact by his close bond with his brother and Vincent's suicide was a death-dealing blow to his already poor health. In January 1891, six months after Vincent's death, Theo, aged 34, died.

Conclusion

Vincent had a spontaneous emotional honesty which was reflected in his letters to his brother, Theo. He had fulfilled his passion through observing, imagining and creating his pictures. His passionate dedication to painting allowed Vincent what inner stability he could obtain. He wanted to paint. He needed to paint to express his inner visions, the emotions and pathos of his soul, in order to survive life. Vincent realized that it was painting which gave him a huge incentive to get out of mental hospitals. Vincent's lifelong quest for immersion through art in the beauty and power of Nature was a displacement of his unremitting quest for closeness, union, affective acknowledgement and loving acceptance that he felt he had continually been denied in his relationship with his mother and with his father (Meissner 1997: 143).

Throughout his adult life Vincent remained always fully aware that, although giving creative expression to his inner life was helpful to him, artistic activity could not be a substitute for loving intimacy with another human. One of his most moving paintings was *The First Steps* (After Millet) finished in 1890 (van Gogh 1991: 291) in which he depicted a one-year-old being lovingly supported by the mother as the child took the first steps into the father's arms. This seemed a representation of an unfulfilled wish for a loving internal and external couple to support him in his journey through life ... and a wish for a family in which he could have a part.

Theo was Vincent's closest and perhaps only friend and the family member in whom he confided. Theo was his long-distance companion. Vincent shared his thoughts for 18 years with him in his almost daily letters. Writing was also a means of having an interior monologue; however, Vincent wanted more. He also wanted to be loved by a woman and have the completion of a deep sexual, emotional, loving union with her.

He was never able to achieve this and each disappointment in love upset him profoundly, leading more unconscious hostility to be projected to internal figures and sometimes to external figures, for after being rejected he rowed with many others around him. This resulted in Vincent becoming increasingly depressed, saying in a letter to his sister-in-law in 1882, 'I ... feel an inexpressible melancholy inside, which I cannot possibly describe' (van Gogh 2005). At times he was delusional and hallucinating. In fact, Vincent seemed to be holding onto life by a thread when he wrote to his sister-in-law, Jo.

The previous blow of Gauguin departing on 23 December 1889 exacerbated Vincent's unconscious sense of rejection in response to Theo's devotion to his new wife and son. Theo's devotion to his family and mother felt more important than Vincent's need to see Theo. This was all too much and seemed to provoke Vincent's unconscious aggression which he turned towards his own body. This was an aggression which he dared not acknowledge and express to Theo, for he depended on and needed Theo so much. When Vincent lay dying and Theo was reunited with him, Theo said he wished to help Vincent so he would be spared so much despair. Vincent responded, 'The sadness will last forever' (van Gogh 1890).

Perhaps Vincent's inner world, the difficulties he faced and his intense need to be loved fuelled his passion for painting. He frequently asserted that 'Throwing himself into his work was his salvation' (Lubin 1972: 26). It is possible to say that Vincent was a genius who was able to develop by overcoming hard obstacles through the power of his love for his art (Du Quesne van Gogh 1913). However, his loneliness, his disappointment, and his sense of rejection seemed to cause too much pain for him to bear staying alive.

Jo, Theo's wife, may have been the one woman who kept lovingly connected to Vincent in her mind, for she preserved as many of his 2000 paintings as she could and collected and published his letters to Theo. After Vincent's suicide, it was Jo who cared enough about Vincent to ensure that his paintings be exhibited and sold. Sadly, Vincent did not survive long enough to know that his hope for his paintings to be accepted and valued by others was realized. He painted for only ten years, but he lives on in the minds of many others all over the world who admire his determination and passion and his emotionally expressive and deeply impressive works of art.

CONCLUSION

Jeanne Magagna and Murray Jackson

The aim of the book has been to increase understanding of creativity and psychotic states through describing the lives of Nash, Nijinsky, Saramago and van Gogh. The accounts invite the reader to further understand psychological issues which both promote and interfere with development of the human personality. Certain experiences and ways of thinking are common to all four men.

Curiosity coupled with the capacity to be alone

Each of the four men showed an intense innate curiosity for life. Saramago (1998) described it beautifully when he said he received 'no help or guidance except curiosity and the will to learn'. The willingness to learn through one's creative endeavours was particularly emphasized in his words:

> In one sense it could even be said that, letter-by-letter, word-by-word, page-by-page, book after book, I have been successively implanting in the man I was the characters I created. I believe that without them I wouldn't be the person I am today; without them maybe my life wouldn't have succeeded in becoming more than an inexact sketch, a promise that like so many others remained only a promise, the existence of someone who maybe might have been but in the end could not manage to be. Now I can clearly see those who were my life-masters, those who most intensively taught me the hard work of living, those dozens of characters from my novels and plays that right now I see marching past before my eyes, those men and women of paper and ink, those people I believed I was guiding as I the narrator chose according to my whim obedient to my will as an author, like articulated puppets whose actions could have no more effect on me than the burden and the tension of the strings which with I moved them.
>
> (Saramago 1998)

The capacity to be alone in order to satisfy this innate curiosity was also apparent in the lives of all four men. Perhaps it was having a specially gifted mind and such an innate depth of sensitive intuition that made it so enticing at an early age to choose primarily solitary activities over friendships. As a young child and adolescent Nash spent time reading the encyclopaedia and scientific books as well as conducting scientific experiments and later solving mathematical problems. Van Gogh became absorbed in carefully observing nature. Saramago essentially taught himself through reading the newspaper. He also learned about politics, literature and the French language through reading any book he could find. Nijinsky had poor communication skills, withdrew from social contact and felt depressed and isolated, but for hours he would practise dancing, leaping and doing special exercises to strengthen his calf muscles and toes. These solitary activities may also have been less conflictual than being with other people for each of them, apart from Saramago, is described as being wilful, wanting to have his own way and having temper tantrums. Of the four, only Saramago did not seem to have so much difficulty in forming peer relationships, but he does describe being intensely bullied in his early childhood.

Emotional and intellectual capacity

But there was something more than curiosity present in these men's lives. It may be that, unless they had the emotional and intellectual capacity to conceive of what did not yet exist, there would have been nothing towards which they would have been able to direct their motivation to create. They seem to have had capacity to develop an empty inner space, and to devote time, motivation and effort to developing imagination and creativity. They each spent many hours pursuing their creative activities.

Freedom from excessive internal and external criticism

They seem also to have had an internal and external situation free of domination by negative, critical voices that would have made them so fearful of doing something badly that they would not have attempted to do anything creative. Both the lack of intense critical voices and absence of excessive intellectual control leave artists such as these men free to receive guidance from their imagination and from the mistakes made in their creating (Liu and Noppe-Brandon 2009: 189).

Many a creative person has been inhibited by the negative destructive criticism of family, friends and self. Listening to these destructive criticisms can keep one safely secure in its prison guard grip so that no creative enterprise is undertaken. Other factors which have been shown to inhibit creativity include inhibition of aggression through obsessional activities involving over-control, premature attempts to eliminate fantasy activity, premature overemphasis on certain verbal skills, over-emphasis in conforming to the proposed curriculum for classroom learning, coercive pressure to conform to the group's way of thinking and being, emphasis on achieving immediate success rather than on simply using and practising developing one's various capacities in the best way one can (Torrance 1963).

It seems relevant here that much of Nash, Saramago, van Gogh and Nijinsky's learning and creative process came through self-discovery at home rather than through formal learning in educational establishments.

Passionate immersion in the creative process

Motivation to create seems to have come from their passion, a penetrating immersion into their creative tasks and a remarkable aliveness as they made order out of chaos. Van Gogh, Saramago and Nash were all overwhelmed with the beauty of nature. Van Gogh described work on his pictures *The Poet's Garden*, *The Starry Night* and *The Sunflowers*: 'I have a terrible lucidity at moments, these days when nature is so beautiful, I am not conscious of myself any more, and the picture comes to me as in a dream' (van Gogh-Bonger 1913: xliii). '"The Poet's Garden" had arrived to him completed almost as in a visual hallucination. He was awed by "nature being so extraordinarily beautiful"' (van Gogh-Bonger 1913: XLIII).

By the age of four, Nijinsky loved executing complex dance steps taught by his father. He was an incautious risk-taker and his passion for dance led him to be particularly innovative. Alexander Benois described how Nijinsky underwent a personal transformation as he entered wholeheartedly into his role when he put on his costume:

> At these moments ... Vaslav became nervous and capricious ... he gradually began to change into another being ... He became reincarnated and actually entered into his new existence, as an exceptionally attractive and poetical personality.
>
> (Benois 1941: 289)

In spite of their difficulties or in connection with them, all four men were able to create an internal space in which they could courageously choose the unexplored, uncertain, risk-taking path of openness to deep inner experiences which was necessary for creative activity to evolve and develop to such a high degree. The challenge for each of them was to remain sensitively open to the inner world when the external world and aspects of their inner worlds presented obstacles which might have evoked massive and rigid defences against being in touch with their inner worlds of phantasies and imaginative narratives. One can imagine anxieties which might interfere with using creative imagination. One fear might be of losing oneself completely in one's fantasies or in deep unconscious feelings accessed in a creative moment. There might also be a fear of breaking new ground, facing change and transforming one's ideas into something unfamiliar to oneself. A creative act involves an attempt to find some expression of an unfamiliar inner conflict and, thus, more mental conflict and tensions may occur in the process of delving into the deeper unconscious part of the personality.

CONCLUSION

Identifications with loved and healthy aspects of family members

Although family influences on creativity are not always clearly present, the influence of the family on the creativity of Nash, Nijinsky, Saramago and van Gogh is strikingly obvious.

Rothenberg (1990) stated that the creative person often strives to fulfil a parent's 'implicit, unrealized yearnings'.

Nash's father was a university professor in engineering and subsequently an electrical engineer. His mother was a school teacher for ten years before marrying. Both of Nash's parents and his grandparents gave him science books and were involved in sharing their interests and knowledge about the books with him. Although they encouraged Nash to socialize with his cousins and friends, something which he didn't particularly find satisfying, they permitted him to stay at home reading the encyclopaedia, conducting his experiments and solving his mathematical problems.

Nijinsky's parents were professional ballet dancers themselves and they enthusiastically helped Vaslav and his siblings learn to dance before they were four. To be an exceptional dancer seen, loved and appreciated by the audience seemed to inspire all five Nijinskys and, in particular, both Nijinsky and his mother. The wish to be loved by the public seemed linked with their shared disadvantage of having very depressed, emotionally unavailable mothers and absent fathers. Nijinsky's mother lost her own mother when she was eight.

Saramago's grandparents and mother were illiterate, but the art of storytelling was very highly valued. Saramago both loved and idealized his grandfather and his wisdom. He particularly remembered his grandfather 'telling him stories of fights and adventure as they lay together under the fig tree and the stars came out in its branches' (Saramago 2009). Saramago wrote for a long time before he developed his unique style and voice, which blossomed as he rediscovered his identification with his storytelling grandfather. In an interview regarding *Raised from the Ground* (Saramago 1980) he said:

> I was ... not very happy with it, when I realized how it could be written. I saw that I would only be able to write it if I did so as if I were actually telling the story. That could not be done by putting so-called oral language into writing, because that's impossible, but by introducing into my writing a mechanism of apparent spontaneity, apparent digression and apparent disorganization in the discourse.
>
> (Jull Costa 2011)

Saramago at a certain point in his life began writing like his grandfather spoke, without the constraints of traditional punctuation, with the freedom of adventurous, sometimes page-long sentences (Jull Costa 2011).

Van Gogh's family interest in art works consisted of a sculptor from a previous generation, artists through marriage and a series of art dealers. He shared his mother's interests: a deep love of nature, a gift for expressing her thoughts on paper and her pleasure in making drawings of plants and flowers.

In later youth and adulthood, in the absence of 'good enough parents', siblings can sometimes provide intimacy through empathic understanding and reliable support. Such supportive love and understanding which fostered their brothers' creative endeavours was shown by Bronislava, the sister of Nijinsky, and Theo, the brother of van Gogh.

Identifications with possible inadequacies in parental containment

Winnicott (1958) describes how parents provide a cocoon of receptivity to the baby's wishes and needs so that the baby's basic genetic need for protective, nurturing parents is satisfied. Fonagy and Target state:

> The child's mental state must be represented sufficiently clearly and accurately for the child to recognize it, yet sufficiently playfully for the child not to be overwhelmed by its realness; in this way he can ultimately use the parent's representation of his internal reality as the seed of his own symbolic thought, his representation of his own representations.
> (Fonagy and Target 1996: 472)

Sometimes each of these men experienced an absence of the necessary emotional containment and this may have fostered the disturbances that they showed alongside their creativity. Certainly their mothers and fathers experienced interference with parenting through grief and/or severe marital violence and may have had other difficulties in meeting the very special requirements of their sensitive, easily frustrated and exceptionally gifted children. It is conceivable that the high intellect combined with extreme emotional vulnerability of these men made them more readily able to perceive loss, grief and hostility. Whatever the external factors, each of the four seemed to have difficulties in integrating loving and hating feelings, and a fragile internal psychic structure which could not tolerate overwhelming internal or external experiences.

Psychotic states of mind, maybe even in the case of Saramago in his early childhood experiences, then functioned in a way which stopped them thinking more directly about their overwhelmingly intense and painful emotional experiences.

Hallucinating and delusional thinking may suggest innate human capacities which initially have a survival function, and can become a way of dealing with some overwhelming emotions. As in a wish-fulfilling dream, a hallucination can provide solace. For example, trapped starving miners have hallucinated someone giving them food. In his need for company, John Nash hallucinated a college roommate who didn't exist. However, when there is an excess of hostility, and it is directed towards the internalized figures, the hallucinatory space becomes filled with figures holding one's projected hostility. Then, as the tendency to hallucinate become more embedded in the personality, the hallucinations arrive when the individual is experiencing intensely anxiety-provoking moments.

The hallucinations can be frightening, threatening and work against a person staying in touch with the real external world. In fact, their function at times may be partially to avoid staying in touch with the real external world. Of course, a frightening hallucination may represent splitting off negative emotions when it feels safer than having the hostile emotions integrated within the self. Often there may be a fragmentation of the mind when a person is endangered by painful feelings.

For all four men hostility was split off from external people and projected onto internalized figures and this may at times have prevented them from being violent to someone externally. Splitting off and projecting such figures from the internal world to the external world may then be a safeguard to the self in response to an excess of feeling. Problems come, though, when a hallucination or delusion brings back the projected hostility, now located in unhelpful or frightening hallucinatory figures or delusions. A person in a psychotic state is then subject to threatening paranoid delusions of being attacked in various ways in his external world and may actually become violent to innocent external people to defend himself. Such paranoid delusions were experienced by Nash, who feared that the CIA were out to get him, Nijinsky who felt he was receiving orders to kill himself, and van Gogh who feared he was being poisoned. Saramago as a child had recurrent night terrors, nightmares and hallucinations, and slept on the floor of his parents' room experiencing hallucinatory terrors of images which he felt were external to him. They were of 'indescribable beings stirring and threatening to leap out and devour' him (Saramago 2009: 61). The monsters had 'great clawed hands and threatened him with their diabolical grimaces' (Saramago 2009: 61). He also had a recurring nightmare of claustrophobic terror depicting his being locked in a triangular room with nothing ... but a 'something' 'gradually growing in size while a piece of music played . . . and the thing grew and grew' until he was trapped in one corner, feeling terrified that he would be crushed to death (Saramago 2009: 35–36). His traumatic experiences and his hostility towards a sometimes violent father and bullies seem to have led him to feel trapped in an internal space with damaged and persecutory monsters (Rey 1994: 24–25). This claustrophobic terror sometimes led to hallucinations but was often contained within his nightmares. Sleeping in the bedroom with his violently arguing parents for much of his early childhood could only have promoted the severity of his childhood anxieties.

From early childhood Nash, Nijinsky and van Gogh had more obviously unusual personalities with severe temper tantrums and violent rages, which perhaps were suggestive of early mental disturbance. It seems that they each could be seen as desiring fusion with the object of their love and feeling enormous hostile Oedipal rage about sharing the loved person's space with a third person. Nash wanted to be his wife's baby and he felt the fetus was an intruder; Nijinsky could not tolerate his sister's pregnancy nor any perceived separation from his daughter, Kyra, or his wife, Romola; van Gogh could be seen as desiring fusion with his loved women and feeling hatred when anyone had a different opinion (representing separation from him by 'a third') from his own. Van Gogh also seemed to feel unconscious hostility towards Theo (representing the mother in the infantile transference) for having other wishes besides the need to be close to him. Saramago's hostility to his brother may have been to a lesser degree, but perhaps his brother's subsequent death may have resulted in intensification of his persecutory anxieties.

Saramago seems to have found some mental stability through externalizing and pondering over his inner terrors as he wrote his novels describing the actual external terrors of both the Salazar regime and worldwide Fascist activities. However, Nash's delusions stopped him from making sense in solving mathematical problems. Nijinsky's psychotic states of mind interfered completely with his dancing, while not dancing exacerbated his illness. Van Gogh was clear about how his depression impeded his work as an artist and he rarely painted through his psychotic states except after 1890, when he did so to a limited extent. In one of his letters to his sister, Wilhelmina, he complained:

> As for me, I am rather often uneasy in my mind, because I think that my life has not been calm enough; all those bitter disappointments, adversities, changes keep me from developing fully and naturally in my artistic career.
> (van Gogh 1999c: 451)

At present there is no evidence that family disturbance, lack of containment or mental disturbance are linked to or correlate with creativity. The only important personality factor is the intense degree of motivation to create (Rothenberg 1990: 160). In fact, it appears from this book, and from research (Rothenberg 1990) that family relationships which promote mental illness often become a decided hindrance to creativity.

Recreational drugs and alcohol are sometimes thought to be helpful to creativity, but this does not seem to be true for writers and visual artists. Drinking alcohol may have been used to numb both van Gogh's personal emotional anguish and his stress from the laborious effort he often had to put into his painting. At times alcohol may have heightened his emotions too, but it made it difficult for him to keep his mind and his emotions in balance. Both starving and drinking may have contributed to van Gogh's epileptic seizures and psychotic states. Nash felt that medication stopped him from being able to speculate creatively and certainly Nijinsky's creative capacities were dampened both by his psychological conflicts and the overuse of medication. By today's standards the amount of medication he received was staggering – it included chloral hydrate, insulin, bromides, opiates, neuroleptics, scopolamine and barbiturates (Moore 2013).

Except for some initial disinhibiting effects, there seems to be no facilitative benefit of alcohol abuse on literary creativity. The same is true for other substances, including marijuana, and for inspiration or success in the visual arts and poetry. On the other hand, musicians may feel that sedative and inhibition-releasing properties of drugs and alcohol could have some facilitative role in producing innovative and interesting temporal and rhythmic patterns in music (Rothenberg 1990: 157).

CONCLUSION

Loss and its effects on the four artists' creativity

> Writers create worlds for themselves in their books and offer allegories of the Self ... When they express these in the form of fiction or poetry or drama we have the work of a transfiguring imagination which uses symbolic statement and myth to disguise autobiography.
> (Edel 1975: 279)

The creative product can show evidence of the loss, the type of mourning process utilized (Pollock 1989: 547).

At times the creative act is an identificatory act, such as Saramago's writing in his grandfather's storytelling style without punctuation and Nijinsky's dancing with gestures of the people who had been resident in the psychiatric hospital with his dead brother before he died. Or the creative act can be a reparative act, such as paintings of the colourful flowers depicted in some of van Gogh's paintings for his mother after his father died.

These are examples of the effect of visible external loss of important family members, but it seems possible that Nijinsky, Saramago and van Gogh also attempted to repair 'the internalized mother' that was damaged and unavailable. She was damaged and unavailable both through her mourning for a lost child and also by the artist's hostility towards her for her inability to provide empathic maternal care and deal with his hostility adequately. For this reason each of the three could not internalize a mother who fully saw and accepted him as a unique individual. In the lives of Nijinsky and Saramago, absent, unsupportive and violent fathers may have exaggerated any harmful impact of the mothers' mourning for dead or damaged children. An indication of attempting repair of a depressed 'internal mother' is described in van Gogh's 1988 letter to Theo saying: 'I am doing a portrait of Mother for myself. I cannot stand the colourless photograph, and I am trying to do one in a harmony of colour, as I see her in my memory' (van Gogh 1999c: 69).

There is a sense of van Gogh also attempting repair of his 'damaged internal objects' when he writes to his sister saying:

> I should like to paint portraits which appear after a century, to people living then, as apparitions. By which I mean that I do not endeavour to achieve this through photographic resemblance, but by means of impassioned emotions – that is to say using our knowledge and our modern taste for colour as a means of arriving at the expression and the intensification of the character.
> (Cleveland Museum of Art 2007: 67)

These words may reflect van Gogh's wish to give life rather than to destroy it.

Fostering creativity

By providing emotional containment of a child's feelings, the parents foster the development of an internal space in which the imagination can flourish. With the development of a sufficiently good internal psychic structure the child's experiences can be transformed into symbolic forms. Then, with thought and feeling freely intermingling, a creative act can occur! The child makes a narrative of his inner emotional experiences. In speaking about this experience a seven-year-old child said:

> My bird comes out at night in the full moon.
> He flies through the sky.
> At night you can never see him. He is in you.
> His name is imagination.
> He lives in a place called heart brain body.
> It is in everyone.
> Some adults think it is childish, but it will never leave you even if you hide it.
>
> (Liu and Noppe-Brandon 2009: 190)

> The dream is possibly the most spontaneous expression of the human being, a piece of art that we chisel out of our lives ... Every aspect of the dream is part of the dreamer ... but a part that to some extent is disowned and projected into other objects.
>
> (Perls *et al.* 1951: 27)

It is conceivable that every artistic creation, including the dream, involves the pursuit of truth (Meltzer 1983) by means of allowing thoughts and feelings to spontaneously intermingle. The artistic creation, including the dream, provides an opportunity for the mind to be enriched and developed through creating visual dramas of lived emotional experience.

Personal creativity may not necessarily achieve the genius status of that achieved by Nash, Nijinsky, Saramago and van Gogh, but it does seem important to reach towards creative acts. Marion Milner (1950) stresses how in order to create symbols there is the need for constant oscillations between the more logical, differentiating practical, common-sense states and merging with the object through blurring of boundaries. She believes that many insecure people find themselves desperately clinging to the raft of rational thinking for security rather than travelling through the rough sea of imagination. Milner also feels that one can regain lost parts of the self through the use of the imagination and symbolization. In her book *On Not Being Able to Paint* (1950) she describes how one has to sacrifice the old self one knows and plunge into an empty space from which one develops a trust that, out of the unconscious, something new and valuable can grow. She advocates a kind of introspection which involves observing fleeting thoughts, which she calls 'butterfly thoughts' for they leave the mind so quickly. Observing fleeting thoughts and catching them through drawing, writing, dance, music and becoming more deeply aware of one's sensory experiences promotes growth of both the imagination and the self.

To use one's spontaneous imagination one has to let go of facts seen or known and to look at things as though they could have been otherwise. To have an imaginative insight one has to believe in oneself, to put total trust in one's thought. Belief in Self is connected with having a secure inner space in which thoughts and feelings can spontaneously combine and emerge. The goal of freedom is to think thoughts that are one's own (Symington 1990).

Creativity, psychoanalysis and psychotic states of mind

The best psychoanalytic psychotherapy or psychoanalysis is a creative process between the individual and the psychotherapist. Its goal is to integrate split-off parts of the personality, develop a better understanding of the whole personality and facilitate reaching a healthier emotional state. The aim of psychotherapy may not be to eliminate barriers to creativity, but it tends to function to enhance creativity of all types (Rothenberg 1990: 179).

There is an idea that psychoanalysis will be detrimental to creativity. There also still remains a popular notion that severely disturbed people are too ill for psychoanalysis and should only be given medication. These two notions are both untrue and harmful to the creative artist searching for emotional stability and integration of lost parts of the self.

Unfortunately when Nijinsky embarked on some kind of psychotherapy, there was limited understanding of psychoanalytic methods for helping people suffering psychotic states. One problem in his treatment seems to have been that the treatment team did not comprehend his developing dependence on the analyst and his hatred of abandonment between the sessions (see Chapter 2). For this reason the team felt nonplussed by his rage about separation from his psychiatrist.

Van Gogh seemed to have been treated only with medication. Had anyone been able to comprehend his infantile dependent transference relationship with his brother Theo they would have realized that his courage to live with his psychological instabilities had been seriously damaged by Theo's refusal to holiday with him. Just before he shot himself he voiced his sense of rejection and hatred in his letters to both Theo and his sister-in-law. Nowadays, hopefully, there is a more sophisticated understanding of the very worrying potential impact of separation in a relationship of emotional closeness and dependence.

Nash on several occasions prematurely abandoned his psychoanalytic psychotherapy and it is not clear what the reasons were. One of the many reasons one can imagine is that abandonment, a prominent feature of Nash's life, may have re-emerged in the transference relationship to the therapist.

Saramago seems to have had a sufficiently supportive internal psychological structure to enable him, with the help of external relationships, to survive both personal and political adversities.

Psychoanalysis has moved on from the days of Nijinsky and van Gogh. Herbert Rosenfeld (1965), Henri Rey (1994) and Murray Jackson (1994 – with Paul Williams, 2001) were pioneers in the treatment of psychotic states of mind. They emphasized the importance of developing a therapeutic milieu and treatment team which can provide psychoanalytic therapy along with the necessary security to face and resolve turbulent emotional states.

In *Weathering the Storms* (Jackson 2001) it is suggested that the sooner people suffering from psychotic states receive the constructive assistance of psychoanalysis or psychoanalytically based psychotherapy with well-trained clinicians, the better their outlook will be. When a person is entering or about to enter a psychotic state, a psychoanalytic assessment which makes emotional contact with the sane part of the mentally ill person can be crucial.

> All people having a psychological assessment should have the right to tell their life story from the first time of contact if possible. The practitioner has an obligation to encourage the person to do so as well as learning to listen with as high a degree of understanding as possible.
> (Jackson and Williams 1994)

Such a psychoanalytic assessment needs to be followed by a multidisciplinary effort to make an appropriate individualized treatment plan combining psychoanalytic, psychosocial and biological approaches. Such multidisciplinary effort is likely to be the best way to foster the mental health of a person suffering a psychotic state. In addition, changes in family environment which reduce expressed emotion have been shown to reduce the chances of relapse (NICE 2014).

Pharmacological treatment alone does not eliminate aspects of psychotic functioning. Without psychotherapy a person's emotional stability will always remain potentially at risk of being endangered by unmodified, psychotic processes involving overwhelming, unthinkable anxieties and a serious impairment of the individual's capacity to remain in contact with reality.

Long-term intensive psychoanalytic treatment can provide possibilities for an individual to have a more meaningful existence characterized by more love for the self and the other and less domination by the destructive forces prompting debilitating psychotic functioning. Psychoanalytic healing involves the therapist receiving the individual's projections while examining his own countertransference experience in the *here and now* of the encounter. Unconditional acceptance, tolerance and withstanding of the patient's communications is now coupled with the therapist using their countertransference, to intuit in a sophisticated way states of a person's mind not yet symbolized and given meaning. The therapist then tries to convey a truthful narrative of the experience of *the present moment* in the interaction with the patient.

The stance of the therapist involves characteristics similar to that of the artist awaiting experiences for artistic creations. This stance includes: receptivity at the perceptual level, noting all the incoming impressions; emotional and empathic receptivity which allows the analyst to experience within himself whatever the person in analysis may be experiencing; and unconscious receptivity through feelings, representations, ideas which appear and may or may not have emotional significance (Houzel 1999: 44).

Through this psychoanalytic encounter help is given to the individual,

> to reduce his use of projective identification, withdraw projections from others, recover and integrate lost parts of the self while recognizing and tolerating his unwanted and feared impulses, his hatred, his love and his wishes. Part of the challenge is that in therapy people have to relinquish their primitive protections against anxiety which may have been solidified over the years and are initially trusted more than the therapist. If the person is able to let go of the protections and bear the psychic pain of reality, he can hope to acquire a new and more stable sense of identity and a capacity to think for himself about himself and, ultimately, to be able to take more responsibility for his own mind.
> (Jackson 2001: 305)

In psychoanalytic psychotherapy the search for meaning and understanding may be thought of as an attempt to help a sane and cooperative part of the patient's mind to acquire an interest in how the patient's mind works. Levander and Cullberg (1993) have demonstrated the impressive results achieved by psychodynamic treatment.

The lives of Nash, Nijinsky, Saramago and van Gogh suggest that creative activities can at times support working through unbearable emotional states and allow the individual to feel some rational control over mental life. At other times, personal relationships and psychotherapy are an absolute necessity to create a psychological space for thinking 'with an empathic, understanding other'. For a person experiencing psychotic states, psychoanalytic psychotherapy can provide meaning where meaning was absent, and permit a depth of compassionate comprehension hitherto unrealizable, and without this the person's life can become severely impoverished, too painful and perhaps meaningless, as we saw ultimately in the lives of van Gogh and Nijinsky.

Concluding comments

This book is intended to encourage professionals, family members and others to see the world through the mind of a person experiencing psychotic states of mind in the hope that they might find that there is an existential coherence and emotional logic to the way in which the person in a psychotic state is communicating.

Psychoanalytic understanding offered in this book hopefully adds depth and appreciation of what it is to be human, trying to find one's authentic self. Illustrated here are four individuals' struggles with the need to love and be loved and to use creative capacities to the fullest while entertaining feelings of rejection, jealousy and envy which can interfere with these desires. There has been an attempt to elucidate the factors that both led to their success in understanding themselves and loving others and those impasses which interfered with working creatively and forming loving relationships.

CONCLUSION

Freud suggested that psychological health implies having the capacities to work and to love. In their personal writings, Nijinsky and van Gogh acknowledged that, although artistic creativity was extremely important to them, creative expression could not replace loving and being loved. John Forbes Nash also movingly acknowledged this in his Nobel Prize Speech when he said:

> I've always believed in numbers and the equations and logics that lead to reason.
> But after a lifetime of such pursuits, I ask,
> 'What truly is logic?'
> 'Who decides reason?'
> My quest has taken me through the physical, the metaphysical, the delusional – and back.
> And I have made the most important discovery of my career, the most important discovery of my life: It is only in the mysterious equations of love that any logic or reasons can be found.
> I'm only here tonight because of you [to his wife, Alicia].
> You are the reason I am.
> You are all my reasons.
> Thank you.
>
> (Nash 1994)

Hopefully this book, *Creativity and Psychotic States in Exceptional People*, has lent meaning to four individuals' personal quests to become the artists of their own lives.

GLOSSARY
Useful psychoanalytic concepts

The following pages describe some key psychoanalytic concepts used in this book. Further exploration of psychoanalytic concepts including these terms with current relevancy can be located in *The New Dictionary of Kleinian Thought* (Bott-Spillius *et al.* (eds) 2011).

Concrete thinking   This state of mind is characterized by a failure in the capacity to form symbols necessary for thinking about feelings. As phantasies are not distinguished from actions, what is happening in one's phantasy is felt to be happening in the external world (Rustin *et al.* 1997: 272).

Containment   This concept is based on the model of a mother as a container for the infant's projected feelings, needs and unwanted aspects of the self. Using reverie the mother receives the baby's projections and conveys to him the sense that his anxieties and communications are bearable and have meaning. It is through the internalizing of a mindful caregiver that the infant gradually develops the capacity for mentalization. A child has a sense of containment when he believes that his feelings, though sometimes painful and frightening, are manageable and will not overwhelm or drive away the external parents (Dallos 2006: 118). Having internalized containing parents, a child then has the capacity to experience his own feelings as manageable. He regulates his feelings through lending thought to them, rather than experiencing them as overwhelming and requiring projection into others or the use of some other defence mechanism, such as primitive omnipotence.

Countertransference   This concept refers to the whole of the therapist's feelings, bodily sensations and unconscious reactions occurring in the encounter with the person in therapy. Insofar as it is a response to the person's transference to the therapist, the countertransference can provide the therapist with valuable information about unconscious feelings in the patient that are not yet in symbolic form permitting language and thought. Feelings aroused by psychotic people can be powerful and disturbing and thinking about them constitutes a major part of therapeutic work.

Delusions   A theory or belief, which is held with conviction despite evidence and arguments to the contrary, and which is not explained by the person's cultural background. Delusions often have important meaning and a hidden emotional charge. Examples of some of the most common types of delusions are:

- *Delusions of persecution or paranoia* – Belief that others (often a vague 'they') are a source of danger. Persecutory delusions may involve bizarre ideas and plots (e.g. 'The Italian waiter is trying to poison my soup'). Persecutory delusions represent retaliatory consequences in the mind for hostile, envious and acquisitive wishes.
- *Delusions of reference* – A neutral event is believed to have a special and personal meaning. For example, a person might believe that the broadcaster he is watching on the TV screen is in love with him and sending him special messages through her eyes.
- *Delusions of grandeur* – Belief that one is a famous or important figure, such as the Messiah. Alternately, delusions of grandeur may involve the belief that one has unusual powers that no one else has, such as the ability to become invisible.
- *Delusions of control* – Belief that one's thoughts or actions are being controlled by outside, alien forces. Common delusions of control include thought broadcasting ('Hitler is planting thoughts in my head').

The analyst's task is to understand a person's emotional experience of living with the delusional belief and the functions it serves before proceeding into any further therapeutic activity in relation to it.

Denial The process of denial can involve disposing of limitations of the self and the importance of the people upon whom one depends. It can also involve obliteration of perceptions, particularly of bad parts of the self or the other.

Depressive anxieties and the depressive position The depressive position is a state of mind characterized by the bringing together of split feelings, so that a person recognizes that the idealized and hated mother are the same person. Relationships then are felt to be with whole people for whom both love and hate are felt (Klein 1935). Depressive anxieties occur when there is the recognition that the good internal object has been and can be attacked and destroyed. This recognition sets in train the mourning process, with its cortege of depressive anxieties and guilt feelings, which awaken in turn the urge to repair, which entails hope (Etchegoyen 1991: 674). A deepening of love for the object accompanies this process. Omnipotent control over the object diminishes. In the depressive position anxiety is also felt on behalf of the object. Recognition of the other as separate from oneself encompasses the other's relationships; thus awareness of the Oedipal situation inevitably accompanies the depressive position.

Attainment of the capacity for depressive anxiety is considered a necessary quality for the forming or maintaining of mature object relationships, since it is the source of generosity, altruistic feelings, reparative wishes, and the capacity to tolerate the object's ultimate separateness.

(Jackson 1994: 189)

Dissociation This refers to a partial or complete disruption of the normal integration of a person's consciousness. Dissociation can be a protective response to trauma for it allows the conscious self to distance itself from overwhelming experiences that are too much for the psyche to process.

Envy The envious wish to own the possessions, qualities or good fortunes that the object is seen or believed to have and that the subject does not have, may generate admiration and a desire to emulate and acquire through personal effort. This represents the life-affirming impulse and positive side of envy. In the case of destructive envy there exists a wish to deprive the object of his possession or to spoil it by devaluation or other hostile means. Klein suggests it is a common feature in mental illness (Jackson 2001: 325).

Inner world and internal objects or figures There is the external world with external figures, and there is the internal world of internal objects or figures formed by the introjective identification with important loved and hated external figures distorted by phantasies and feelings projected onto them. The person's internal world provides the impetus for re-enactment in relation to external figures.

Internalization/introjection These mechanisms involve taking in aspects, qualities and skills of the parents and other important people in one's life. Very early internalization of good-containing objects leads to the ensuing experience of an internal sense of goodness, self-confidence and mental stability. Internalization of a good-containing object is important for integration of the self. Internalization of the bad object also occurs and this can be felt to endanger the person.

Introjective identification This concept describes a process of being in a relationship with someone and taking in aspects, qualities or skills of the person in such a way that they are gradually identified with and inform the character of an individual. This process is the way in which a person develops in an emotionally healthy way with a capacity to think about emotional experiences. Introjection of bad qualities also occurs.

Jealousy In contrast to envy, jealousy involves three parties, and it is the third who, feeling excluded, suffers the emotion of jealousy. Jealousy is related to possessiveness of the other. Jealousy is often an important pathogenic factor in some types of mental illness (Jackson 2001: 329).

Manic defences Klein used the term manic defences to describe a series of defensive mental operations aimed at escaping mental pain. Omnipotent thinking and a belief in personal omniscience characterize these defences.

They comprise denial of psychic reality and devaluation of the importance of the object, associated with an attitude of contempt and triumph. Intense excitement and a pathological sense of well-being are often present.

Mentalizing   This is the process by which we make sense of each other and ourselves. It involves mental activity which is attentive to and imagines what other people might be thinking or feeling. It implies perceiving and interpreting behaviour as combined with intentional mental states. It involves analysing one's emotional experiences (Bateman and Fonagy 2006: 2).

Narcissism   Narcissism is caused by disturbance in relation to the mother. There is a withdrawal of love from an object that has disappointed through either the threat of loss or some kind of slight, back to the more secure love of the self (Bott Spillius *et al.* 2011: 409–414).

Pathological narcissism involves an omnipotent idealization of the destructive or bad parts of the self, which are directed against any dependence on a positive loving object relationship (Rosenfeld 1971: 246).

Object   Freud initially used the technical term 'object' to refer to the person or thing upon which energy was discharged for the purpose of obtaining some satisfaction and relief. Later, Freud and others looked at the psychological aspects of the relationship to the object. A significant person towards whom one might feel love or hate would be referred to as an 'object' (Bott Spillius *et al.* 2011: 424).

Object relations   This theory implies that people are seeking to have relationships with an object. The concept relates to a psychoanalytic style of thinking about phantasies in relation to an object. These may include oral, anal and genital loving and hostile phantasies in relation to an object (Bott Spillius et al. 2011: 419–420).

Omnipotence   This is a concept referring to a notion that one's thoughts have a power to protect the self from harmful anxieties. For a person using primitive omnipotence there is a turning to one's phantasies as powerful and controlling protections. Omnipotence is used rather than facing the reality of one's persecutory fears and depending on the caregivers necessary for one's emotional development.

Paranoid-schizoid position and paranoid anxieties   The paranoid-schizoid position is a state of mind characterized by the splitting of objects into extremely good (ideal) and extremely bad ones (Klein 1946). Schizoid defences involve splitting of love and hate, good and bad, to diminish pain and threats to the ego by severing disturbing portions of experience from awareness. Paranoid anxieties are characterized by persecutory anxieties concerning survival of the self (Bott-Spillius *et al.* 2011: 456). Paranoid and depressive anxieties fluctuate from birth onwards.

Klein suggests that the infant splits both his ego and his object and projects out separately his loving and hating feelings (life and death instincts) into separate parts of the mother (or breast). The result is that the maternal object is divided into a 'bad' breast (mother that is felt to be frustrating, persecutory and is hated) and a 'good' breast (mother that is loved and felt to be loving and gratifying). Both the 'good' and the 'bad' objects are then introjected and a cycle of re-projection and re-introjection ensues. Omnipotence and idealization are important aspects of this activity; bad experiences are omnipotently denied whenever possible and good experiences are idealized and exaggerated as a protection against the fear of the persecuting breast.

This 'binary splitting' is essential for healthy development as it enables the infant to take in and hold on to sufficient good experience to provide a central core around which to begin to integrate the contrasting aspects of the self. The establishment of a good internal object is thought by Klein to be a prerequisite for the later working through of the 'depressive position' where love and concern for the object are present (Klein 1946).

Phantasy 'There is no impulse, no instinctual urge or response, which is not experienced as unconscious phantasy' (Isaacs 1973: 83). 'Unconscious phantasy is in a constant interplay with external reality, both influencing and altering the perception or interpretation of it and also being influenced by it' (Box *et al.* 1994: 258).

Primary process thinking 'A psychic apparatus possessing only the primary process does not exist ... but primary processes are present in the psyche from the beginning of life' (Freud 1991: 330).

According to Freud, primary process thinking is the visual, unstructured logic typical of one's id (an unconscious, instinctual part of the psyche). Some features of primary process include ignoring of time sequence and its relation to causality, alogical forms of causality and concrete thinking in which words and thoughts are dealt with in exactly the same way as objects and equated exactly with the substances or the objects or the modes of action that they are meant to represent. This mode of thought is typical in children, in dreams and in those suffering from psychotic states (Meltzer 1994: 66).

Projection This can be a phantasy of expelling a part of the self into the other. It can also involve externalizing internal conflicts and putting them into external objects. In early infancy there is a wish to eject from the self everything that is bad (Bott-Spillius, *et al.* 2011: 424).

Projective identification In projective identification, through the way he is behaving or speaking an individual projects aspects of his experience into another person, who is affected by this experience. This process is an essential part of normal development in a parent–infant relationship where the mother or father feels and understands those experiences and is able to contain them, and make them bearable for the infant. Projective identification becomes problematic when an individual loses unwanted parts of the self in the other and then fears that the significant other is relating with those projected parts of self. However, good parts of the self may also be projected into the other.

Herbert Rosenfeld talks about various motives for projective identification: a wish to communicate; a wish to evacuate something unpleasant; a wish to control the mind of the other and a wish to get rid of an awareness of envy (Bott-Spillius *et al.* 2011: 126–143).

Psychoanalysis This method of psychological therapy originated with Sigmund Freud and uses free association, dream interpretation and analysis of resistance and transference to explore repressed or unconscious impulses, anxieties and internal conflicts in order to free psychic energy for mature love and work. Psychoanalysis generally involves four or five sessions weekly over a substantial period.

Psychodynamic and psychoanalytic psychotherapy Psychodynamic and psychoanalytic therapies aim to reveal the unconscious content of a client's psyche in an effort to alleviate psychic tension. In this way, they are similar to psychoanalysis. They draw on the same body of theory as psychoanalysis, such as the work of Freud, Klein, object relations theorists such as Winnicott, Guntrip and Bion, as well as Jung, Lacan, Kohut and many others.

However, these forms of therapy uses psychoanalysis adapted to a less intensive style of working, usually at a frequency of once or twice per week. Psychodynamic and psychoanalytic psychotherapy are sometimes used interchangeably, though the term psychoanalytic therapy is also sometimes used to refer to more intense therapy than once or twice weekly sessions. Psychodynamic and psychoanalytic approaches are used in individual psychotherapy, group psychotherapy and family therapy and to understand and work with institutional and organizational contexts.

Psychotic states and psychotic anxieties Psychotic states are associated with disturbance of the sense of reality and often with delusions, hallucinations and disruption of a sense of personal identity. The term 'psychotic organization' (Steiner 1993) refers to an anti-emotional and anti-thought system in the mind, developed from a background of early trauma and deprivation, a system that is dedicated to destroying any thinking that might revive past mental pain.

Psychotic anxieties involve dread and terror, often described as intolerable confusion, dissolution of the sense of self, or fear of disintegrating and falling to pieces or of ceasing to exist (Jackson 2001: 335).

Re-enactment 'An essential element in this concept is replacement of recollection (or any form of mental realization) by a blindly repeated pattern of events' (Britton 1994: 86).

Regression This is a process involving emotionally returning to an earlier stage of psychological development rather than handling an emotional crisis in an age-appropriate way.

Reparation When the object loved is also seen to be the same object as the object hated, then some integration of the personality can occur and there is some feeling of concern for the damage done to the loved object and a sense of responsibility to repair harm done to it. Reparative wishes bring the possibility of beneficent change, of putting things right when possible

GLOSSARY

and of mourning when impossible and of emotional growth. Efforts to repair internal as well as external objects permit the working-through of feelings of regret, remorse and mourning, even if the victim of the destructive attacks is long dead (Jackson 2001: 337).

Splitting   This process occurs as part of normal development, but also in later life. It involves separating the gratifying experiences linked with an attuned experience with a person and keeping them apart from the persecuting, frustrating negative experiences. This leaves an idealized object and a hostile persecutory object relation until the splitting is replaced by integration of the good and bad aspects of the loved object.

Superego   An internal structure or part of the self that, as the internal authority, reflects on the self, makes judgements, exerts moral pressure and is the seat of conscience, guilt and self-esteem. In Kleinian thinking, the superego is composed of a split-off part of the ego into which is projected death instinct fused with life instinct and good and bad aspects of the primary and also later objects. It acquires both protective and threatening qualities.

Transference   Transference implies that there are impulses and phantasies which are aroused and made conscious during the progress of the therapy. A transference experience is part of an ongoing internal relationship to internal figures that is being re-experienced in relation to the therapist.

Working through   Working through in therapy is the process of the patient moving from an initial awareness of emotional experience, often through the therapist's interpretation, to a stage of consolidated change where the insight is accepted with conviction. Working through links emotional insight or awareness and intellectual insight or the ability to put experience into words. It often involves repeated re-experiencing and interpretation over a period of time.

APPENDIX
List of publications by Murray Jackson

Jackson, M. (1946) A case of juvenile essential hypertension with encephalopathy, *Medical Journal of Australia*, 2(17): 599–600.

Jackson, M. (1949) Familial lumbosacral syringomyelia and the significance of developmental errors of the spinal cord and column, *Medical Journal of Australia*, 1(14): 433–439.

Jackson, M. and Plaut, A. (1954) Psychological aspects of ulcerative colitis in childhood, *Archives*, Middlesex Hospital, 5(1): 21–34.

Jackson, M. (1956) Hysteria and the general practitioner, *Royal Society of Medicine Medical Press*, 7 Nov.: 434–438.

Jackson, M. (1958) A short history of psychotherapy, by Nigel Walker, Routledge and Kegan Paul, 1957, p. 185. *Journal of Analytic Psychology*, 3: 177–178.

Jackson, M. (1958) Schools of psycho-analytic thought, by Ruth L. Munroe. Hutchinson, 1957, p. 670. *Journal of Analytic Psychology*, 3: 178–179.

Jackson, M. (1960) Jung's 'archetype': clarity or confusion?, *British Journal of Medical Psychology*, 33(2): 83–94.

Jackson, M. (1960) Jung's 'archetypes' and psychiatry, *Journal of Mental Science*, 106: 1518–1526.

Jackson, M. (1960) Family influences and psychosomatic illness: an inquiry into the social and psychological background of duodenal ulcer, by E. M. Goldberg. London: Tavistock Publications, 1958, p. 308. *Journal of Analytic Psychology*, 5: 82–83.

Jackson, M. (1961) Communication or conflict, Mary Capes (ed.). London: Tavistock Publications, 1960, p. 228. New York: Association Press. *Journal of Analytic Psychology*, 6: 181–182.

Jackson, M. (1961) Chair, couch, and counter-transference, *Journal of Analytical Psychology*, 6(1): 35–43.

Jackson, M. (1962) Jung's later work: the archetype, *British Journal of Medical Psychology*, 35(3): 199–204.

Jackson, M. (1963) Technique and procedure in analytic practice with special reference to schizoid states, *Journal of Analytic Psychology*, 8: 51–63.

Jackson, M. (1963) The manipulation of human behaviour, A. D. Bidermann and H. Zimmer (eds). London, New York: John Wiley, 1961, p. 323. *Journal of Analytic Psychology*, 8: 93–94.

Jackson, M. (1963) Symbol formation and the delusional transference, *Journal of Analytical Psychology*, 8(2): 145–159.

Jackson, M. (1963) Reply, *Journal of Analytic Psychology*, 8: 164–166.

APPENDIX

Jackson, M. (1964) The importance of depression emerging in a therapeutic group, *Journal of Analytical Psychology*, 9(1): 51–59.

Jackson, M. (1971) Children as individuals, by Michael Fordham. London: Hodder & Stoughton, 1969, p. 223. *International Journal of Psycho-Analysis*, 52: 327–328.

Jackson, M. (1972) Psychosomatic factors in disease, *King's College Hospital Gazette*, Nov.

Jackson, M. (1973) Integration of psychosomatic medicine in a teaching hospital: Experiences with a discussion seminar, *Psychotherapy and Psychosomatics*, 22(2): 205–218.

Forth, M. W. and Jackson, M. (1975) Group psychotherapy in the management of bronchial asthma, *British Journal of Medical Psychology*, 49: 257–260.

Jackson, M. (1977) Psychopathology and 'pseudo-normality' in ulcerative colitis, *Psychotherapy and Psychosomatics*, 28: 179–186.

Jackson, M. (1979) *Psychosomatic Medicine: The Mysterious Leap from the Psychic to the Somatic*. London: Institute of Psychiatry.

Jackson, M. (1982) Psychoanalysis, somatisation and pseudo-normality, *Bulletin of the British Psychoanalytical Society*, 7: 28–36.

Jackson, M. and Jacobson, R. (1983) Psychoanalytic hospital treatment the application of psychoanalytic principles, in P. Pichot, P. Berner, R. Wolf et al. (eds), *Psychoanalytic Hospital Treatment in Psychiatry: The State of the Art. Vol. 4*, pp. 209–216. New York: Plenum Press.

Jackson, M. (1985) A psycho-analytical approach to the assessment of a psychotic patient, *Psychoanalytic Psychotherapy*, 1(2): 11–22.

Jackson, M. and Pines, M. (1986) The borderline personality, *Neurologia et Psychiatria*, 9(2): 54–67.

Jacobson, R., Jackson, M. and Berelowitz, M. (1986) Self-incineration: a controlled comparison of in-patient suicide attempts: clinical features and history of self-harm, *Psychological Medicine*, 16(1): 107–116.

Jackson, M. (1987) Understanding psychosis: a psychoanalytical contribution, *Midland Journal of Psychotherapy*, 1 (June): 11–23.

Jackson, M. (1989) Discussion: a Kleinian perspective, *Psychoanalytic Inquiry*, 9: 554–569.

Jackson, M. and Tarnopolsky, A. (1990) Borderline personality, in R. S. Bluglass and P. M. A. Bowden (eds), *Forensic Psychiatry*. London: Churchill Livingstone, Chapter 27.

Jackson, M. (1990). Psychosomatic symptoms: psychodynamic treatment of the underlying personality disorder, C. Philip Wilson and Ira L. Mintz (eds), London and Northvale, NJ: Jason Aronson, 1989, p. 460. *International Review of Psycho-Analysis*, 17: 388–390.

Jackson, M. (1991) Psychotic disorders, in J. Holmes (ed.), *Textbook of Psychotherapy in Clinical Practice*. London: Churchill Livingstone.

Jackson, M. (1992) Learning to think about schizoid thinking, *Psychoanalytic Psychotherapy*, 6(3): 191–203.

Jackson, M. and Cawley, R. (1992) Psychodynamics and psychotherapy on an acute psychiatric ward: the story of an experimental unit, *British Journal of Psychiatry*, 160: 41–50.

Jackson, M. (1993) Psychoanalysis, psychiatry, psychodynamics: training for integration, *Psychoanalytic Psychotherapy*, 7(1): 1–14.

Jackson, M. (1993) Manic-depressive psychosis: psychopathology and individual psychotherapy within a psychodynamic milieu, *Psychoanalytic Psychotherapy*, 7(2): 103–133.

Jackson, M. and Williams, P. (eds) (1994). *Unimaginable Storms: A Search for Meaning in Psychosis*. London: Karnac Books.

Jackson, M. (2001) Psychoanalysis and the treatment of psychosis, in P. Williams (ed.), *The Language of Psychosis*, Chapter 2. London: Whurr.

Jackson, M. (2001). *Weathering the Storms: Psychotherapy for Psychosis*. London: Karnac.

Steiner, J. and Jackson, M. (2001). Henri Rey (1912–2000), *International Journal of Psycho-Analysis*, 82: 397–399.

Jackson, M. (2002) Need adapted treatment for psychosis: past, present and future, *Folia Psychiatria Aboensia*, Finland, 7: 1, 22–39.

Jackson, M. (2008). A psycho-analytical approach to the assessment of a psychotic patient, *Psychoanalytic Psychotherapy*, 22: 31–42.

Jackson, M. (2009) A beautiful mind, *Bulletin of the British Psychoanalytical Society*, 45, 8: 59–64.

Jackson, M. (2009) The contribution of Kleinian innovations to the treatment of psychotic patients, in Y. Alanen, M. Gonzalez de Chavez, A.L. Silver and B. Martindale (eds), *Psychotherapeutic Approaches to Schizophrenic Psychoses*, Chapter 8, 78–92. Hove: Routledge.

Award

ISPS Lifetime Achievement Award for Outstanding Contribution to the Psychotherapy of Schizophrenia.

BIBLIOGRAPHY

Abenheimer, K. M. (1946) The diary of Vaslav Nijinsky: a pathographical study of a case of schizophrenia, *Psychoanalytical Review*, 33: 257–284.
Akhtar, S. (1997) *The Seed of Madness*, Madison, CT: International Universities Press.
Alanen, Y. O. (1997) *Schizophrenia: Its Origins and Need-adapted Treatment*, London: Karnac Books.
——. (2002) Vulnerability to schizophrenia: an integrated view, *Psychiatria Fennica*, 33: 11–30.
Allende, I. (1988) *Eva Luna*, London: Penguin.
Arieti, S. (1974) *Interpretation of Schizophrenia*, London: Basic Books.
Art Experts (2013) *Vincent van Gogh (1853–1890)*. Available online at: http://www.artexpertswebsite.com/pages/artists/van_gogh_bio.php [16 August 2013].
Auden, W. H. (1938) 'O Tell Me the Truth About Love', reprinted in *Tell Me the Truth About Love: Ten Poems* (1994), London: Vintage.
Bakker, N., Jansen, L. and Luijten, H. (2010) *Van Gogh's Letters: Windows to a Universe*, Hove, UK: Psychology Press.
Balint, M. (1968) *The Basic Fault: Therapeutic Aspects of Regression*, Evanston, IL: Northwest University Press.
Barnes, M. and Berke, J. (1971) *Mary Barnes: Two Accounts of a Journey Through Madness*, New York: Other Press.
Barrosso, D. (1998) José Saramago: Art of Fiction No. 155, *Paris Review of Books*, Winter: p. 149.
Bateman, A and Fonagy, P. (2006) *Mentalization Based Treatment for Borderline Personality Disorders: A Practical Guide*, Oxford: Oxford University Press.
——. (2010) Mentalization based treatment for borderline personality disorders, *World Psychiatry*, 9: 11–15.
——. (2011) *Handbook of Mentalizing in Mental Health Practice*, Arlington, VA: American Psychiatric Publishing.
Bell, D. (2003) *Ideas in Psychoanalysis: Paranoia*, Cambridge: Icon Books.
Bell, E. T. (1937) *Men of Mathematics*, New York: Simon & Schuster.
Benois, A. (1941) *Reminiscences of the Russian Ballet*, London: Putnam.
Berke, J. (1989) *The Tyranny of Malice*, London: Simon & Schuster.
Bernard, B. (ed.) (1991) *Vincent by Himself*, London: Macdonald & Co.
Bick, E. (1968) The experience of the skin in early object relations, *International Journal of Psychoanalysis*, 49: 484–486.
Bion, W. R. (1954) Notes on the theory of schizophrenia, *International Journal of Psychoanalysis*, 3: 113–118.

——. (1957) Differentiation of the psychotic from the non-psychotic personalities, *International Journal of Psychoanalysis*, 38: 266–275; republished in *Second Thoughts* (1967), London: Heinemann; and also in E. Bott-Spillius (ed.) (1988) *Melanie Klein Today*, Vol. 1, London: Routledge.

——. (1961) *Experiences in Groups*, London: Tavistock.

——. (1963) *Elements of Psycho-Analysis*, London: William Heinemann.

——. (1965) *Transformations*, London: William Heinemann, reprinted London: Karnac Books, 1984.

——. (1967) *Second Thoughts*, London: Heinemann.

——. (1970) *Attention and Interpretation*, London: Tavistock Publications, reprinted London: Karnac Books, 1984.

——. (1992) *Cogitations*, F. Bion (ed.), London: Karnac Books.

Bleuler, M. (1978) *The Schizophrenic Disorders: Long-Term Patient and Family Studies*, New Haven, CT: Yale University Press.

Bleurer, E. (1911) *Dementia Praecox or The Group of Schizophrenias*, New York: International Universities Press.

Blom, J. D. (2010) *Dictionary of Hallucinations*, London: Springer.

Bloom, H. (2005) *José Saramago*, Philadelphia: Chelsea House.

Bott-Spillius, E., Milton, J., Garvey, P., Couve, C. and Steiner, D. (2011) *The New Dictionary of Kleinian Thought*, London: Routledge.

Bowlby, J. (1969) *Attachment and Loss, Vol. 1: Attachment*, London: Hogarth Press and the Institute of Psychoanalysis.

——. (1973) *Attachment and Loss, Vol. 2, Separation: Anxiety and Anger*, London: Hogarth Press and the Institute of Psychoanalysis.

——. (1980) *Attachment and Loss, vol. 3. Loss: Sadness and Depression*, London: Hogarth Press and the Institute of Psychoanalysis.

Box, S., Copley, B., Magagna, J. and Smilansky, E. (eds) (1994) *Crisis at Adolescence*, London: Jason Aronson.

Bradshaw, P. (2008) Blindness, *The Guardian, Culture*, 21 Nov. 2008. Available online at http://www.theguardian.com/film/2008/nov/21/blindness-julianne-moore-film-review? INTCMP=SRCH [1 April 2013].

Brazelton, T. B. (2006) *Touchpoints: Birth to Three: Your Child's Emotional and Behavioral Development*, Boston: Da Capo Press.

Britton, R. (1994) Re-enactment as an unwitting professional response to family dynamics, in S. Box, B. Copley, J. Magagna and E. Smilansky (eds) *Crisis at Adolescence*, Northvale, NJ and London: Jason Aronson.

——. (1998) *Belief and Imagination*, London: Routledge.

Buckle, R. (1975) Nijinsky, in A. Carter and J. O'Shea (2010) *The Routledge Dance Studies Reader*, London: Taylor & Francis.

Camus, A. (1960) *Resistance, Rebellion and Death*, London: Hamish Hamilton.

Capozzi, P. and De Masi, F. (2001) The meaning of dreams in the psychotic state, *International Journal of Psychoanalysis*, 82: 933–952.

Caron, N. A., Thormann, L. L., Diesel, M. and Lopes, R. C. S. (2013) Life, hanging by a thread, *Psychoanalysis and Culture – of Revista de Psicanálise da Sociedade Psicanalítica de Porto Alegre*, Aug., 22(2): 314–347, Brazil: Porto Allegre.

Charles, M. (2003) A Beautiful Mind – review of the film, *The American Journal of Psychoanalysis*, 63: 21–37.

Cleveland Museum of Art (2007) *Manet to Dali: Impressionism and Modern Masterworks from the Cleveland Museum of Art*, Cleveland: Cleveland Museum of Art.

Coleridge, S.T. (1797) 'The Rime of the Ancient Mariner', in *Lyrical Ballads and Other Poems of Wordsworth and Coleridge* (2003) London: Oxford University Press.

Cook, J. (2013) *Van Gogh*. Available online at: http://www.jeanninecook/blog/ [12 Oct. 2014].

Cooper, H. and Magagna, J. (2004) The development of self-esteem in infancy, *Intimate Transformations: Babies with their Families*, London: Karnac.

Cox, P. (2001) *The Diaries of Vaslav Nijinsky* [DVD], Albert Park, Australia: Illumination Films.

Cullberg, J. (2002) One-year outcome in first episode psychosis patients in the Swedish Parachute project, *Acta Psychiatrica Scandinavica*, 106: 276–285.

——. (2006) *Psychoses: An Integrative Perspective*, East Sussex: Routledge.

Dallos, R. (2006) *Attachment Narrative Therapy*, Maidenhead, UK: Open University Press.

De Masi, F. (1997) Intimidation at the helm: superego and hallucinations in the analytic treatment of a psychosis, *International Journal of Psychoanalysis*, 78: 561–576.

——. (2000) The unconscious and psychosis: some considerations on the psychoanalytic theory of psychosis, *International Journal of Psychoanalysis*, 81: 1–20.

——. (2003) On the nature of intuitive and delusional thought, *International Journal of Psychoanalysis*, 84: 1149–1169.

Du Quesne van Gogh, E. (1913) *Personal Recollections of Vincent van Gogh*, Boston: Houghton Mifflin.

Dumas, A., Meedendorp, T., Vergeest, A. and Zwikker, R. (2010) *The Real van Gogh: The Artist and His Letters*, London: Royal Academy.

Edel, L. (1975) Portrait of the artist as an old man, in D. D. van Tassel (ed.) *Aging, Death and the Completion of Being*, Philadelphia: University of Pennsylvania Press.

Eksteins, M. (2000) *The Rites of Spring: The Great War and the Birth of the Modern Age*, New York: Houghton Mifflin.

Etchegoyen, A. and Trowell, J. (2002) *The Importance of Fathers: A Psychoanalytic Re-Evaluation*, London: Karnac.

Etchegoyen, H. (1991) *The Fundamentals of Psychoanalytic Technique*, London: Karnac.

Fairbairn, W. R. (1952) *Psychoanalytical Studies of the Personality*, London: Henley & Boston; Routledge & Kegan Paul.

Ferro, A. (1939) *Salazar*, London: Faber.

Fonagy, P. and Target, M. (1996) Playing with reality I: theory of mind and the normal development of psychic reality, *International Journal of Psychoanalysis*, 77: 217–233.

Fonagy, P., Steele, H., Moran, G., Steele, M. and Higgit, A. (1991) The capacity for understanding mental states: the reflective self in parent and child and its significance for security of attachment, *Infant Mental Health Journal*, 13: 200–217.

Fonagy, P., Gergely, J., Elliot, L. and Target, M. (2002) *Affect Regulation, Mentalisation, and the Development of the Self in Psychiatry*, London: Free Association Books.

Freedman, D. and Adatto, C. (1968) On the precipitation of seizures in an adolescent boy, *Psychosomatic Medicine*, 30, 4: 437–447.

Freeman, T. (1994) On some types of hallucinatory experience, *Psychoanalytic Psychotherapy*, 89, 3: 273–281.

——. (1998) *The Psychoanalyst in Psychiatry*, London: Free Association Books.

Freud, S. (1893) *The psychotherapy of hysteria, SE2*, London: Hogarth.

BIBLIOGRAPHY

——. (1900) *The Interpretation of Dreams, SE5*, London: Hogarth.
——. (1910) *Leonardo da Vinci and a Memory of his Childhood, SE11*, London: Hogarth.
——. (1911) *Psycho-Analytic Notes on an Autobiographical Account of a Case of Paranoia, SE12*, London: Hogarth.
——. (1917) *A Childhood Recollection from Dichtung und Wahrheit, SE17*, London: Hogarth.
——. (1920) *Beyond the Pleasure Principle, SE18*, London: Hogarth.
Fromm-Reichman, F. (1964) *I Never Promised You a Rose Garden: An Account of Hannah Green*, New York: Rinehart & Winston.
Fuller, P. (1988) *Art and Psychoanalysis*, London: Hogarth Press.
Gabbard, G. O. (ed.) (2001) Psychoanalysis and film, *International Journal of Psychoanalysis Key Paper Series*, London: Karnac.
Gaddini, E. (1992) A psychoanalytic theory of infantile experience: conceptual and clinical reflections, *The New Library of Psychoanalysis No. 16*, London: Tavistock/Routledge.
Gedo, J. (1989) *Portraits of the Artist: Psychoanalysis of Creativity and its Vicissitudes*, New York: Guilford.
Gill White, P. (2006) *Sibling Grief*, New York: Universe.
Gorlitz, P. C. (1890) Letter by P. C. Gorlitz to Frederik van Eden, in V. van Gogh (1999c) *The Complete Letters of Vincent van Gogh, Vol. III*, London: Thames & Hudson.
Greenacre, P. (1957) The childhood of the artist, in P. Greenacre (1971) *Emotional Growth, Vol. 2*, New York: International Universities Press.
Grotstein, J. S. (1997) The psychoanalytic concept of schizophrenia, *International Journal of Psychoanalysis*, 58: 403–542.
——. (2000) *Who is the Dreamer Who Dreams the Dream?*, London: The Analytic Press.
Grotstein, J. S. and Rinsley, D. B. (1994) *Fairbairn and the Origins of Object Relations*, London: Free Associations Books.
Harding, C., Brooks, G., Ashikaga,T., Strauss, J. and Brier, A. (1987) The Vermont longitudinal study of persons with severe mental illness, *American Journal of Psychiatry*, 144: 727–735.
Harding, C. M. (2002) Beautiful Minds Can Be Recovered, *New York Times*, 10 March.
Hauptmann, E., (1927) *Till Eulenspiegel*, Gütersloh: C. Bertelsmann.
Haziot , D. (2010) *Van Gogh*, Brazil: L&PM Editores.
Heimann, P. (1942) A contribution to the problem of sublimation and its relation to processes of internalization, *International Journal of Psycho-Analysis*, 23: 8–17.
Hendrick, I. (1940) Psychoanalytic observation on the aurae of two cases with convulsions, *Psychosomatic Medicine*, 2(1): 43–52.
Hinshelwood, R. D. (1989) *A Dictionary of Kleinian Thought*, London: Free Association Books.
Hobson, P. (2002) *The Cradle of Thought*, London: Macmillan.
Holmes, J. (1996) *Attachment, Intimacy, Autonomy*, New York: Jason Aronson.
——. (2000) Fitting the biopsychosocial jigsaw together, *British Journal of Psychiatry*, 177: 93–94.
Houzel, D. (1999) A therapeutic application of infant observation in child psychiatry, *International Journal of Infant Observation and its Applications*, 2(3), 42–53.
Howard, R. (2001) *A Beautiful Mind*.[DVD] Hollywood: Universal Pictures/Universal Studios.
Isaacs, S. (1973) The nature and function of phantasy, *Developments in Psychoanalysis*, 43: 67–121.
Jackson, M. (1993) Manic-depressive psychosis: psychopathology and individual psychotherapy within a psychodynamic milieu, *Psychoanalytic Psychotherapy*, 7(2): 103–133.

——. (2001) *Weathering the Storms; Psychotherapy for Psychosis*, London: Karnac; New York: Other Press.

——. (2009) The contribution of Kleinian innovations to the treatment of psychotic patients, in Y. Alanen, M. Gonzalez de Chavez, A. L. Silver and B. Martindale (eds) *Psychotherapeutic Approaches to Schizophrenic Psychoses*, Hove: Routledge.

Jackson, M. and Cawley, R. (1992) Psychodynamics and psychotherapy on an acute ward: the story of an experimental unit, *British Journal of Psychiatry*, 160: 41–50.

Jackson, M. and Williams, P. (1994) *Unimaginable Storms: A Search for Meaning in Psychosis*, London: Karnac Books.

Jamison, K. R. (1993) *Touched with Fire: Manic-depressive Illness and the Artistic Temperament*, New York: The Free Press.

——. (1995) *An Unquiet Mind: A Memoir of Moods and Madness*, New York: Alfred A Knopf.

Jethani, S. (2009) *The Divine Commodity: Discovering a Faith Beyond Consumer Christianity*, Grand Rapids, MI: Zondervan (eBook).

Johns, C., Nazroo, J. Y., Bebbington, P. and Kuipers, E. (2002) Occurrence of hallucinatory experiences in a community sample and ethnic variations, *British Journal of Psychiatry*, 180: 174–178.

Johnson, S. and Ruszczynski, S. (1999) *Psychoanalytic Psychotherapy in the Independent Tradition*, London: Karnac Books.

Jones, E. (1931) The problem of Paul Morphy: a contribution to the psycho-analysis of chess, *International Journal of Psychoanalysis*, 12: 1–23.

Jull Costa, M. (2011) *José Saramago: A Celebration*. Available online at: http://www.granta.com/New-Writing/saramago [16 August 2013].

Jung, C. (1979) Aion: Researchers into the phenomenology of the self, in *Collected Works of C. G. Jung*, Vol. 9, Part 2, New York: Bollingen Foundation.

Karon, B. P. (2003) The tragedy of schizophrenia without psychotherapy, *Journal of the American Academy of Psychoanalysis and Dynamic Psychiatry*, 31(1): 89–118.

King, P. and Steiner, R. (1991) *The Freud–Klein Controversies 1941–1945*, London: Routledge.

Klein, M. (1927) Criminal tendencies in normal children, in *Love, Guilt and Reparation and Other Works: The Writings of Melanie Klein, Vol. 1*, London: Hogarth.

——. (1929) Infantile anxiety situations reflected in a work of art and in the creative impulse, *International Journal of Psychoanalysis*, 10: 436–443.

——. (1930) The importance of symbol formation in the development of the ego, *International Journal of Psychoanalysis*, 11: 24–39.

——. (1935) A contribution to the psychogenesis of manic depressive states, in *Love, Guilt and Reparation and Other Works: The Writings of Melanie Klein, Vol. 1*, London: Hogarth.

——. (1940) Mourning and its relation to manic depressive states, *International Journal of Psychoanalysis*, 21: 125–153.

——. (1946) Notes on some schizoid mechanisms, *International Journal of Psychoanalysis*, 26: 137–142.

——. (1959) Our adult world and its roots in infancy, in *Envy and Gratitude and Other Works, Vol. 3*, London: Hogarth.

——. (1975) *Envy and Gratitude and Other Works*, London: Hogarth.

Klein, S. (1980) Autistic phenomena in neurotic patients, *International Journal of Psychoanalysis*, 61: 295–402.

BIBLIOGRAPHY

Lacan, J. (1997) *Ecrits*, New York: W.W. Norton.

Laing, R. D. (1967) *The Politics of Experience and the Bird of Paradise*, London: Penguin Books.

Leff, J., Kuipers, L. and Berkowitz, R. (1982) A controlled trial of social intervention in the families of schizophrenic patients, *British Journal of Psychiatry*, 131: 121–134.

LeGuin, U. K. (2006) The plague of blank ballots, *The Guardian, Culture*, 15 April. Available online at: http://www.theguardian.com/books/2006/apr/15/featuresreviews.guardianreview16 [1 April 2013].

Leichsenring, F. and Rabung, S. (2011) Long-term psychodynamic psychotherapy in complex mental disorders: update of a meta-analysis, *British Journal of Psychiatry*, 199: 15–22.

Levander, S. and Cullberg, J. (1993) Sandra: successful psychotherapeutic work with a schizophrenic woman, *Psychiatry*, 6: 284–293.

Lewontin, R. C. (1993) *The Doctrine of DNA: Biology as Ideology*, London: Penguin Books.

Lidz, T. (1964) August Strindberg: a study of the relationship between his creativity and schizophrenia, *International Journal of Psychoanalysis*, 45: 399–406.

Likierman, M. (2001) *Melanie Klein: Her Work in Context*, London: Continuum.

Liu, E. and Noppe-Brandon, S. (2009) *Imagination First*, San Francisco, CA: Jossey Bass.

Lotterman, A. (1996) *Specific Techniques for the Psychotherapy of Schizophrenic Patients*, Madison, CT: Madison International Universities Press.

——. (2015, in press) *Psychotherapy for People Diagnosed with Schizophrenia: Specific Techniques (Formerly Specific Techniques for the Psychotherapy of Schizophrenic Patients)*, Hove: Routledge.

Lubin, A. J. (1972) *Stranger on the Earth: A Psychological Biography of Vincent van Gogh*, New York: Holt, Rinehart & Winston.

Lucas, R. (2003) The relationship between psychoanalysis and schizophrenia, *International Journal of Psychoanalysis*, 84: 39.

McDougall, J. (1980) *Plea for a Measure of Abnormality*, New York: International Universities Press.

Magagna, J., Bakalar, N., Cooper, H., Levy, J., Norman, C. and Shank, C. (eds) (2004) *Intimate Transformations: Babies with their Families*, London: Karnac.

Mahler, M., Pine, F. and Bergman, A. (1975) *The Psychological Birth of the Human Infant: Symbiosis and Individuation*, New York: Basic Books.

Main, M. (1991) Metacognitive knowledge, metacognitive monitoring, and singular (coherent) vs multiple (incoherent) model of attachment: findings and directions for future research, in C. M. Parkes, J. Stevenson-Hinde, and P. Marris (eds) *Attachment Across the Life Cycle*, London: Tavistock/Routledge.

Martindale, B., Bateman, A., Crowe, M. and Margison, F. (eds) (2000) *Psychosis: Psychological Approaches and their Effectiveness*, London: Gaskell.

Matte-Blanco, I. (1998) *Thinking, Feeling and Being*, London: Routledge.

Meirelles, F. (2008) *Blindness*, USA: Miramax.

Meissner, W. W. (1993) Vincent: the self-portraits, *Psychoanalytic Quarterly*, 62: 74–105.

——. (1995) Creativity and symbiosis in Vincent van Gogh, *Contemporary Psychoanalysis*, 30: 323–347.

——. (1997) *Vincent's religion: The search for meaning*, New York: Peter Lang.

Meltzer, D. (1967) *The Psychoanalytic Process*, London: Heinemann.

——. (1968) Terror, persecution and dread, *International Journal of Psychoanalysis*, 49(2): 391–401.

——. (1983) *Dream Life*, Perthshire: Clunie Press.
——. (1988) *The Apprehension of Beauty*, Perthshire: Clunie Press.
——. (1992) *The Claustrum: An Investigation of Claustrophobic Phenomena*, London: The Clunie Press.
——. (1994) *Sincerity and Other Works*, A. Hahn (ed.), London: Karnac.
Michels, R. (2003) The relationship between psychoanalysis and schizophrenia by Richard Lucas – A commentary, *International Journal of Psychoanalysis*, 84: 9–12.
Milner, M. (1950) *On Not Being Able to Paint*, London: Heinemann Educational Books.
Milnor, J. (1998) *John Nash and 'A Beautiful Mind'*, Notices of the AMS, 45, 10: 1329–1332.
Milton, J. (1608–1674). 'On His Blindness', in *The Oxford Book of English Verse*, A. T. Quiller-Couch (ed.) (1919), Oxford: Clarendon.
Mitchell, J. (2000) *Mad Men and Medusas*, London: Penguin.
——. (2003) *Siblings*, London: Karnac.
Moore, L. (2013) *Nijinsky: A Life*, London: Profile Books.
Morgan, D. and Ruszczynski, S. (eds) (2007) *Lectures on Violence, Perversion and Delinquency*, London: Karnac.
Moustaki, E. (1981) Glossary in S. Box, B. Copley, J. Magagna and E. Moustaki (eds) *Psychotherapy with Families*, London: Routledge.
Music, G. (2012) *Nurturing Natures*, London: Routledge.
——. (2014) *The Good Life: Wellbeing and the New Science of Altruism, Selfishness and Immorality*, London: Routledge.
Nagera, H. (1969) The imaginary companion, *Psychoanalytic Study of the Child*, 24: 165–196.
Nasar, S. (1994) The lost years of a Nobel Laureate, *New York Times*, 13 November.
——. (1998) *A Beautiful Mind*, London: Faber & Faber.
Nash, J. (1994) In (2002) John F. Nash Jr. – Autobiography, Nobel e-Museum. Available online at: http://www.nobel.se/economics/laureates/1994/nash-autobio.html [1 April 2013].
——. (1996) Plenary lecture to the 10th Congress of Psychiatry, Madrid, reported in *The Times, Foreign News*, 28 August.
——. (2002a) *A Brilliant Madness*, television programme, Public Broadcasting Service, America, 27 March.
——. (2002b) Interview with John Nash: How does recovery happen?, *American Experience*. Available online at: http://www.pbs.org/wgbh/amex/nash/sfeature/sf_nash_14.html [1 April 2013].
Newton, P. M. (1995) *From Youthful Dreams to Mid-Life Crisis*, New York: Guilford Press.
NICE (2014) *Psychosis and Schizophrenia in Adults: Treatment and Management*, National Collaborating Centre for Mental Health.
Nijinsky, B. (1981) *Early Memories*, New York: Holt, Rinehart & Winston.
Nijinsky, R. (1934) *Nijinsky by his Wife Romola Nijinsky*, New York: Simon & Schuster.
Nijinsky, V. (1936) *The Diary of Vaslav Nijinsky*, R. Nijinsky (ed.), New York: Simon & Schuster.
——. (1999). *The Diary of Vaslav Nijinsky*, J. Acocella and K. Fitzlyon (eds), New York: Farrar, Strauss and Giroux.
——. (2006) *The Diary of Vaslav Nijinsky*, J. Acocella (ed.), USA: University of Illinois Press.
O'Connor, J. J. and Robertson, E. F. (2002) *John Forbes Nash*. Available online at: http://www-history.mcs.st-andrews.ac.uk/Biographies/Nash.html [4 April 2013].
Ogden, T. H. (1989) *The Primitive Edge of Experience*, London: Jason Aronson.
Oldham, J. M. and Russakoff, L. M. (1987) *Dynamic Therapy in Brief Hospitalisation*, Northvale NJ: Aronson.

BIBLIOGRAPHY

Ostwald, P. (1985) *Schumann: The Inner Voices of a Musical Genius*, Boston: Northeastern University Press.

——. (1991) *Vaslav Nijinsky: A Leap into Madness*, London: Robson Books.

——. (1997) *Glenn Gould: The Ecstasy and Tragedy of Genius*, New York: Norton.

Pao, P.N. (1979) *Schizophrenic Disorders: Theory and Treatment from a Psychodynamic Point of View*, New York: International Universities Press.

Perls, F., Hefferline, R. F. and Goodman, P. (1951) *Gestalt Therapy*, New York: Julian Press.

Pestalozzi, J. (2003) The symbolic and concrete: psychotic adolescents in psychoanalytic psychotherapy, *International Journal of Psychoanalysis*, 82: 515–532.

Pickvance, R. (1992) *A Great Artist is Dead: Letters of Condolence on Vincent van Gogh's Death*, Waanders: Zwolle.

Pollock, G. (1989) *The Mourning–Liberation Process, Vol. II*, Madison, CT: International Universities Press.

Proust, M. (1989) *In Search of Lost Time (A la recherché du temps perdu)*, Paris: Gallimard (Folio).

Pylkkanen, K. (1989) A quality assurance programme for schizophrenia, *Psychoanalytic Psychotherapy*, 4: 13–22.

Rank, O. (1989) *Art and Artist*, New York and London: W.W. Norton.

Rather, L. (2001) Collaborating with the unconscious other: the analyst's capacity for creative thinking, *International Journal of Psychoanalysis*, 82: 515–532.

Read, J. and Ross, C. A. (2003) Psychological trauma in psychosis: diagnosed schizophrenics must be offered psychological therapies, *Journal of the American Academy of Psychoanalysis and Dynamic Psychiatry*, 31: 247–268.

Reid, M. (2013) Grief in the Mother's Eyes, unpublished talk given to the Washington Institute of Psychoanalysis, 5 April 2013, Washington DC.

Rey, J. H. (1979) Schizoid phenomena in the borderline, in J. le Boit and A. Capponi (eds) *Advances in the Psychotherapy of Borderline States*, New York: Jason Aronson.

——. (1994) *Universals of Psychoanalysis in the Treatment of Psychotic and Borderline States*, J. Magagna (ed.), London: Free Association Books.

Riviere, J. (1955) The unconscious phantasy of an inner world reflected in examples from literature, in M. Klein, P. Heimann and R. Money-Kyrle (eds) *New Directions in Psychoanalysis*, London: Hogarth Press.

Robbins, M. (1993) *Experiences of Schizophrenia*, London: The Guilford Press.

Roddenberg, G. (1979) *Star Trek* [DVD] Hollywood: Paramount Pictures.

Romme, M., Honig, A., Noorthoorn, E. O. and Escher, A. D. (1992) Coping with hearing voices: an emancipatory approach, *British Journal of Psychiatry*, 161: 99–103.

Rosenfeld, D. (1992) *The Psychotic: Aspects of the Personality*, London: Karnac Books.

Rosenfeld, H. A. (1965) Notes on the psycho-analysis of the superego conflict in an acute schizophrenic patient, in *Psychotic States*, London: Hogarth Press.

——. (1971) A clinical approach to the psychoanalytical theory of the life and death instincts: an investigation into the aggressive aspects of narcissism, *International Journal of Psychoanalysis*, 52: 169–178.

——. (1987) *Impasse and Interpretation*, London: Tavistock Publications.

Rothenberg, A. (1990) *Creativity and Madness*, Baltimore, MD: Johns Hopkins University Press.

Rushdie, S. (1990) *Haroun and the Sea of Stories*, London: Puffin.

Rustin, M., Rhode, M., Dubinsky, A. and Dubinsky, H. (eds) (1997) *Psychotic States in Children*, London: Duckworth.

Ruszczynski, S. and Johnson, S. (1999) *Psychoanalytic Psychotherapy in the Kleinian Tradition*, London: Karnac Books.

Rycroft, C. (1968) *Imagination and Reality*, London: Hogarth Press.

Sacks, O. (1995) *An Anthropologist on Mars*, London: Picador.

Samels, M. (2003) *The American Experience: A Brilliant Madness*. [television] Arlington, VA: PBS.

Saramago, J. (1980) *Levantado do Chao* (*Raised from the Ground*), Madrid: Punto de Lectura.

——. (1992) *The Year of the Death of Ricardo Reis*, London: HarperCollins.

——. (1996) *The History of the Siege of Lisbon*, New York: Harcourt, Brace.

——. (1997) *Blindness*, London: Harvill Press.

——. (1998) *How characters became the masters and the author their apprentice*, Nobel Lecture. Available online at: http://www.nobelprize.org/nobel_prizes/literature/laureates/1998/saramago-lecture.html [4 April 2013].

——. (1999) *All the Names*, San Diego: Harvest, Harcourt.

——. (2005) *The Double*, London: Vintage.

——. (2006) *Seeing*, San Diego, CA: Harvest, Harcourt.

——. (2008) *Death at Intervals*, London: Vintage.

——. (2008) *The Gospel According to Jesus Christ*, London: Vintage.

——. (2009) *Small Memories*, London: Vintage.

——. (2010) *The Notebook*, London: Verso.

——. (2011) *Cain*, Boston: Houghton Mifflin Harcourt.

Sawa, A. and Kamiya, A. (2003) Elucidating the pathogenesis of schizophrenia, *British Medical Journal*, 327, 7416: 632–633.

Schapiro, M. (1956) Leonardo and Freud: an art-historical study, *Journal of the History of Ideas*, 17: 147–148.

Schejen, S. (2010) *Diaghilev: A life*, London: Profile Books.

Schore, A. (2003) *Affect Regulation and Repair of Self.* New York: W.W. Norton.

Segal, H. (1952) A psychoanalytical approach to aesthetics, *International Journal of Psychoanalysis*, 33: 196–207.

——. (1972) A delusional system as a defence against the emergence of a catastrophic situation, *International Journal of Psychoanalysis*, 52: 393–401.

——. (1979) *Klein*, London: Fontana.

——. (1981) Notes on symbol formation, in *The Work of Hanna Segal*, New York: Jason Aronson.

——. (1991) *Dream, Phantasy and Art*, London: Routledge.

Seikkula, J., Alakare, B., Aaltonen, J., Haarakangas, K., Keränen, J. and Lehtinen, K. (2006) Five years experiences of first-episode non-affective psychosis in Open Dialogue approach: treatment principles, follow-up outcomes and two case analyses, *Psychotherapy Research*, 16: 214–228.

Seikkula, J., Alakare, B. and Aaltonen, J. (2011). The comprehensive open-dialogue approach (II). Long-term stability of acute psychosis outcomes in advanced community care: the Western Lapland Project, *Psychosis*, 3: 1–13.

Sinason, M. (1993) Who is the mad voice inside?, *Psychoanalytic Psychotherapy*, 7: 207–221.

——. (2003) On film review essay: *Fight Club*, *International Journal of Psychoanalysis*, 83, 6: 1442–1444.

Spillius, B. E., Milton, J., Garvey, P., Couve, C. and Steiner, D. (2011) *The New Dictionary of Kleinian Thought*, New York: Routledge.

BIBLIOGRAPHY

Star Trek (1966) Desilu Productions, America.

Stein, A. et al. (1991) The relationship between post-natal depression and mother–child interaction, *British Journal of Psychiatry*, 158: 46–52.

Steiner, J. (1993a) Commentary in 'The analyst at work', *International Journal of Psychoanalysis*, 83(5): 1012–1015.

——. (1993b) *Psychic Retreats*, London: Routledge.

Stern, D. (1985) *The Interpersonal World of the Infant: A View from Psychoanalysis and Developmental Psychology*, New York: Basic Books.

Strindberg, A. (1979) *The Inferno*, Penguin Classics.

Sullivan, H. S. (1962) *Schizophrenia as a Human Process*, New York: W.W. Norton.

Suomi, S. J. (1997) Early determinants of behaviour: evidence from primate studies, *British Medical Bulletin*, 53(1): 170–184.

Sweetnam, A. (2007) Are you a woman – or a flower?: the capacity to experience beauty', *International Journal of Psychoanalysis*, 88(6): 1491–1506.

Symington, N. (1990) The possibility of human freedom and its transmission (with particular reference to the thought of Bion), *International Journal of Psycho-Analysis*, 71: 95–106.

Tienari, P. (1992) Implications of adoption studies on schizophrenia, *British Journal of Psychiatry*, 18: 52–58.

Torrance, E. P. (1963) *Education and the Creative Potential*, Minneapolis: University of Minnesota Press.

van Gogh-Bonger, J. (1913) Memoir of Vincent van Gogh, in V. van Gogh (1999), *The Complete Letters of Vincent van Gogh, Vol I*, London: Thames & Hudson.

——. (1958) *Memoir of Vincent van Gogh*, in J. van Gogh-Bonger (ed.) *The Complete Letters of Vincent van Gogh, Vol. I*, Greenwich, CT: New York Graphic Society.

van Gogh, V. (1890) *Letter to Elisabeth van Gogh, written 5 August 1890 in Paris*, R. Harrison (trans. and ed.). Available online at: http://www.vangoghletters.org/vg/letters/let898/letter.html [July 23 2013]

——. (1958) *The Complete Letters of Vincent van Gogh, 1st edn*, London: Thames & Hudson.

——. (1959) *The Complete Letters of Vincent van Gogh, 2nd edn, Volume 3*, Greenwich, CT: New York Graphic Society.

——. (1991) *Vincent by Himself*, B. Bernard (ed), London and Sydney: Macdonald.

——. (1995) *Dear Theo: The Autobiography of Vincent van Gogh*, I. Stone (ed.) New York and London: Penguin Group.

——. (1999a) *The Complete Letters of Vincent van Gogh, Vol. I*, London: Thames & Hudson.

——. (1999b) *The Complete Letters of Vincent van Gogh, Vol. II*, London: Thames & Hudson.

——. (1999c) *The Complete Letters of Vincent van Gogh, Vol. III*, London: Thames & Hudson.

——. (2005) *Biography of Vincent van Gogh*. Available online at: https://www.exp-vangogh.com/2.cfm [28 May 2005].

Volkan, V. D. (1995) *The Infantile Psychotic Self and its Fates: Understanding and Treating Schizophrenics and Other Difficult Patients*, Northvale, NJ: Jason Aronson.

Volkan, V. D. and Akhtar, S. (eds) (1997) *The Seeds of Madness*, Madison, CT: International Universities Press.

Volkan, V. D. and Ast, G. (1997) *Siblings in the Unconscious and Psychopathology*, Madison, CT: International Universities Press.

BIBLIOGRAPHY

Whipp, G. (2001) 'Mind' games: Ron Howard, Russell Crowe aim for the truth, but missed facts, *Los Angeles Daily News*, 26 December.

Williams, A. H. (1960) *A Psychoanalytic Approach to the Treatment of a Murderer*, London: Oxford.

——. (1998) *Cruelty, Violence, and Murder: Understanding the Criminal Mind*, London: Karnac.

Williams, P. (2010) The 'beautiful mind' of John Nash: notes towards a psychoanalytic reading, in *Invasive Objects: Minds under Siege*, New York: Routledge.

Williams, T. (1979) 'A Cavalier of Milady', *The Traveling Companion and Other Plays* (2008), New York: New Directions.

Willick, M. S. (2001) Psychoanalysis and schizophrenia: a cautionary tale, *Journal of the American Psychoanalytical Association*, 49: 27–56.

Willoughby, R. (2001) The dungeon of thyself: the claustrum as pathological container, *International Journal of Psychoanalysis*, 82(5): 917–931.

Winnicott, D. W. (1958) *Collected Papers: Through Paediatrics to Psychoanalysis*, London: Tavistock.

Wyndham, J. (1951) *The Day of the Triffids*, London: Penguin.

Zemel, C. (1997) *Van Gogh's Progress: Utopia, Modernity, and Late-Nineteenth-Century Art*, Berkeley: University of California Press.

INDEX

Abenheimer, Karl, on Nijinsky 26
abstract thinking 50; Nash 6
Acocella's version of Nijinsky's diary
  (2006) 2, 26
Adler, Alfred 45–6
Afternoon of a Faun 25, 31
alcohol 120–1
aliens, Nash's 6, 9, 15, 16
All the Names 83
alone, curiosity and capacity to be 114–15
*American Experience: A Brilliant
  Madness, The* 5
anger *see* rage and anger
antipsychotics *see* medication
anxiety: depressive 74, 128–9; psychotic
  see psychotic anxiety
Arles, van Gogh's move to 104
asylums *see* mental and psychiatric
  institutions
auditory hallucinations (hearing voices):
  Nash 13, 16, 17, 20; Nijinsky 39

baby *see* infant–parent relationships;
  penumbra baby
ballet and dancing, Nijinsky's 2, 3, 25,
  28–32, 34, 36–8, 40, 47, 48, 57, 61,
  62, 115
Ballets Russes 25, 27, 29, 30, 31, 34, 36,
  43, 62
Beautiful Mind, A: book xx, 5, 6, 18; film
  xx, 5, 9–11, 17
Bellevue sanatorium 41, 42, 43, 44, 46, 47
Berceuse 107
bereavement and mourning 80; in sibling
  death *see* sibling death
binary splitting 131
Binswanger, Kurt 43, 44, 45, 46, 47,
  49, 63

Binswanger, Ludwig 41, 42–3, 43
bisexuality, Nijinsky's 29
Bleuler, Eugen 41, 42, 46, 55, 56
Blindness 1, 67, 71–82, 84–5, 86, 88
breast-mother 131; Nijinsky 58
brother(s): Freud's (Julius) 83; Nijinsky's
  (Stanislav) 27, 28, 34, 39, 45, 51, 61;
  Saramago's (Francisco) 68, 82–4, 85,
  88; van Gogh's (still-born – also called
  Vincent) 92; van Gogh's (Theo) 3, 92,
  93, 94, 97, 98, 99, 100, 100–1, 102,
  103, 104, 106, 107, 108–11, 112, 113;
  see also sibling death

Cain 85, 86, 87, 88
car thief in *Blindness* 75–6
Carnival 34
catastrophe in Saramago's writings
  71, 85
catatonia, Nijinsky's 42, 43
causes (origins) of psychotic disorders
  50–3; *see also* precipitating factors;
  vulnerability
childhood (and early years) 119;
  emotional growth and development *see*
  emotional growth and development;
  Nash 6–7, 8; Nijinsky 26–8, 30, 45,
  52, 54, 60; Saramago 67–9, 70, 84, 85,
  118; van Gogh 91–5
Christ, Jesus: Nijinsky and 59, 63; van
  Gogh and 96, 110, 111, 112; *see also*
  Messiah
claustrophobia: Nash 16; Saramago
  84, 119
Cold War Russia and Communism, Nash
  and 7, 15, 16
Coleridge's *Rime of the Ancient Mariner*
  79–80

148

INDEX

Communist Russia and Cold War, Nash and 7, 15, 16
concrete thinking 127; Nijinsky 58, 63
conflicts (in psychotic states): Nash 14–15; Nijinsky 35, 50, 53, 57, 61, 62; Saramago's *Blindness* 65, 73, 76, 81, 85, 87
containment (parental) 118–20, 127; Nash 1, 20, 118, 119, 120; Nijinsky 119, 120; Saramago 119, 120; van Gogh 119, 119–20
control, delusions of 128
countertransference 124, 127; Binswanger (Kurt) 44, 45
criticism, internal and external, freedom from 115
curiosity and capacity to be alone 114–15

dancing and ballet, Nijinsky's 2, 3, 25, 28–32, 34, 36–8, 40, 47, 48, 57, 61, 62, 115
daughters: Nijinsky's (Kyra) 35–6, 39, 44, 46, 54, 57, 58, 62, 119; Nijinsky's (Tamara) 26, 45, 46, 62
death: Nash's father 14; Nijinsky 26, 48–9; sibling *see* sibling death; van Gogh 108–12, 113; van Gogh's father 102, 104; *see also* bereavement and mourning; loss
delusions 118, 128; of grandeur *see* grandeur; omnipotence; Nash 9, 10, 11, 12, 13, 15–16, 17, 21, 107; Nijinsky 42, 49, 63, 64; paranoid/persecutory *see* paranoia
denial 128
depression (depressive/moods and illness) 74; Nash 13, 20; Nijinsky 27, 29, 32, 35, 36, 39, 57, 58, 62; Saramago's writings 80; van Gogh's 92, 95–6, 98, 101–2, 108, 110, 120; van Gogh's lover (Sien) 101, 102; van Gogh's mother 92, 93
depressive anxiety 74, 128–9
depressive guilt 74, 76
depressive position: Nash 17–18, 19; in Saramago's writings 79, 84
despair, van Gogh's 102, 104, 107, 108, 109, 111, 113
Diaghilev, Sergei 2, 25, 29–30, 31–2, 33, 34, 35, 36, 36–7, 38, 46, 55, 59, 60, 61, 62
diary of Vaslav Nijinsky 54–8, 63; Acocella's (2006) 2, 26; Romola's (1936) 26

dissociation 129; splitting and 51, 52
dreams and Saramago's *Blindness* 80–2; *see also* nightmares
drugs: recreational 120; therapeutic *see* medication

ear, van Gogh's cutting-off 107
emotional capacity 115
emotional growth and development 49; Nijinsky and siblings 28; Saramago's writings 75, 87–8, 88
encapsulation: Nijinsky's 53, 56; van Gogh 103
environmental factors 51
envy 129; Nash 14, 15; Nijinsky 33; van Gogh 111
external criticism, freedom from 115
extraterrestrial beings/aliens, Nash's 6, 9, 15, 16
eye for an eye (law of talion) 74, 75

family: identifications with loved and healthy aspects of members of 117–18; loss of member of 121; Nijinsky's separation 46–7; relationships 3, 117–19
father(s): Nash's 7, 8, 9, 12, 14, 18, 117; Nijinsky's (Thomas) 27, 28, 29–30, 51, 52, 60, 61; Nijinsky's wife's (Charles) 32, 33, 35, 40, 41, 42, 43, 44, 53, 54, 62; Saramago 67, 68, 69; sibling death and 84; van Gogh's 91, 92, 96, 98, 102, 104
First Steps 112
First World War prisoner, Nijinsky 36
flower drawing and paintings of van Gogh 93, 104, 105, 116, 118, 121
Fokine, Michel 30, 31, 32, 34, 36
fostering creativity 121–3
Frenkel, Hans 39
Freud, Sigmund 15, 35, 41, 73, 74, 83, 95; brother Julius 83; Nijinsky's wife consulting 45
Fromm-Reichmann (von Reichmann), Frieda 45, 48

Gachet, Doctor 110
game theory 7, 18
Gauguin, Paul 3, 104–7, 110, 112, 113
genetic factors 50–1
God: Nijinsky and 33, 39, 40, 43, 57, 60; 'Nijinsky the God' 26, 30–1
good Samaritan in *Blindness* 72, 75

INDEX

Gorlitz, P.C. 96
government: Nash and 16; Saramago's writings 72, 85–6, 88
grandeur, delusions of 128; *see also* omnipotence
grandmother, Nijinsky's 27, 28
grandparents, Saramago 68, 69, 71, 80, 83, 88, 117, 121
guilt 74–6; Nijinsky's 35, 57, 61; persecutory *see* persecutory guilt

hallucinations 118, 118–19; auditory *see* auditory hallucinations; Nash 13, 16, 17, 20, 118; Nijinsky 39, 40, 43, 44, 49, 57, 58, 64; Saramago 70, 80; van Gogh 107, 113
Head of a Peasant Woman in a Black Cap 102
hearing voices *see* auditory hallucinations
History of the Siege of Lisbon 84
homicidal/murderous feelings and wishes, Nijinsky 42, 53–4, 57, 58, 59, 60
homosexuality: Nash 8, 11, 12; Nijinsky's 29, 33
Hoornick, Christina Maria (Sien) 100–1
hospitals, psychiatric *see* mental and psychiatric institutions
hostility 118, 119; Nash 7; Nijinsky 44, 52, 56; van Gogh 92–3, 109, 112, 120, 121
How Characters Became the Masters and the Author Their Apprentice 67

identification(s): introjective 129; with loved and healthy aspects of family members of 117–18; with possible inadequacies in parental containment 118–920; projective 125, 131–2
independent self, Nijinsky's search 32
infant (baby)–parent relationships 51; Nijinsky 52, 56–7; van Gogh and depressed mother and 92, 93, 94; *see also* penumbra baby
inferno: Nash's 16, 17; Saramago's *Blindness* 84
inner world 20, 80, 116, 129; Nash 16; Nijinsky 53, 58; Saramago and his writings 71, 74, 83; van Gogh 102, 113
insanity (lunacy): Nijinsky's ballets about 40, 61; recovery from *see* recovery
insight, Saramago's *Blindness* 78, 81

insulin coma/insulin shock therapy: Nash 12; Nijinsky 47–8
intellectual capacity 115
internal criticism, freedom from 115
internal objects/figures 128, 129, 131; Nash 11; *Rime of the Ancient Mariner* 79; van Gogh 121
internalization/introjection 121, 129; Nijinsky 36, 52, 60, 121; Saramago 72, 82; van Gogh 91, 92, 93, 121
introjection *see* internalization
introjective identification 129
involuntary memory 80

Jackson, Murray xvii–xiii; *Weathering the Storms* 124
Jacob B (Mr B) and Nash 7, 11, 12, 13, 14
jealousy 129; Nash 7, 8, 11, 14, 15; Nijinsky 2, 26, 27, 33, 38, 43, 52, 54, 61, 62; van Gogh 109, 111
Jesus Christ *see* Christ
Jeux 25, 31

La Berceuse 107
Landscape with Pollard Willows 102
law of talion 74, 75
Lifar, Serge 47, 49
Lisbon, Saramago and his brother 69, 83
Lloyd George, David 59
London, Nijinsky's final years in 48–9
loss of family member 121; *see also* death
love 117–18; identifications with loved family members 117–18; Nash's feelings/need for 14; Nijinsky's for daughter Kyra 34; van Gogh's for brother Theo 108–11; van Gogh's first love (Eugenie Loyer) 95–7; van Gogh's mother's unlovingness for him 92; van Gogh's second love (Kee Vos-Stricker) 97–9; van Gogh's third love (Sien) 99–101
Loyer, Eugenie, van Gogh's first love 95–7
lunacy *see* insanity
Lvov, Prince Pavel 29, 30
lying and Saramago 69

Madrid, Nijinsky in 35, 38
manic defences 129–30; Nijinsky 57
masturbation, Nijinsky 31, 35–6, 64
mathematics, Nash 6, 7, 9, 11, 13, 15
Mauve, Anton 99

INDEX

meaning, search for 125; Saramago 86
medication (pharmacological treatment with psychoactive drugs incl. antipsychotics) xx, 64, 124; Mijinsky 64, 120; Nash (and its rejection) 6, 12, 13, 17, 18, 19; van Gogh 120
memory, involuntary 80
mental and psychiatric institutions/hospitals/asylums 21; Nash 12, 13, 20; Nijinsky 41–2, 42, 43, 44, 45, 47, 48, 62, 64; Nijinsky's brother 27, 39; Saramago's *Blindness* 72, 75, 76, 82; van Gogh 107, 109, 110, 112
mentalizing 130
Mephisto Waltz 37
Messiah, Nash as saviour or 13, 15, 16; *see also* Christ
Milner, Marion 122
Mr Jacob B and Nash 7, 11, 12, 13, 14
mistress, Nash's (Eleonor) 7–8, 13, 14
mother(s): containment by *see* containment; infant relationship with *see* infant; Nash's 7, 8, 11, 13, 18; Nijinsky's (Eleonore) 27, 28, 29, 39, 51, 52, 121; Nijinsky's wife's (Romola's) 32, 33, 34, 35, 36, 52–3, 53, 60, 61; Saramago's 3, 67, 68, 117; sibling death and 84; van Gogh's 3, 91, 92, 93, 94, 102, 103, 104, 111; *see also* breast-mother
motivation to create 115, 116–17
mourning *see* bereavement and mourning
Muller, Dr Max 47, 48
murderous/homicidal feelings and wishes, Nijinsky 42, 53–4, 57, 58, 59, 60

Narcisse 37
narcissism 5, 10, 130; Nash 10, 11
Nasar's biography of Nash (*A Beautiful Mind*) book xx, 5, 6, 18
Nash, John xx, 1–2, 4–22, 117, 118–19; conflicts 14–15; containment 1, 20, 118, 119, 120; curiosity and capacity to be alone 115; delusions 9, 10, 11, 12, 13, 15–16, 17, 21, 107; depressive position 17–18, 19; early years 6–8; evolution of psychosis 11–14; father 7, 8, 9, 12, 14, 18, 117; hallucinations 13, 16, 17, 20, 118; identifications with loved and healthy aspects of family members 117; internal objects 11, 121; medication (and its rejection) 6, 12, 13, 17, 18, 19; omnipotence delusions 15–16; psychoanalysis 12, 20, 123; recovery 2, 5, 6, 11, 13, 18–19, 19–20, 20–1, 21; repentingness oscilloscope 17–18; search for sanctuary and claustro-agoraphobic dilemma 16; 'self-cure'/return to sanity 18–19; superego 10, 13, 18, 75
Night Café 105
nightmares: Saramago's and his writings 68, 80–2, 85, 86, 119; van Gogh's 107
Nijinsky, Vaslav 2, 24–64, 117, 119, 120, 123; ballet and dancing 2, 3, 25, 28–32, 34, 36–8, 40, 47, 48, 57, 61, 62, 115; breakdown 40–1; childhood 26–8, 30, 45, 52, 54, 60; containment 119, 120; curiosity and capacity to be alone 115; daughters *see* daughters; death 48–9; delusions 42, 49, 63, 64; diary *see* diary; early years 26–8; encapsulation complex 53; family members' separation 46–7; genetic influences 51; guilt 35, 57, 61; identifications with loved and healthy aspects of family members 117; insulin coma/insulin shock therapy 47–8; internalization 36, 52, 60, 121; jealousy 2, 26, 27, 33, 38, 43, 52, 54, 61, 62; in London, final years 48–9; mother (Eleonore) 27, 28, 29, 39, 51, 52, 121; passion for creating 116; precipitating factors 61–2; prisoner of war 36; projection 51, 53, 56, 57, 59, 60, 61, 64; psychoanalysis and 45, 49–50, 123; psychotherapy/taking therapy 41–2, 43, 44–5, 49; psychotic anxiety 2, 53; rage and anger 32, 42, 43, 44, 47, 52–3, 53–4, 56, 62, 64, 119, 123; red roses and 59–60; regression 53–4, 57–8, 64; search for independent self 32; Switzerland 39–40, 42, 44, 46; vulnerability/predisposition 25, 33, 35, 52–3, 53, 54, 61; wife (Romola Pulszky) 26, 32–48, 54, 58, 62, 64; writings on 26
Notebook 89

object 130; internal *see* internal objects; relations/relationships with 130
Oedipal relationships 119; Nash's 11, 14; Nijinsky's 52, 60, 61
omnipotence (delusions of) 10, 130; Nash 15–16; Nijinsky 55, 57, 58, 64

INDEX

On Not Being Able to Paint 122
origins (causes) of psychotic disorders 50–3; *see also* precipitating factors; vulnerability
Ostwald, Peter, on Nijinsky 26, 30, 35, 36, 39, 40, 41, 45, 46, 58, 61, 63

paranoia (paranoid or persecutory delusions) xxi, 80, 119, 128; Nash 7, 11, 15, 18, 19, 20, 107; Nijinsky 53; Saramago's *Blindness* 82, 84
paranoid-schizoid position 130; Saramago's *Blindness* 84
parents: containment by *see* containment; internalization/introjection *see* internalization/introjection; relationship between infant and *see* infant; *see also* father; mother
passion (motivation) for creating 115, 116–17
Peasant Woman, Kneeling Seen from the Back 103
Peasant Woman Digging 102
peer relationships: Nash's 7
penumbra baby, van Gogh as 92
persecutory delusions *see* paranoia
persecutory guilt 74, 83; Nash 18; Nijinsky 61; Saramago and his writings 68, 75, 85
personality transformation *see* transformation
phantasies 116, 131; Nash 11, 14, 16, 21; Nijinsky 28, 35, 38, 39, 50, 53, 56, 58, 59, 60, 61; Saramago (and his writings) 67, 80, 83; van Gogh 101, 111
pharmacological treatment *see* medication
Pieta 110, 111
Portrait of Doctor Gachet 110
Potato Eaters 102
precipitating factors: Nash 5, 8, 14; Nijinsky 61–2; *see also* causes; vulnerability
predisposition *see* vulnerability
primary process thinking 131; Saramago and 81, 81–2
Princeton University, Nash at 1, 13, 18
prisoner of war, Nijinsky 36
projection 119, 124, 131; Nash 15; Nijinsky 51, 53, 56, 57, 59, 60, 61, 64; van Gogh 3, 92, 94
projective identification 125, 131–2

prostitutes: Nijinsky and 29, 31, 39; Saramago's *Blindness* 75; van Gogh and 99–100, 103, 104
Proust, Marcel 2, 31, 80
psychiatric institutions *see* mental and psychiatric institutions
psychoactive drugs *see* medication
psychoanalysis 21–2, 49–50, 123–5, 132; glossary of useful concepts 127–33; Jackson and xviii; Nash 12, 20, 123; Nijinsky 45, 49–50, 123; promising contemporary approaches 21–2; Saramago and his writings 73–4, 123
psychodynamic and psychoanalytic psychotherapy 132
psychotherapy (talking therapy) 49; Nijinsky 41–2, 43, 44–5; psychoanalytic *see* psychoanalysis; psychodynamic and psychoanalytic 132; risks/dangers in exposure of psychotic core xx, 22; therapist's stance 124; working through 19, 45, 81, 125, 131, 133
psychotic anxiety 1, 132; Nijinsky 2, 53
psychotic state, definition 132

rage and anger: Nijinsky's 32, 42, 43, 44, 47, 52–3, 53–4, 56, 62, 64, 119, 123; van Gogh's 92, 98, 102, 107
Reaper 102–3, 109
recovery/return to sanity: commentary author (Dr Clive Hathaway) xx, xxi; Nash 2, 5, 6, 11, 13, 18–19, 19–20, 20–1, 21; van Gogh's 97, 101
recreational drugs 120
red roses and Nijinsky 59–60
redemption (in *Blindness*) 76–80
re-enactment 132
reference, delusions of 128
regression 57, 132; Nijinsky 53–4, 57–8, 64
reparation 133
repentingness oscilloscope: Nash's 17–18
Rime of the Ancient Mariner 79–80
Rimsky-Korsakov's *Schéhérazade* 30, 37
Rite of Spring 25, 31
Rosenfeld, Herbert 5, 10, 17, 64, 123, 132
roses (red) and Nijinsky 59–60
Russia, Communist (and Cold War), Nash and 7, 15, 16

INDEX

St Moritz, Nijinsky in 39–40, 40, 44
Samaritan in *Blindness* 72, 75
sanity, return to *see* recovery
Saramago, José 2–3, 66–89, 117, 119, 120, 123; *Blindness* 1, 67, 71–82, 84–5, 86, 88; childhood 67–9, 70, 84, 85, 118; claustrophobia 84, 119; containment 119, 120; curiosity and capacity to be alone 114, 115; early years 67–9; identifications with loved and healthy aspects of family members 117; internalization 72, 82; nightmares 68, 80–2, 85, 86, 119; *Seeing* 85–6, 86
saviour or Messiah, Nash as 13, 15, 16
Schéhérazade 30, 37
schizoid defences 130
schizophrenia: Bleuler's invention of term 41; Nijinsky and 42, 49, 64
search for meaning *see* meaning
Seeing 85–6, 86
self-harm, van Gogh 3, 107
self-independence, Nijinsky's search 32
sexual assault on Saramago 2, 68
sexual intercourse, Saramago's account of surprising a couple in a field 69–70
sexuality and sexual relationships: Diaghilev's 31; Nash's 7–8; Nijinsky's 29, 30, 33, 35–6; van Gogh's 100, 103, 112; *see also* masturbation; prostitutes
sibling death (and bereavement) 83–4; Freud's brother (Julius) 83; Nijinsky's brother (Stanislav) 39, 61; Saramago's brother (Francisco) 68, 82–4; van Gogh's brother (also Vincent) 3, 92, 111; *see also* brother; sister
sin 74–6
sister(s): Nash's (Martha) 7, 14; Nijinsky's (Bronislava) 27, 28, 29, 32, 33, 34, 38, 39, 43, 51, 54, 118; Nijinsky's wife's (Tessa) 32, 33, 35, 46; van Gogh's (Wilhelmina) 92, 109, 120; *see also* sibling death
Small Memories 67, 68, 69, 70–1, 82, 86
sons: Nash's first son (John) 8, 13, 18; Nash's second son (also John) 8, 13, 18
Sorrow 100
South America, Nijinsky in: first tour 32; second tour 38–9
Sower 105

Spectre of the Rose 37
splitting 109, 133; binary 131; dissociative 51, 52; Nijinsky 44, 51, 52, 56; van Gogh 3, 93
Starry Night 105
Starry Sky over the Rhone 105
Strauss, Richard 36
Stravinsky, Igor 25, 31, 34, 59
suicide, van Gogh 108–12, 113
Sunflowers 105, 116
superego 10, 133; Nash 10, 13, 18, 75
Switzerland, Nijinsky in 39–40, 42, 44, 46
symbolic thinking, loss: Nash 15; Nijinsky 63

talion, law of 74, 75
talking therapy *see* psychotherapy
taxi-driver in *Blindness* 72, 75
therapist's stance in psychotherapy 124
three-person (triangular) relationships, Nijinsky 43, 53, 56, 63
Till Eulenspiegel 36, 37, 40
Tolstoy, Leo 37, 38
transference 133
transformation (in personality): Nash 6, 18; Nijinsky 116; Saramago's *Blindness* 76–80
triangular (three-person) relationships, Nijinsky 43, 53, 56, 63

unconscious, siblings in 82–4
United States, Nijinsky in: first tour 36–7; second tour 37–8

van Gogh, Vincent xxi, 3, 90–113, 117–18, 119–20, 120, 123; alcohol 120; containment 119, 119–20; curiosity and capacity to be alone 115; early years 41–5; first exhibition 104; Gauguin and 3, 104–7, 110, 112, 113; hostility 92–3, 109, 112, 120, 121; identifications with loved and healthy aspects of family members 117–19; internal objects 91, 92, 93, 121, 121; internalization 91, 92, 93, 121; loves *see* love; splitting 3, 93; suicide 108–12, 113
Vienna, Nijinsky in 36, 45, 48
von Reichmann (Fromm-Reichmann), Frieda 45, 48
Vos-Stricker, Kee 97–9

153

INDEX

vulnerability and predisposition (to psychological problems) 50, 118; Nash's 8, 9, 21; Nijinsky's 25, 33, 35, 52–3, 53, 54, 61; *see also* causes; precipitating factors

Weathering the Storms 124
Wenger, Dr Marta 56–7
Wheatfield under Clouded Sky 111
Wheatfield with Crows 111
wife: Nash's (Alicia) 8, 9, 10, 12, 13, 14, 17, 18, 19; Nijinsky's (Romola Pulszky) 26, 32–48, 54, 58, 62, 64; Saramago's first wife 70; Saramago's second wife (Pilar) 70, 88
working through 19, 45, 81, 125, 131, 133
World War 1 prisoner, Nijinsky 36